ARCTIC OCEAN

NORWEGIAN SEA

White S

NORTH SEA

Baltic Sea

Irish Sea

Celtic Sea

English Channel

Adriatic Sea

Black Sea

Tyrrhenian Sea

Ionian Sea

Aegean Sea

MEDITERRANEAN SEA

Madeira

MARITIME STRATEGY AND EUROPEAN SECURITY

COMMON SECURITY STUDIES NO. 2

Also available from Brassey's

WINDASS & GROVE
The Crucible of Peace: Common Security in Europe
Common Security Studies No. 1

CHARTERS & TUGWELL
Deception Operations:
Studies in the East-West Context

HIGGINS
Plotting Peace

CORBETT
Some Principles of Maritime Strategy

Brassey's Sea Power: Naval Vessels, Weapons Systems and Technology Series

Volume 6 KIELY
Naval Surface Weapons

Volume 8 PAKENHAM
Naval Command & Control

Volume 9 PEARSALL
Merchant Shipping

Volume 10 KAY
Technology and the Law of the Sea

One of the most significant naval events of the 1980s was the deployment in 1987-8 of a concerted Western European naval presence to sustain European and wider Western interests in the Gulf during the Iran-Iraq War. The ships of five nations were directly involved and two more countries gave support. Here the Italian Maestrale class frigate *Grecale* gives close protection to an Italian container ship. (US Naval Institute)

MARITIME STRATEGY AND EUROPEAN SECURITY

COMMON SECURITY STUDIES NO. 2

ERIC GROVE

BRASSEY'S (UK)

(A member of the Maxwell Pergamon Publishing Corporation plc)

LONDON · OXFORD · WASHINGTON · NEW YORK · BEIJING
FRANKFURT · SÃO PAULO · SYDNEY · TOKYO · TORONTO

UK (Editorial)	Brassey's (UK) Ltd., 24 Gray's Inn Road, London WC1X 8HR, England
(Orders, all except North America)	Brassey's (UK) Ltd., Headington Hill Hall, Oxford OX3 0BW, England
USA. (Editorial)	Brassey's (US) Inc., 8000 Westpark Drive, 4th Floor, McLean, Virginia 22102, USA
(Orders, North America)	Brassey's (US) Inc., Front and Brown Streets, Riverside, New Jersey 08075, USA Tel (toll free): 800 257 5755
PEOPLE'S REPUBLIC OF CHINA	Pergamon Press, Room 4037, Qianmen Hotel, Beijing, People's Republic of China
FEDERAL REPUBLIC OF GERMANY	Pergamon Press GmbH, Hammerweg 6, D-6242 Kronberg, Federal Republic of Germany
BRAZIL	Pergamon Editora Ltda, Rua Eça de Queiros, 346, CEP 04011, Paraiso, São Paulo, Brazil
AUSTRALIA	Brassey's Australia Pty. Ltd., P.O. Box 544, Potts Point, NSW. 2011, Australia
JAPAN	Pergamon Press, 5th Floor, Matsuoka Central Building, 1-7-1 Nishishinjuku, Shinjuku-ku, Tokyo 160, Japan
CANADA	Pergamon Press Canada Ltd., Suite No. 271, 253 College Street, Toronto, Ontario, Canada M5T 1R5

First edition 1990

Library of Congress Cataloging-in-Publication Data

Grove, Eric.
Maritime strategy and European security/Eric Grove.—1st ed.
p. cm.—(Common security studies: no. 2)
1. Sea-power—Europe. 2. Europe—National security.
3. North Atlantic Treaty Organization—Armed Forces.
I. Title. II. Series.
VA450.G.76 1990 359'03'094—dc20 89-71287

British Library Cataloguing in Publication Data

Grove, Eric.
Maritime strategy and European security—(Common security studies: no. 2)
1. Europe. Naval policies
I. Title
359.03094

ISBN 0-08-037702-5

Printed in Great Britain by B.P.C.C. Wheatons Ltd., Exeter, South Devon

To Masha

Contents

Glossary of Abbreviations ix

List of Plates xi

List of Tables xiii

List of Maps xv

Introduction xvii

Foreword xix

1. Europe's Maritime Security Interests 1

2. The Forward Maritime Strategy and Extended Deterrence 15

3. The Atlantic Link—NATO's Merchant Fleets and Extended Deterrence 29

4. Europe's Premier Navy: Problems and Prospects 40

5. NATO's Continental Navies 48

6. The Gulf Precedent—Birth of a Western European Navy? 59

7. Soviet Naval Policy in the Gorbachev Era 67

8. Conventional Arms Control in Europe—The Naval Dimension 72

9. Maritime Forces and European Security—The Future 86

Appendix I. Adderbury Conversations on Naval Strategy and Arms Control, 30-31 July 1988 91

Appendix II. Moscow Conversations on the Limitation of Naval Activities and Confidence Building Measures at Sea, February 1989 105

Appendix III. Adderbury Maritime Strategic Dialogue 17-19 November 1989 Report of Conversations 115

Notes 161

Index 165

Glossary of Abbreviations

AAW	Anti-Air Warfare
ASROC	Anti-Submarine Rocket
ASTOR	Anti-Submarine Torpedo
ASW	Anti-Submarine Warfare
AUS	Assistant Under Secretary of State
BPK	Large Anti-Submarine Ship (Russian)
CBM	Confidence Building Measure
CFE	Negotiations on Conventional Armed Forces in Europe
CNO	US Chief of Naval Operations
CONMAROPS	NATO Concept of Maritime Operations
CSBM	Confidence and Security Building Measures
CVSA	Anti-Submarine Support/Attack Aircraft Carrier
C^3I	Command Control Communications Intelligence
DDG	Guided Missile Destroyer
DNI	Director of Naval Intelligence
DSA	NATO Defence Shipping Agency
DWT	Dead Weight Tonnage (the carrying capacity of a vessel)
EASTLANT	Eastern Atlantic Command
EC	European Community
FAMS	Family of Anti-Air Missilc Systems
FOC	Flag of Convenience
FOFA	Follow-on Forces Attack (a NATO concept)
FROD	Functionally Related Observable Difference
GIUK	The passages through the gaps between Greenland, Iceland, the Faeroes and the United Kingdom
GLCM	Ground Launched Cruisc Missile
GNP	Gross National Product
GRT	Gross Register Ton (100 cu.ft.; 218 cu.metres)
ICBM	Inter Continental Ballistic Missile
LPD	Landing Platform Dock (Assault ship)
LPH	Landing Platform Helicopter
MC	Military Committee (of NATO) document
MCM	Mine Counter Measures

MCMV	Mine Counter Measures Vessel
MNC	Major NATO Commands (Europe, Atlantic and Channel)
NAAWS	NATO Anti-Air Warfare System
NATO	North Atlantic Treaty Organisation
NAVOCFORMED	Naval On Call Force Mediterranean
NNA	Neutral and Non Aligned
PAN	Porte Avions Nucleaire
PBOS	NATO Planning Board for Ocean Shipping
PLARB	Russian term for SSBN (QV)
POC	Points of Contact (WEU officers concerned with Gulf matters)
Re-Re	Reinforcement and Resupply
RFA	Royal Fleet Auxiliary
Ro-Ro	Roll on-Roll off ship
SACLANT	Supreme Allied Command(er) Atlantic
SACEUR	Supreme Allied Commander Europe
SCEPC	NATO Senior Civil Emergency Planning Committee
SLCM	Sea Launched Cruise Missile
SNA	Sous-marin Nucleaire d'Attaque
SSBN	Nuclear Powered Ballistic Missile Firing Submarine
SSC	Coastal Submarine
SSG	US Navy Strategic Studies Group
SSK	Conventionally Powered Hunter-Killer Submarine
SSN	Nuclear Powered Attack Submarine
START	Strategic Arms Reduction Talks
STOVL	Short Take-Off and Vertical Landing (aircraft)
SUBROC	Submarine Launched Rocket
SNFL	Standing Naval Force Atlantic
TLAM-C	Tomahawk Land Attack Missile—Conventional
UN	United Nations
WEU	Western European Union

List of Plates

Frontispiece. Italian frigate *Grecale* escorting a container ship

1. USS *America*
2. USS *Samuel Elliot Morison*
3. HMS *Phoebe*
4. HMS *Turbulent*
5. HMS *Intrepid*
6. Norwegian Type 207 submarine *Kya*
7. Bundesmarine contingent visiting the United Kingdom
8. British, Dutch and Belgian mine countermeasures vessels
9. Dutch minehunter *Hellevoetsluis*
10. Portuguese corvette *Alfonso Cerqueira*
11. French Task Force 623
12. Italian ships *Vittorio Veneto*, *Audace* and Stromboli
13. Italian mine countermeasures vessels
14. Greek destroyers *Apostolils* and *Sachtouris*
15. Greek submarine *Poseidon*
16. Captain Alexander Pavlov of the *Kerch* briefs his guests
17. Ratings' accommodation on the *Kerch*
18. Ratings' recreation space
19. Soviet twin-tubed chaff rocket launchers

List of Tables

1.1 Merchant Fleets as at 30 June 1988 — 4

1.2 The Decline in British Merchant Tonnage — 9

1.3 Index of Relative Sea Dependence of European Nations — 10

3.1 United States Funded Resources Available for Military Sealift — 31

3.2 European NATO's Resources Available for Military Sealift — 32

3.3 Annual Economic Shipping Requirements for North America and NATO Europe — 34

List of Maps

1. The North Atlantic (front end-paper)
2. NATO Maritime Campaigns (rear end-paper)
3. Norway 18
4. Soviet Naval Concerns 138

Introduction

Over the last two years, under the auspices of the Foundation for International Security, the author has been directing a research project designed to explore the often neglected maritime dimensions of European Security. Usually, the security of Europe, which for the purposes of this study means Western Europe, is defined almost purely in terms of nuclear weapons and land-air warfare on the Central Front. Western Europe's dependence on the use of the seas in peace, crisis and war is little understood and often just ignored. For various reasons, some good, some bad, naval arms control is also a relatively unexplored area in an era of START and CFE. Yet maritime forces are deployed in large quantities in and around Western Europe. Moreover, they are fundamental to the defence of the continent. NATO is a maritime alliance: without the 'Atlantic', NATO quite literally falls apart. Flexible response relies on maritime force projection not only on the flanks but also on the Central Front. Moreover, the countries of Western Europe are highly dependent upon the sea for their economic prosperity. This gives them interests which it is sometimes appropriate to defend with maritime forces. The continuing European interest in maritime security has tended to be disguised by the decline of Europe's empires. These have not entirely disappeared, however, even in formal terms, as the British found in 1982. That one must be very careful indeed in using evidence from the imperial past to demonstrate a continuing wider role for European maritime forces, only makes the correct formulation of the 'out of area' European naval role the more challenging.

As in *The Crucible of Peace* (Brassey's 1988), the first book in this series, the emphasis in this book will again be on 'common security', a vision of the future in which East and West progressively cease to rely on destabilising threats to each other's security but in which each side uses military power in necessary and responsible ways to maintain its legitimate security interests. The progressive winding down of the East-West confrontation, in which some measures to mitigate that confrontation at sea will be necessary, is bound, however, to create instabilities that maritime forces have traditionally proved themselves good at controlling. As well as suggesting ways in which we ought to go to maintain security in Europe therefore, this study will also consider in what frameworks and in what ways maritime forces might maintain Europe's security in the wider world.

The author must acknowledge the generous help of the Leverhulme Trust who funded this two year study from May 1987 to May 1989. Many officers, officials and academics, Eastern as well as Western, have been helpful in sharing their perspectives, often with such frankness that it is necessary not to mention any of them by name. To those who have generously given of their time to our discussions I must offer my sincerest thanks. Three colleagues, however, must be mentioned by name: Stan Windass, Director of the Foundation for International Security, without whose inspiration this project would not have been undertaken; Rear Admiral Richard Hill RN (retd) with whom I have been sharing ideas on naval arms control to a degree that makes our concepts sometimes hard to disentangle; and, last but by no means least, Jean Hollis who has typed and re-typed draft papers and reports with her usual extraordinary patience and skill. None of the above are in any way responsible for the defects of anything that follows but without them all this book would not have existed. The author must also express his thanks to Commander Michael Ranken and the British Maritime Charitable Foundation for their unstinting help in providing information on merchant shipping and for commissioning the original work that provided the basis for Chapter 3.

An earlier version of Chapter 2 was presented as a paper to the Annual Conference of the International Studies Association in London in 1989; Chapter 3 is an extended, revised and up-dated version of a paper *The Merchant Fleet and Deterrence* that appeared under the auspices of the British Maritime Charitable Foundation in 1988; Chapter 4 is based in part on a memorandum prepared for the House of Commons Defence Committee enquiry into *Future Size and Role of the Royal Navy's Surface Fleet*; Chapter 4 is a very extensively amended and revised version of an article that appeared in the special 'Naval Balance' issue of *Naval Forces* Vol. IX, No. II, 1988; and Chapter 8 is the final draft of a paper first drafted for the Moscow discussions in February 1989, re-written for the Barnett Hill Arms Control Conference of the International Institute of Strategic Studies in May 1989 and extensively revised subsequently.

ERIC GROVE

Morden, October 1989

Foreword

by Rear Admiral Jeremy Larken, DSO (Assistant Chief of Defence Staff (Overseas), Ministry of Defence, Whitehall)

Eric Grove has been thinking about what was, until recently, the unthinkable. We owe the colloquial use of this awesome phrase to Herman Kahn. It became current in 1962, the year of the Cuban missile crisis, in association with Kahn's seminal work on the effects and consequences of thermonuclear war.

This book is seminal too, but here the unthinkable is back through the looking glass. From the terrifying possibilities which Kahn tried to tame intellectually, Eric Grove returns us to a curiously familiar environment—in which old wisdoms have suddenly regained their youthful vigour. We are able at last to turn our minds a little from a hybrid world in which thermonuclear war on the scale feared by Kahn and once confronted by President Kennedy has been our mainstream strategic consideration. In its place we are entering an age 'in which nuclear weapons have not gone away but in which they are regarded as having little or no operational utility and in which their overall deterrent effect is, therefore, more subtle and elusive.' In consequence our circumstances require a great deal of rethinking, and as a matter of some urgency. Eric Grove has made a distinguished contribution to this process, and we quickly find that maritime matters are a crucial element of the refreshing situation that confronts us in 1990.

It is well understood that we are moving rapidly from a relatively simple two-bloc strategic system towards a more polycentric global arrangement. The Soviet Union faces an extremely uncertain future, including a degree of instability exceedingly disturbing in a nation still possessed of huge armed forces and a superpower nuclear arsenal; beyond question, however, it is attempting to come to terms with its impaired economic situation. Eastern Europe is in disarray, with all the worries attendant upon such uncertainty. The USA has emerged in a military class of its own. Those concerned that unbalanced martial power is inclined by its nature to be unhealthy will be relieved that fiscal imperatives are already bearing upon the US military establishment. This process is induced particularly by the economic power of Japan—now judged upon several criteria to be the world's foremost economy. Europe too is making somewhat elephantine progress, not just economically but towards a degree of identity which could become national, subject to the evolution of the new German dimension. Some other nations are gaining increased prominence, notably China and India, if not Brazil. Prospective groupings need also to be considered. Perhaps some formal Muslim understanding could develop, possibly against elements of the old West and a reformed Russia, or simply around the Indian Ocean to counter the growing power of India itself. A loose coalition of prosperous Pacific-rim states could serve to balance the different pressures of China and of Japan. At the other end of the scale, sub-Saharan Africa is showing marked signs of becoming an underclass of backward nations, some rich in resources but the whole quite possibly in the process of extensive depopulation due to AIDS. From all this, a fresh coherence is beginning to emerge. The form is not totally unfamiliar, even if the geography itself is novel. It is the revival of the classical Balance of Power as the basic substance of world politics, confined in this new incarnation by the limits of the global envelope itself.

In a world where the imperatives of the strategic nuclear balance and the rigid bi-polar East/West axis are becoming less sharply focussed, there is no time to be lost in reviewing the strategic principles pursued by Marlborough, the Pitts, Canning and Edward Grey, and which found their clearest maritime articulation in Mahan and Corbett. We are reminded that we are an island race, and whereas we are increasingly bound to Europe it is important that we realise the degree to which in economic terms Europe itself is an island. It is heavily dependent upon imported fuel, and although largely self-sufficient for food requires substantial imports of phosphates for fertilisers. Equally Europe remains import-dependent for a range of key non-fuel minerals; and although wise stockpiling can moderate strategic vulnerability the significance remains. So we must secure our air and sea routes, remembering that basically people move by air and materials by sea; some 99.5 per cent by weight of all trans-ocean cargo is carried in ships; and the spare capacity that can be taken up by bulk air freight is relatively minute. Moreover, our continent depends on the sea fundamentally for its security.

Accordingly the book moves into an illuminating study of the current NATO Forward Maritime Strategy and Extended Deterrence, passing rather lightly over the UK contribution to its inception and early development. Eric Grove reminds us, quoting the famous Maritime Strategy brochure (published by the US Institute Proceedings in January 1986), that 'Although deterrence is most often associated with strategic nuclear warfare, it is a much broader concept. To protect national interests we must deter threats ranging from terrorism to nuclear war'. This duly leads us to his own observation that in NATO terms 'the main future roles of naval forces in underpinning extended deterrence are ... the synergistic projection of conventional power to the flanks of Atlantic sea lines of communications so that conventional hostilities can be continued as long as required'. This in fact expresses an ancient principle. It is, moreover, complementary to two fundamental demands of warfare and its deterrence; logistics and sustainability.

If one accepts this thesis and that in-place forces in Europe may be reduced substantially, it follows that trans-Atlantic reinforcement will become even more important to European security. In these circumstances, it will be necessary to re-examine the degree to which the robust exercise of the Forward Maritime Strategy will necessarily insulate our shipping from the risk of hazard by well-equipped ill-wishers. Indeed, the logic will be the same for any maritime theatre in which, for one reason or another, we may become involved. Quiet submarines, especially nuclear powered with a sustained speed advantage over merchant ships, are a very dangerous proposition. In some future maritime conflict, therefore, greater emphasis may need to be placed on the classical convoys around which the anti-submarine battles will come to be fought. The practice of convoying has not been abandoned: the doctrine is kept up to date and exercised occasionally. But the fact is that the flotillas of smallish escorts that may be best suited for close protection of convoys do not now exist in Western navies. History records that during World War II we needed literally hundreds of them. The Royal Navy (which Eric Grove refers to as Europe's premier navy) has become, in the terms of the order-of-battle of the two world wars, substantially a light-cruiser navy, with three light aircraft carriers and a small amphibious force which can achieve some modest power projection, and nuclear submarines as capital strike units.

There are, moreover, worries about nationally-owned European sealift capacity. Notwithstanding some recent encouraging developments it is clear, set against a fairly precise measure of requirements, that the shortage of both ships and seafarers is critical. Yet we are reminded that wartime shipping requirements have always proved to be greatly underestimated in peacetime. Eric Grove recalls a striking observation by Adam Smith himself: that the national security requirements made shipping a special case in his free market economy.

The events in the Persian Gulf during the Iran/Iraq war are used by Eric Grove to illustrate the weight and subtlety of these points to a nicety. Here my own comment must be constrained by a continuing personal involvement. This has, however, been a classical deterrent campaign to protect our vital shipping interests. Intriguingly these interests were, from our point of view, almost as much European as national. I underline, at its face value, the proposition that this crisis 'may be the catalyst for the beginning of a 'European Navy', not some grandiose bureaucratic structure, but a flexible framework of cooperation between separate national forces'. As a current practitioner in the conduct of contingency operations, I cannot emphasise strongly enough that a fundamental divide exists between the mounting of a polyglot force to underpin some ceasefire or disengagement process under reasonably benign conditions, which a miscellaneous group of nations under UN auspices can reasonably undertake, and actual intervention or other forceful peacekeeping military operations (in this context maritime). The latter can only be achieved on the basis of joint doctrines, frequent practice amongst the forces concerned and firm command and control arrangements. Operation CALENDAR, the joint UK/Netherlands/Belgian mine clearance operation in the Gulf, demonstrated this very clearly. Only NATO, or alternatively the WEU, and their close friends are within reach of this sort of capability; perhaps some time in the future it will gather some measure of UN authority.

This brings me to the final major point which Eric Grove has developed. He and I would together boast that we British, and in their slightly different way the French, excel at entrepreneurial diplomacy and problem solving. We also share with them, the Dutch, the Belgians, the Danes, the Norwegians and the Portuguese, and even with the Germans, Spanish and Italians, a measure of common naval heritage, albeit that it has sometimes been adversarial. Like him I feel increasingly convinced, in this reviving international structure of global balances of distributed power, that good sense dictates we should make common cause with our neighbours as best we may, contributing our foremost talents whilst accepting theirs. In the famous words of Benjamin Franklin at the signing of the Declaration of American Independence, 'We must hang together, or, most assuredly, we shall hang separately'.

A final section of the book and the appendices are devoted to Maritime Arms Control; and the report of the Adderbury Maritime Strategic Dialogue 17-19 November 1989 brings the reader right up to date. Here again I have a personal involvement, but it is a refreshing feature of the current arms control process that much of it is evolving in open forum—such as Adderbury. Eric Grove is personally engaged in this debate, and he has a profound grasp of the far-reaching implications involved. I must agree that in principle more good than harm can come from non-committal debate about maritime arms control. It is certainly true that 'discussing matters of mutual concern is a confidence building measure in itself'. But readers will find ample material in the book, and indeed I hope in this short foreword, to remind them that unfettered use of the sea is essential to the West as a whole, for Europe in particular. The sea is our main highway for much of the trade that constitutes the life-blood of our well-being, indeed of our civilisation. Accordingly we must be prepared to defend this facility with a level of capability sufficient to ensure, through the well-tried principles of deterrence, that any contemplated warlike challenge to the UK—or indeed to a Europe which encompasses us—will be an unattractive option.

CHAPTER 1

Europe's Maritime Security Interests

Europe depends fundamentally on the use of the sea for its security. At any one time the sea gives cover for 400 European assigned American submarine launched ballistic missile warheads, at least one British ballistic missile firing submarine and three French, the strategic nuclear firepower that would certainly be brought into play if war in Europe escalated uncontrollably. Apart from mine countermeasures cover, as the SSBNs enter and leave harbour, these forces are otherwise undefended: they rely on the ocean itself for their security.

Despite protestations to the contrary by some of their owners, these forces are only really of certain utility in deterring strategic nuclear strikes. Although they do provide some 'nuclear uncertainty', thus making a resort to major hostilities of any kind more dangerous, it is easy to overstate the deterrence thus provided. Deterring conventional attack requires as robust a conventional capability as can be afforded, and some linkage between events on the land battlefield and the overall strategic nuclear balance. Maritime forces, by definition, are unsuitable for the latter role, a point that will be explained later and which points to the 'tactical denuclearisation' of navies. As far as conventional defence is concerned, however, maritime power plays an absolutely fundamental role. Without massive maritime reinforcement (see Chapter 3), NATO's conventional forces cannot fight effectively on the Central Front. On the flanks, especially in the north, maritime power projection is even more vital. The Norwegian case is especially interesting. Here a situation of low tension in peacetime requires rapid maritime reinforcement in crisis in order to move from that stability obtained by the mutual confidence that neither is going to attack, to the stability given by the confidence that an attack will meet a powerful defence. What makes the Norwegian case so crucial is that fighting in this area will greatly enhance the security of the shipping carrying the reinforcements to the Central Front.

The next chapter will examine in more detail the role played by American and NATO Alliance maritime strategy in maintaining extended deterrence in Europe. We shall now go on briefly to examine Europe's wider interest in peaceful uses of the sea. First, Europe is more dependent on seaborne trade than either of the Superpowers. The Soviet Union, and to a much greater extent the United States, both choose to import large quantities of seaborne supplies to maintain their economic well-being but the absolute requirement for these overseas supplies is a matter of debate. This is not to say that America would not have to import large quantities of raw materials in wartime to exert its full conventional military strength but Western European states are significantly more involved in and dependent upon maritime trade than either Superpower in peace as well as in war. In 1982 the ports of the European Community (plus Spain and Portugal) loaded 458,221 million tonnes of goods and unloaded 1,576,598 million tonnes, 23 per cent of world tonnage. North America's proportion was only 13 per cent, Japan's 9 per cent, and Comecon's 6 per cent.[1] As far as exports by sea are concerned, the Netherlands, Norway, and United Kingdom all export over 20 per cent of their GNP by sea. France, West Germany and Italy export between 10 per cent and 20 per cent—a level comparable to Japan. Both the United States and the Soviet Union export under 10 per cent by sea.[2]

As for import dependence, Europe imports all or most of its supplies of a number of non-fuel materials such as columbium, manganese, sheet mica, bauxite and alumina, cobalt, platinum, tantalum, chromium, tin, zinc, nickel, tungsten, silver, mercury, silenium, gold, copper, silicon, iron ore, lead and molybdenum. Import dependence for certain materials, for example, bauxite and alumina or potash, is less than America's but for a wide range of other materials it is more, for example, chromium, tin, nickel, tungsten, silver, mercury, silenium, gold, copper, silicon, iron ore, sulphur and lead.[3] One can argue about the strategic importance of such dependence given stockpiling, substitution and the possibility of opening up currently uneconomic domestic production but, given problems of dislocation, it does demonstrate Europe's continued ties of economic security, largely by sea, to the wider world.

Europe's clearest and most crucial import dependence is that for supplies of energy. Europe either extracts oil from the sea bed or imports it in tankers from abroad. Western Europe (that is to say, the European Community plus Norway and the neutrals) is the largest individual regional importer of oil and oil products, 303.8 million tonnes of crude in 1987 plus another 84.6 million tonnes of oil products.[4] The equivalent figures for the United States were 229.2 plus 77.6 million tonnes and for Japan 159 plus 44.2 million tonnes. Almost half of Western Europe's supplies came from the Middle East, 167.3 million tonnes with 77.7 million from North Africa, 68.4 million from the Soviet Union and 41.6 million tonnes from West Africa. Imports were two thirds of European consumption although the two main European North Sea oil producers, the United Kingdom and Norway, produced far more than they consumed

(125.6 million tonnes production for UK against 75.2 million tonnes consumption and 51.9 million tonnes production for Norway against 9.5 million tonnes consumption—all of course from the sea bed). Otherwise Western Europe depends almost wholly on overseas supplies. In relation to overall primary energy demand, oil provides just under half the overall energy consumption of Western Europe, in 1987 about 45 per cent. Middle East oil therefore provides some 13 per cent of the total energy consumption of Europe, a significant proportion. Middle East oil provides only 3 per cent of the United States' total energy demands although the figure for Japan is as high as 35 per cent. Certain individual European countries are more oil dependent than others. West Germany, France and the Netherlands all rely for about 43-44 per cent of their total energy demand. Italy, however, is 61 per cent oil dependent, thanks to a 55 per cent reliance on oil for electricity production. (Oil producing Britain, by comparison, is only 37 per cent dependent on oil for total energy.) Moreover, oil is not the only imported energy source. Europe ships in significant quantities of coal and in 1987 almost 40 per cent more energy from coal was consumed than came from the coal Europe produced.

Europe is now more or less self-sufficient for food; indeed, as is well known, she produces substantial surpluses. Cereals, once a major import, are now exported; the surplus in 1984-5 was 32 million tonnes out of production of 151 million tonnes.[5] Production depends heavily on imported energy however. Fertilisers are also heavily in demand and require substantial imports of phosphates. Without seaborne imports therefore, Europe's new found food self-sufficiency would wither away, probably rapidly.

Although much of Europe's vital maritime trade is carried in non-European shipping, all the European states maintain substantial merchant fleets. In mid-1988, the European Community's merchant fleet comprised 13,429 vessels of 58.5 million gross register tons (GRT) compared to 6,442 American ships of 20.8 million GRT and 8,520 Comecon (6,744 Soviet) of 35.9 million GRT. Japan had the world's largest national merchant fleet—over 9,804 vessels of just over 32 million GRT. This gives the European Community the largest collective mercantile marine in the world (15 per cent of the world's total shipping). Norway added another 2,078 vessels of almost 9.35 million tons. In terms of ships owned by nationals of European states, the European fleet is even more impressive. In 1987 the states of the European Community owned over 161 million deadweight tons of shipping as against Japan's 89 million, America's 65 million and the Warsaw Pact's 42 million (28.5 million Soviet). Of the European tonnage, 63 per cent was 'own flag', the rest 'flag of convenience'. Table 1.1 shows the position (including the fleets of European dependencies) in more detail.[6]

Sadly, Europe's fleets have been in precipitate decline because of the

Table 1.1 *Merchant Fleets as at 30 June 1988*

	OIL TANKERS	ORE & BULK CARRIERS	GENERAL CARGO PASSENGER CARGO	CONTAINER SHIPS	FERRIES AND PASSENGER SHIPS	TRADING TOTALS	FISHING VESSELS	SUPPLY SHIPS AND TENDERS	RESEARCH VESSELS	GRAND TOTALS
EEC BELGIUM	35 700,601	19 871,538	24 120,811	8 200,067	17 33,987	103 1,927,004	117 21,851	6 3,915	5 1,962	344 2,118,422
DENMARK	78 2,158,767	3 162,813	351 566,549	27 1,007,454	86 326,192	545 4,221,775	564 201,942	16 11,762	4 1,011	1,240 4,501,727
FRANCE	71 2,156,691	20 698,449	118 618,841	19 560,036	63 170,495	291 4,204,512	383 133,942	25 13,293	19 18,980	930 4,506,237
WEST GERMANY	91 598,764	9 176,374	611 1,100,083	99 1,654,065	113 196,744	923 3,726,030	93 38,532	34 34,391	30 35,350	1,233 3,917,257
GREECE	329 9,564,566	413 9,077,379	540 2,287,384	20 233,772	280 651,661	1,582 21,814,762	115 39,844	3 19,820	6 3,665	1,874 21,978,820
IRISH REPUBLIC	7 21,922	— —	43 58,549	8 15,199	8 33,166	66 128,836	75 28,388	7 6,603	— —	169 172,768
ITALY	315 4,010,640	53 1,543,317	298 974,784	16 265,892	238 570,910	920 7,365,543	243 68,478	25 22,041	6 4,781	1,583 7,794,247
NETHER-LANDS	81 702,703	9 295,423	428 1,379,622	19 579,214	25 234,841	562 3,191,803	435 143,624	29 25,457	13 8,878	1,265 3,726,464
PORTUGAL	16 492,172	10 266,581	40 85,186	2 6,975	8 3,966	76 854,880	194 119,535	1 3,467	— —	306 988,844
SPAIN	104 1,907,916	44 988,033	335 658,810	28 96,568	42 125,451	553 3,776,778	1,584 538,406	5 4,151	1 660	2,343 4,415,122
UNITED KINGDOM	255 3,341,781	34 1,043,426	393 814,272	49 1,340,594	139 696,312	870 7,236,385	395 114,948	259 268,544	34 33,839	2,142 8,260,431

TABLE 1.1 *(Continued)*

	OIL TANKERS	ORE & BULK CARRIERS	GENERAL CARGO PASSENGER CARGO	CONTAINER SHIPS	FERRIES AND PASSENGER SHIPS	TRADING TOTALS	FISHING VESSELS	SUPPLY SHIPS AND TENDERS	RESEARCH VESSELS	GRAND TOTALS
EEC TOTALS	**1,382** **25,656,523**	**614** **15,123,333**	**3,181** **8,664,891**	**295** **5,959,836**	**1,019** **3,043,725**	**6,491** **58,448,308**	**4,198** **1,449,490**	**410** **413,444**	**118** **109,126**	**13,429** **62,380,329**
NATO EUROPE										
ICELAND	4 3,669	— —	31 51,336	— —	4 2,362	39 57,367	343 110,312	1 356	— —	396 174,550
NORWAY	190 6,615,664	32 905,028	576 667,457	6 88,240	390 520,806	1,194 8,797,195	609 268,883	82 99,323	30 34,986	2,078 9,350,303
TURKEY	108 1,156,441	54 1,075,178	473 882,710	— —	127 121,744	762 3,236,873	11 4,307	2 1,256	2 1,183	872 3,281,153
EUROPEAN TOTALS	**1,677** **33,410,375**	**700** **17,103,539**	**4,218** **10,207,845**	**293** **6,032,877**	**1,532** **3,655,471**	**8,420** **70,410,107**	**5,086** **1,804,604**	**488** **507,776**	**150** **145,295**	**16,606** **75,013,567**
NATO N. AMERICA										
CANADA	55 299,812	87 1,569,988	86 171,162	2 16,083	139 328,918	369 2,385,963	489 150,414	40 55,921	39 41,041	1,225 2,902,394
USA	303 9,638,657	105 1,698,711	421 4,111,108	117 3,341,027	73 378,511	1,019 19,168,014	3,207 660,495	589 189,502	142 152,177	6,442 20,832,137
NATO TOTALS	**2,035** **43,348,844**	**892** **20,372,238**	**4,725** **14,490,115**	**412** **9,389,987**	**1,744** **4,362,900**	**9,808** **91,964,084**	**8,782** **2,624,513**	**1,117** **753,199**	**331** **338,513**	**24,273** **98,748,098**
WARSAW PACT										
BULGARIA	19 292,188	37 611,563	62 354,100	2 19,097	15 6,077	135 1,283,025	38 102,597	— —	1 164	201 1,392,381
CZECHO-SLOVAKIA	— —	4 75,072	14 82,831	— —	— —	18 157,903	— —	— —	— —	18 157,903
GERMANY GDR	12 53,426	140 748,632	18 338,408	8 77,620	14 40,645	192 1,258,731	116 153,471	4 1,016	5 1,884	369 1,442,840

TABLE 1.1 *(Continued)*

	OIL TANKERS	ORE & BULK CARRIERS	GENERAL CARGO PASSENGER CARGO	CONTAINER SHIPS	FERRIES AND PASSENGER SHIPS	TRADING TOTALS	FISHING VESSELS	SUPPLY SHIPS AND TENDERS	RESEARCH VESSELS	GRAND TOTALS
HUNGARY	— —	— —	15 76,121	— —	— —	15 76,121	— —	— —	— —	15 76,121
POLAND	21 235,341	88 1,603,918	160 1,257,210	— —	28 42,493	297 3,138,962	317 312,080	4 1,579	4 1,505	714 **3,489,449**
ROMANIA	14 523,306	68 1,667,217	226 1,085,694	— —	3 820	311 3,277,037	64 233,847	5 2,730	1 659	462 3,560,736
USSR	462 5,464,197	174 2,930,933	1,535 7,578,684	60 785,524	255 701,578	2,486 17,460,916	3,318 6,843,309	63 37,932	195 396,796	6,741 25,783,967
WARSAW PACT TOTAL	**528** **6,568,458**	**511** **7,637,335**	**2,030** **10,773,048**	**70** **882,241**	**315** **791,613**	**3,454** **26,652,695**	**3,853** **7,645,304**	**76** **43,257**	**206** **401,008**	**8,520** **35,903,399**
CHINA PRC	197 1,830,099	220 4,391,217	924 5,417,409	50 617,795	67 176,453	1,458 12,432,973	131 66,548	32 25,179	28 53,971	1,841 12,919,876
JAPAN	1,890 12,277,667	195 9,868,142	2,472 3,856,679	145 3,176,320	625 1,135,099	5,327 30,313,907	2,793 1,072,483	69 28,255	28 34,943	9,804 32,074,417
WORLD	**8,721** **161,345,812**	**4,662** **109,605,762**	**19,638** **71,862,646**	**1,403** **26,037,074**	**4,080** **9,666,602**	**38,504** **378,517,896**	**22,706** **13,812,341**	**2,154** **1,386,697**	**786** **1,004,245**	**75,680** **403,406,079**
CROWN DEPENDENCIES CHANNEL ISLANDS										37 14,801
ISLE OF MAN										114 2,137,224
TOTAL										**151** **2,152,025**

Table 1.1 *(Continued)*

	OIL TANKERS	ORE & BULK CARRIERS	GENERAL CARGO PASSENGER CARGO	CONTAINER SHIPS	FERRIES AND PASSENGER SHIPS	TRADING TOTALS	FISHING VESSELS	SUPPLY SHIPS AND TENDERS	RESEARCH VESSELS	GRAND TOTALS
DEPENDENT TERRITORIES										
ANGUILLA	— / —	— / —	10 / 2,679	— / —	1 / 195	11 / 2,874	— / —	— / —	— / —	12 / 3,303
BERMUDA	42 / 3,189,344	12 / 283,939	32 / 192,068	2 / 32,416	1 / 12,343	89 / 3,710,110	4 / 2,187	9 / 8,117	— / —	116 / 3,774,298
BRITISH VIRGIN IS.	— / —	— / —	20 / 4,302	— / —	2 / 752	22 / 5,054	4 / 705	2 / 627	1 / 420	29 / 6,806
CAYMAN ISLANDS	15 / 80,704	5 / 102,700	96 / 192,074	2 / 3,198	2 / 1,766	120 / 380,442	74 / 42,631	15 / 8,213	6 / 28,341	235 / 476,505
FALKLAND ISLANDS	— / —	— / —	3 / 537	— / —	— / —	3 / 537	— / —	— / —	2 / 6,370	5 / 6,907
GIB - RALTAR	27 / 2,651,019	14 / 231,449	55 / 153,915	— / —	1 / 322	97 / 3,036,705	— / —	3 / 2,552	1 / 849	107 / 3,041,811
HONG KONG	67 / 2,131,532	120 / 4,392,924	37 / 273,957	21 / 436,797	98 / 58,384	343 / 7,293,594	7 / 2,104	3 / 20,156	— / —	394 / 7,328,984
MONT-SERRAT	— / —	— / —	1 / 711	— / —	— / —	1 / 711	— / —	— / —	— / —	1 / 711
ST HELENA	1 / 490	— / —	— / —	— / —	1 / 3,150	2 / 3,640	— / —	— / —	— / —	2 / 3,640
TURKS & CAICOS	2 / 890	— / —	7 / 1,828	— / —	1 / 384	10 / 3,102	1 / 124	2 / 258	— / —	14 / 3,963
TOTALS	**154 / 8,053,979**	**151 / 5,011,012**	**261 / 822,071**	**25 / 472,411**	**107 / 77,296**	**698 / 14,436,769**	**90 / 47,751**	**34 / 39,923**	**10 / 35,980**	**915 / 14,646,528**

TABLE 1.1 *(Continued)*

	OIL TANKERS	ORE & BULK CARRIERS	GENERAL CARGO PASSENGER CARGO	CONTAINER SHIPS	FERRIES AND PASSENGER SHIPS	TRADING TOTALS	FISHING VESSELS	SUPPLY SHIPS AND TENDERS	RESEARCH VESSELS	GRAND TOTALS
BRITISH INDIAN OCEAN TERRITORY AND PITCAIRN										151 / 2,152,025
UNITED STATES OVERSEAS TERRITORIES—American Samoa; Guam; Pacific Islands Trust Territory; Puerto Rico; Virgin Islands of the USA										62 / 74,434
DANISH DEPENDENCIES—Faeroes and Greenland							296 / 179,876			296 / 179,876
FRENCH DEPENDENCIES Djibouti			2 / 1,780		1 / 500	4 / 2,280		1 / 202		7 / 3,051
OVERSEAS TERRITORIES—Kerguelen; French Guiana; French Polynesia; Guadeloupe; Martinique; New Caledonia; St Pierre & Miquelon; Wallis & Futuna Islands										119 / 401,957
NETHERLANDS OVERSEAS TERRITORIES—Antilles and Aruba										92 / 432,488
PORTUGUESE OVERSEAS TERRITORIES—Azores; Macao and Madeira										34 / 27,193
SPANISH OVERSEAS TERRITORIES—Canary Islands										107 / 94,670
TOTAL OVERSEAS AND/OR DEPENDENT TERRITORIES										**1,934 / 20,164,623**

Notes: 1. Compiled by Commander Michael Ranken of the British Maritime Charitable Foundation from information in *Statistical Tables*, Lloyds Register of Shipping, London 1988.

2. In each entry the figure in the top left hand corner represents the number of vessels by type. The figure at bottom right is the gross register tonnage.

over-supply of shipping on the world market and the availability of cheaper alternatives. Between 1983 and 1986, Norway lost over half its merchant tonnage. This tendency has only been reversed by Government intervention. The decline of the British fleet has been one of the most notable (figures refer to ships over 500 gross register tons).[7]

TABLE 1.2 *The Decline in British Merchant Tonnage*

Year	Ships	Millions of DWT
1975	1614	50.0
1980	1143	35.7
1985	627	15.9
1986	501	10.6
1987	463	9.5
1988	437	8.6

By 1995 the General Council of British Shipping estimate that there may be as few as 100 British merchantmen of over 500 GRT. As for deep sea vessels, a British Maritime Charitable Foundation study showed a decline from 955 vessels in 1978 to 193 in 1987, a figure likely to fall by another 40-50 per cent by 1990.[8]

The implications of this decline for deterrence and national security will be covered later in Chapter 3. Already, European shipbuilding has been seriously reduced by foreign competition. The only major shipbuilding nations in Europe now are West Germany, Denmark, Spain and Italy. In 1988 the Federal Republic built 55 ships of 521,000 gross register tons, third in the world in terms of tonnage, (4.8 per cent of world tonnage built), Denmark built 38 of 377,000 GRT (3.45 per cent), Spain 126 small ships of 162,000 total GRT (1.5 per cent) and Italy 24 ships of 145,000 GRT (1.3 per cent). By comparison, Japan built 598 ships of over 4 million GRT and South Korea 117 of 3.2 million GRT.[9] In terms of order books, both West Germany and Italy were still high in the world league in 1988, with orders of almost a million GRT each. Even Britain was showing some modest recovery as the Far Eastern shipbuilding giants began to suffer from major cost increases.[10] In 1988 Britain only built 31 ships of 60,000 GRT (0.5 per cent of world shipbuilding), but she rose from seventeenth to fifteenth in terms of orders.[11] On the basis of total build, however, Europe as a whole (in 1988) still commands a very respectable share of the world's shipbuilding market, 489 vessels (second only to Japan in numbers) of 1.73 million tonnes, 15.9 per cent of world output and number three in the world.[12]

The story for fishing is much the same. Britain's fishing industry has declined although European countries retained very significant fishing fleets overall. Norway caught over 1.9 million tonnes of fish in 1986, the world's tenth biggest ocean catch. The largest European Community fishing countries were close behind Denmark with 1.87 million tonnes and Spain with 1.3 million. France and Britain caught 850,000 and 848,000 tonnes respectively, and Britain imported almost a further 820,000 tonnes. Italy and the Netherlands both caught about 500,000 tonnes and 450,000 tonnes respectively (but also imported about the same) and Portugal caught almost 390,000 tonnes. Put together, the European Community catch makes it fourth in the world after Japan, the Soviet Union and China.[13]

Fisheries must form part of any overall index of sea dependence. One of the most interesting indices is that developed by Admiral Hill in *Maritime Strategy for Medium Powers.*[14] This clearly shows that several European states are significantly more sea-dependent than the United States.

The following table has been derived from one in that book. The criteria are seaborne trade in tonnes, merchant marines, fish catches, and both production and stocks of offshore oil and fish: all are related to gross domestic product to give a dependency index.

TABLE 1.3 *Index of Relative Sea Dependence of European Nations*

	Seaborne Trade	Merchant Marine	Fish Catch	Offshore Zone
Belgium	1	2	1	1
Denmark	3	3	4	2
France	2	2	2	1
West Germany	2	2	1	1
Greece	4	5	2	2
Italy	4	1	3	2
Netherlands	5	3	1	1
Spain	2	3	2	2
UK	2	3	1	3
Norway	4	4	4	4
USA	2	2	1	2
Japan	3	3	3	2

The stakes of Western Europe's states in the sea are thus highly significant, although, interestingly, when the figures are weighted for relative GDP they tell a slightly different story. The maritime trade dependence of Europe as a whole is about halfway between those of the United States and Japan, the merchant marine index comparable to the United States, fishing catches about half those of Japan and offshore oil and fish less than either Japan or the United States. This has some interesting implications for the dependence of a united Europe upon the sea. Nevertheless, as things are at present, the figures show quite clearly that Western Europe is a continent highly dependent on the use of the seas and its relationships with overseas countries. Although some of this sea dependence is essentially local, for example, intra EEC trade or fishing within 200 mile economic zones, some is not. Ships flying European flags and/or owned by European companies still ply the oceans of the world in large numbers. European states still have substantial amounts of trade with non-European states overseas. Most important of all, Western Europe still consumes far more energy imported by sea than she produces from her own sea bed and that oil is a vital component of the food production process.

Self-interest therefore might be assumed to dictate the deployment of maritime forces in defence of those interests. A number of countervailing factors, however, have tended to limit, and often to prevent completely, both defence by Europeans of their own maritime interests and the use of maritime forces to defend other interests. Firstly, the diminished relative power of the European states has forced what resources are available to be concentrated on defence closer to home. The end of the European empires, itself a reflection of a loss of relative power, removed the infrastructure, requirement and, perhaps most important, much of the legitimacy of world wide European naval activities. The willingness of European governments to take political or military risks outside Europe is thus significantly diminished.

Public opinion cannot be relied upon to see significiant losses for example, a warship, as anything but the result of serious political error. Also, the post-colonial international system is an environment in which the legal and political obstacles to military action are very great. Many fairly poor states are relatively well armed, in part thanks to the successful efforts of the European arms industries. Moreover, the economic problems of areas vital to Europe provide equally good reasons for leaving well alone as they do for intervention and the risk of serious destabilisation. If two warring states are both important to one's national well being, it is crucial not to appear to be taking sides. States which appear overly committed to one side or the other in a 'Third World' dispute risk economic sanctions at best and, at worst, terrorist outrages.

The continued fragmentation of Europe into small states narrows natural horizons and perceptions of 'national interest'. Norway, for example, Europe's most maritime state, as a 'small nation', feels confined to a very limited role in international affairs. National uses of armed force at any distance from her shores are considered out of the question. The attitudes of larger states are also conditioned by limiting factors. The Federal Republic of Germany, despite its economic strength, feels limited by its basic law, treaty commitments and political traditions from engaging in military activity outside Europe and its contiguous waters. The ex-imperial states, the Netherlands and Belgium and, to a lesser extent, the United Kingdom, all share a reluctance, now that virtually all empires and residual commitments have been discarded, to embroil themselves once more in entanglements overseas. Only France self-consciously retains a military emphasis on overseas intervention, although even she recognises the limitations of her real capabilities and acts accordingly. France, however, tends to define her policies, more than most, in national terms, while the national interests of different European states in extra-European crises are often different, especially in terms of commercial relationships both during a conflict and after it, when reconstruction contracts will be 'up for grabs'. A final factor militating against European action is acceptance of American leadership in the NATO Alliance and dependence on the United States for superpower support against the Soviet Union. These both lead to a reliance on the United States to act as the West's world policeman and a reluctance to be seen to be acting in ways contrary to American policies and perceived interest outside Europe.

As some of these factors are likely to remain persistent, if not to increase, the security relationship with the USA is likely to remain a vital concern in the foreign policies of European states. The decline of Europe's merchant fleets is likely to reduce the dangers to European shipping defined in the strictest of national terms. Small 'Third World' states are likely to become still better armed rather than less and there will be increasing numbers of Europeans in 'Third World' states to be considered hostages for the passive, if not good, behaviour of European governments. Furthermore, the growth of immigrant communities within European states, who might identify with the objects of European government's military actions, might reinforce the potential for terrorist retaliation. Finally, Europe's remaining interest in the 'Third World' could reduce significantly as Japan becomes a still more dominant trading nation.

There are, however, signs that domestic opposition to a more interventionist policy by European governments in overseas affairs may be reducing. The Dutch Government faced significant domestic pressure to send mine clearance forces to the Gulf in 1987. Even Norway considered some maritime contribution in the framework of United Nations action. The Falklands War demonstrated that overseas military operations could, in certain circumstances, be extremely popular domestically and that the resilience of medium powers in the face of losses was significant. The growing dangers to foreign nationals in a disordered world put a premium on limited military capabilities to maintain their safety and at worst evacuate them from overly disordered situations. New forms of threat, notably the laying of mines in international waters create challenges that can only be countered by naval deployment.

As countries are forced to take action where national interests are especially threatened, for example, protecting their tankers from mines in areas from which they import substantial quantities of oil, new avenues begin to open up for international co-operation. Putting naval action into an international context dramatically diminishes several of its major drawbacks. International action prevents the singling out of states for countermeasures such as terrorism or economic discrimination. International action also gives extra political legitimacy to the operation which defuses domestic opposition. A United Nations operation especially would be hard for most domestic political groups to oppose. Casualties also become more acceptable as being sustained in fulfilment of international duty. Support from friends overcomes deficiencies of national capability both in terms of military conflict and logistical support.

International action is, however, not without its own difficulties. Arranging it raises conflicts of national interest and the perception of those interests. The shared common assets at risk have to be very important and clearly perceived as such to overcome these problems. Strictly speaking, the right of self-defence does not extend to a ship of another state in a multinational force. Unless ships are engaged in enforcement action under the terms of Chapter 7 of the United Nations Charter, a warship of one nation might not feel it can legally defend a ship flying another flag. This difficulty should not be over-estimated, however. It has not, as we shall see, precluded bilateral arrangements for mutual support between ships of different navies in the Gulf.

Rules of engagement can also create problems. Multinational forces need rules of engagement that are common to all, or at least which are closely harmonised. It is often difficult to arrange these to suit everyone. This puts a premium on clear political agreement on what a force is intended to achieve.

As the following will make clear, these problems caused difficulties in the Gulf where, in 1987-8, the first major experiment in European naval co-operation took place. Western Europe is much less inhibited by lack of capacity for applying naval power. As will be seen in subsequent chapters, Europe's navies both separately and collectively possess substantial military power and the capacity to project it at considerable distances from their shores. The Royal Navy's retention of afloat support facilities is especially notable, a reflection of its ability to retain much of the flexibility that was built up to sustain its world-wide post-imperial policing role of the period 1957-71. Other European navies, however, have significant numbers of tenders, supply vessels and tankers. This reach, as defined by Admiral Hill, is an asset possessed by few naval forces, if any, other than those of the Superpowers (and Soviet capabilities in this regard are still very limited). Europe's navies are also well equipped with major surface combatants of the destroyer/frigate type capable of ocean going general purpose duties especially in the protection of shipping. They are particularly well supplied with mine countermeasures surface vessels, providing almost all the Western Alliance's capability in such forces. They even deploy a growing number of small aircraft carriers. Europe's navies also possess significant numbers of specialised amphibious vessels, being much better equipped than the Soviet Union in this regard. Finally, most of Europe's navies (including France's) are used to operating together in an integrated NATO team.

Now, however, these forces are primarily orientated to contributing to NATO's forward maritime strategy. It is to this controversial subject that we must first turn therefore in our examination of the present and future contribution of maritime strategy to European security.

CHAPTER 2

The Forward Maritime Strategy and Extended Deterrence

Many debates generate more heat than light and this has certainly been true with the controversy over the American forward 'Maritime Strategy'. Even before it had been publicly articulated in Congressional testimony in 1985, and the infamous 'brochure' issued at the beginning of 1986, it had been heavily criticised. To some extent the United States Navy brought some of this upon itself. The formulation of the 'Maritime Strategy' was part of a renaissance in naval self-confidence that too often was expressed with a robustness that was both over-confident and deliberately provocative. The tendency was to emphasise the more extreme war fighting scenarios at the expense of the more realistic peacetime/crisis aspects, for example, in the brochure headings. The brochure also took a public swipe at 'the superficially appealing manifesto of the self proclaimed defense reformers'.[1]

Nevertheless, on their side, the criticisms were often overdrawn and took the overenthusiasm at face value. Not only was there sometimes a lack of critical sense of proportion, there was also a lack of historical perspective in treating the 'Maritime Strategy' as a new formulation of the 1980s: in fact it is but a re-articulation—with some significant additions—of NATO's maritime strategy dating back to the earliest days of the Alliance. What is interesting about the 'Maritime Strategy', especially in the context of extended deterrence, is how it draws out strands that have always been in NATO's thinking about overall deterrence strategy but which have tended to be overshadowed by the reliance on nuclear weapons and the concomitant assumptions of a short nuclear war. It then re-twines these into what is, in essence, a coherent doctrine for maintaining extended deterrence into the post nuclear age.

What is meant by the 'post nuclear age'? The era we are now entering is one in which nuclear threats, at least threats of first use, are going to have diminished credibility, no matter how hard we try to make them stick. This is not to say that some 'nuclear uncertainty', i.e. the possibility of nuclear use in a particular theatre (notably Europe) leading to a catastrophic full scale nuclear war, will not have a continued role to play in underpinning overall deterrence. The main element in this overall deterrent posture, however, will be the likelihood of one's conventional forces being able to prevent an attacker rapidly gaining his objectives on land. There is a third dimension that needs adding too, 'long war uncertainty', that is to say the possibility that an initial attack may lead to a long conflict which the aggressor would wish to avoid. Long wars are unwelcome but so are nuclear wars. The possibility of either outcome, a nuclear war or conventional conflict of indeterminate duration, being the result of a desperate bid for rapid military success, coupled with the uncertainty of that rapid success which is imposed by the deterrer's conventional counter-blitzkrieg capacity, is a formula for stability, especially if both sides reduce and restructure their forces co-operatively. 'Long war uncertainty', however, requires for NATO a capacity to reinforce and resupply. It also requires a strategy to exert 'leverage' to achieve 'war termination on unfavourable terms'.[2] Certainly it means that the modalities of major conventional war fighting must be thought through in a new, more rigorous manner. As Norman Friedman has put it:

> ... the United States in the late 1980s finds itself in a semi-non-nuclear world in which the lessons of the pre-nuclear past may have gained in their instructive value. The mere existence of survivable nuclear weapons is extremely important because it still inhibits the two Superpowers from violent confrontation. However, it is no longer possible to argue that, should they come to blows, their war would end swiftly as each tried to avoid nuclear escalation. There is no credible war-ending apocalyptic threat. Thus, where NATO has debated whether to build seven or thirty days worth of munitions, it seems more realistic to imagine that should war come it might well last months or, more probably, years.[3]

Such circumstances vindicate the persistent doubts of NATO's maritime commanders about the assumptions that short wars were inevitable and that hence naval forces were irrelevant in the nuclear age. Naval strategy did not die in the post war period. Anglo-American and NATO thinking traditionally postulated the prospect of a long war with a maritime campaign based around a mix of convoy escorts and forward-operating carrier and submarine forces. The carrier striking fleet began to predominate after the setting up of NATO's Atlantic Command in 1952. It was to have the key role of attacking the Soviet Navy at source. Composed of four American and two British carriers, it operated off Vestfjord in Exercise 'Main Brace' in 1952. Admittedly, at this stage, the Striking Fleet was mainly seen as a primarily nuclear armed force which was designed to add to the initial nuclear offensive, but the idea of long drawn out hostilities did not die immediately. Although Britain's dalliance with the concept of 'broken backed war' was brief, she herself became embarrassed that NATO—and by implication the United States—wished to maintain at least the option of a longer conflict. The important

September 1957 'Role of the Navy' paper, that was the culmination of the post Sandys White Paper 'Autumn Naval Re-Think', contains the following instructive passages, written just after the revised strategy document MC 14/2 which set out the principles of massive retaliation in a NATO context.

> The deterrent value of NATO is the knowledge that it will fight, should war be forced upon it. It must, therefore, have plans to do so. The United Kingdom may not always agree with these plans, but if her influence within the Alliance cannot secure their amendment she must do her best to honour them; ... NATO plans take into account the possibility of a war against Russia continuing after the nuclear exchange. They thus call for the Atlantic sea routes to be kept open... Another feature of NATO plans is the operation of the Carrier strike fleet in Northern waters... Her Majesty's Government's view may be that the plan represents something less than the best use of NATO resources, but it is an integral part of NATO planning, and if we were to unilaterally withdraw from this plan it would certainly have serious repercussions within the Alliance.[4]

'Flexible Response' and MC14/3, the document which formulated this concept, re-emphasised the role of maritime forces in NATO's overall deterrent. Shortly before this momentous strategic change, Rear Admiral Richard Colbert USN, Deputy Chief of Plans at Headquarters Supreme Allied Commander Atlantic (SACLANT), disturbed by the growth of Soviet naval capabilities, called for a new concept of maritime strategy that would increase the Alliance's ability to respond quickly and collectively at sea in a crisis and which would recognise the importance of the sea to NATO's overall strategy. SACLANT's staff were evolving the concept of 'Maritime Contingency Forces', to be drawn at short notice from forces earmarked to the Alliance in peacetime to support contingency plans at an early point in a crisis. As part of this process, the 'Standing Naval Force Atlantic' (SNFL) was born at the beginning of 1968 as a multi-national standing contingency force under NATO command. At the same time, after a SACLANT briefing to the North Atlantic Council on the 'World-Wide Soviet Maritime Challenge', Colbert got his wish with a special study commissioned by NATO Secretary General Manlio Brosio. The Brosio study, 'Relative Maritime Strategies and Capabilities of NATO and the Soviet Bloc' carried out by members of the SACLANT staff and presented to the Secretary General in March 1969, set out NATO's maritime strategy in tones that have a remarkably modern ring. Both early forward movement and offensive forward operations were emphasised. In crisis, the Maritime Contingency Forces would be mobilised to provide a controlled response and to deter further escalation. If deterrence failed, however, Western maritime forces would be used to contain and destroy Soviet submarines as far forward as possible while strike carriers would support the land and amphibious operations ashore,

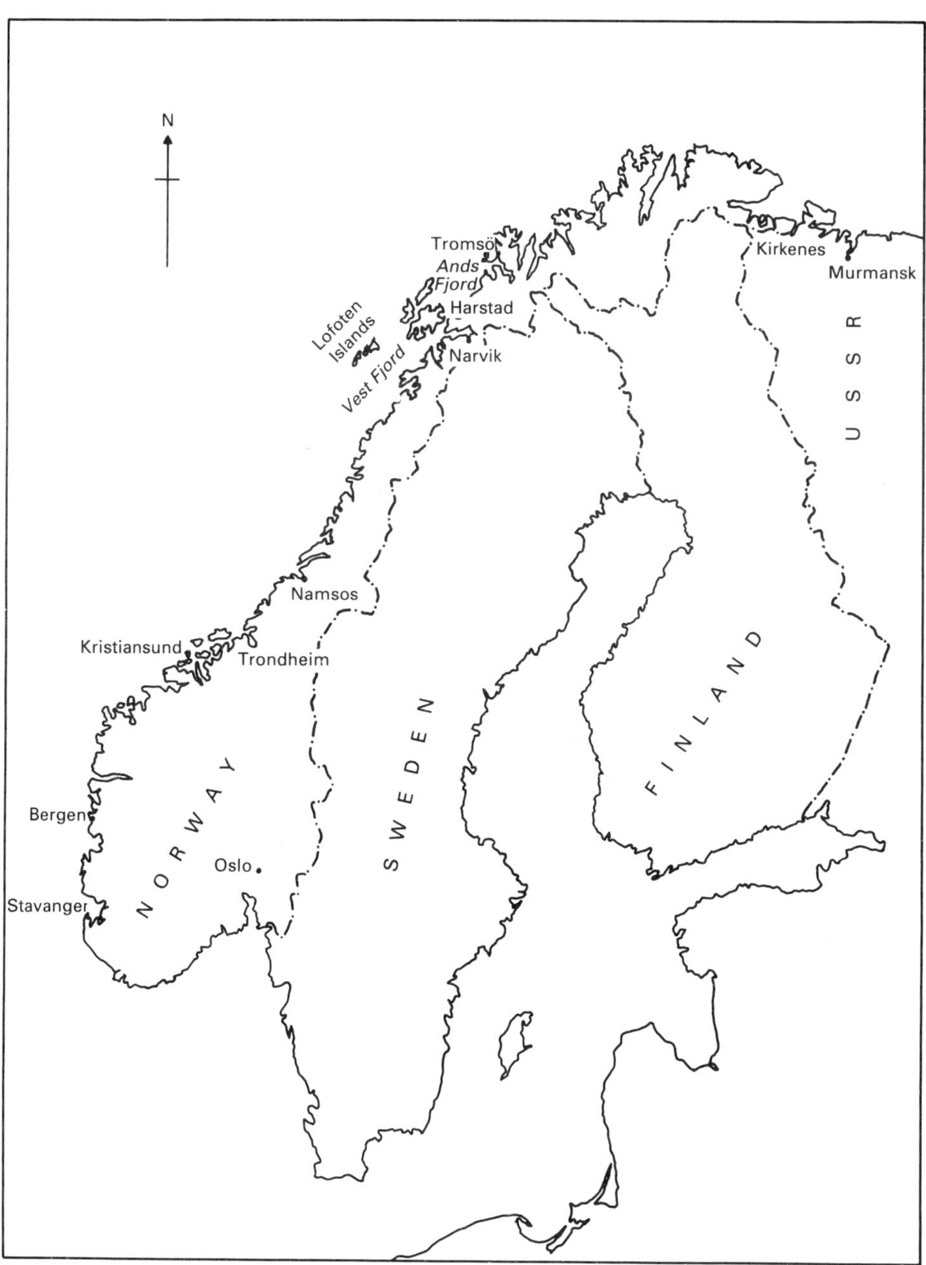
N
Tromsö
Ands
Fjord
Lofoten
Islands
Harstad
Narvik
Vest Fjord
Kirkenes
Murmansk
U S S R
Namsos
Kristiansund
Trondheim
SWEDEN
FINLAND
NORWAY
Bergen
Oslo
Stavanger

Norway

especially on the flanks; defence of shipping would be concerted with an offensive against Soviet maritime forces.

The Brosio study played through a theoretical Norwegian scenario, postulating an invasion of Northern Norway using amphibious and airborne forces. The Alliance used its warning time to bring carrier task forces into the Norwegian Sea, while anti-submarine barriers were set up in the Greenland-Iceland-Faroes-United Kingdom (GIUK) Gap and carrier and convoy escort units deployed in the Atlantic. When the shooting started, the Allied carrier aircraft attacked the Soviet invaders ashore and were engaged in combat by Soviet naval aviation. Most Soviet submarines were held back for defensive purposes and the barriers and convoy escorts defeated the residual attack on shipping. The Allies were able to rotate sufficient carriers into the Norwegian Sea both to defeat the attacks upon them at sea and to allow and ensure the successful interdiction of the land invasion of Norway. The assessment was that after a three month battle at sea, using conventional weapons alone, the war would be won and the Soviets would be faced with the choice of accepting defeat or mounting a major attack on the Central Front. At the Naval War College at Newport, war games began to be held under the name 'Establish Contact' in which a striking fleet of four American carriers and two British took on Soviet opposition in the Norwegian Sea. In the Norwegian Sea itself, in September 1972, Exercise 'Strong Express' saw an Anglo-American carrier striking fleet support an amphibious reinforcement of the defence of Northern Norway.[5]

The Brosio study had warned that although NATO could win a naval battle in 1968 the prospects for the future were less optimistic. Its authors feared that on these current trends, as Western maritime strength declined and Soviet strength increased, sea control in vital areas could no longer be assured in 1977. The reduction in the American carrier force and the disappearance of British strike carriers did indeed make NATO commanders less optimistic about taking on Soviet naval forces in the Norwegian Sea. Although the commitment to reinforce Norway in crisis and war remained, barrier operations at the GIUK Gap, rather than a forward carrier offensive, seemed to receive greater emphasis as the main complement to operations in the Atlantic itself. It even seemed possible that the Striking Fleet might have to go to the Mediterranean to reinforce depleted strength there. The Americans also looked as if they might be moving right away from their strike carrier strategy to build instead small 'sea control ships' to engage in anti-submarine warfare in the gaps and around the sea lines of communication themselves. This in turn reflected the development under Admiral Stansfield Turner's tutelage at the War College of new concepts of 'sea control' for limited time periods in limited areas that openly accepted that in the era of the submarine and aircraft, old fashioned command of the sea was unattainable. Even the ability of the Alliance to carry out amphibious operations against opposition began to be doubted at the highest level. Senior NATO naval commanders began to talk of 'pre-reinforcement' before the shooting started rather than reinforcement against the full might of the Northern Fleet.

In 1977, these doubts led NATO defence ministers to order a major reassessment of the Alliance's position at sea. There was a feeling that NATO's naval concepts were both ill defined and too reactive. Some felt that Western maritime strategy was in danger of becoming fixated with the 'Maginot Line' of the GIUK; a line, moreover, far to the west of Norway. Ministers ordered the Alliance's military commanders and their staffs to draw up a broad statement of principles of how maritime forces should be used in support of the overall NATO strategic concept and its governing principles of deterrence, forward defence and flexible response. The result was the drafting by three major NATO commands (MNCs) of the first edition of NATO's 'Concept of Maritime Operations' (CONMAROPS) that was drawn up in 1980 and approved by the Defence Planning Committee in 1981. This was a thorough-going assessment of the Alliance's maritime interests, the threats to those interests and the types of confrontation to be expected. It has been twice revised in the 1980s and has been used as the basis for revising the maritime contingency plans on a tri-MNC basis. NATO's maritime campaigns are to be conducted on the basis of three principles:

> *Containment*—offensive action to prevent Warsaw Pact forces deploying into open waters;
> *Defence in Depth*—putting the enemy at risk wherever he is operating, not only forward but throughout the NATO area;
> *Keeping the Initiative*—positioning forces early in crisis and handling them in war so that the enemy responds as much as possible to NATO moves rather than vice versa.[6]

This Alliance effort to some extent pre-dated the United States' own national reassessment of its maritime strategy: it certainly paralleled and interacted with that reassessment in a two way process. The American national strategic revision began when Admiral Thomas B Hayward was appointed Chief of Naval Operations (CNO) in 1978. In his previous appointment in the Pacific he had encouraged the development of a 'Sea Strike' concept based on the forward deployment of carrier forces against the periphery of the Soviet Union. On becoming CNO, Hayward brought this return to a more offensive orientation to Washington. He also reorganised the Navy's machinery for strategic planning, notably the creation of annual Strategic Studies Groups (SSGs) housed at the Naval War College. In their initial work in 1981-3, the SSGs looked specifically at the situation in Norway and adjacent waters and emphasised the need to capitalise on Soviet missions and sensitivities. By now, that is to say in the 1970s, the traditional Soviet passion for home defence had acquired a new dimension with the deployment of Soviet ballistic missile firing submarines (SSBNs) with intercontinental ranged missiles that were deployed in defended 'bastions' close to the Soviet Union. Threatening both its homeland bases and the SSBN bastions might well contain the Northern Fleet and keep it away from the Atlantic. This implied forward deployment: the SSGs also called for NATO's 'forward defence' concept to be fully applied at sea in order to get forces forward so that their deterrent effect was enhanced and they would be in the right place if deterrence failed.[7]

The key event in the formulation of the Maritime Strategy was when Lieutenant Commander Stan Weeks and Commander Spencer Johnson of the Navy's Strategic Concepts Branch (Op-603) in the Pentagon were tasked in 1982 with drafting a paper appraising how it was intended the United States Navy was to be used in war. Admiral William N Small, Vice Chief of Naval Operations and a major exponent himself of the need for a new coherence and offensive mindedness in Navy thinking, wanted the paper primarily as an aid in programming and budgeting: he wanted strategy to drive budgeting rather than vice versa. Weeks, the initial action officer, integrated the existing war plans of the United States Commanders-in-Chief, including those of the United States Atlantic Commander, Admiral Harry B Train, NATO's SACLANT into a coherent whole. Thus was existing thinking and planning, including NATO thinking, given a new coherence, emphasis and force. When presented with the Weeks-Johnson briefing in 1983, Admiral Watkins, just appointed CNO, was enthusiastic; his only rider was that it should not become too parochial but instead remain focused on cooperation with allies and the other services. This was after the publication of Robert W Komer's important article 'Maritime Strategy vs. Galition Defense' in the Summer 1982 edition of *Foreign Affairs* which centred its critique on the undue implied unilateralism in the new 'Maritime Strategy'. The internal briefing document thus became the 'Maritime Strategy'. The then Deputy CNO for Plans Policy and Operations, Rear Admiral Moreau, encouraged the new head of the Strategic Concepts Branch, Captain Roger Barnett, and the replacement for the Weeks-Johnson team, Commander Peter Swartz, to develop the thinking in the original paper into a broader statement of strategic priorities. Swartz continued Weeks' methodology of using current operational plans, including NATO defence plans, as his basic sources. When their thinking was briefed back to them, the American Commanders-in-Chief agreed that this was indeed what they had been about all along! The 'Maritime Strategy' was discussed in numerous classified briefings and continuously refined. As stated above, it appeared as a classified document in 1984, was briefed to Congress in open hearings in 1985, re-written by the staff and finally published in the CNO's department, over Admiral Watkins' name, at the beginning of 1986.

In this definitive form the 'Maritime Strategy' mapped out the United States Navy's roles in peacetime, crisis and war. Forward deployments of forces are the key to success in all these contexts. It was argued that they signify interest and a willingness to stand by allies in peace; in crisis they enhance deterrence and control escalation; and in the event of war, they allow the initiative to be seized and the enemy to be put on the defensive. Once seized, the initiative would be pressed home world wide, with carrier battle groups rolling up the Soviets on the flanks and Western attack submarines inflicting attrition on SSBNs. This pressure, it was hoped, would create sufficient leverage on the enemy for the conflict to be concluded on terms favourable to the West before the nuclear threshold was crossed.

The logic was not too different from the classified study of a decade before but 'the rigor inherent in codification', especially when combined with public articulation, proved too much for many. The latter tended to overlook that the emphasis in the Watkins' chapter was on the conventional aspects of extended deterrence and escalation control. For example:

> Although deterrence is most often associated with strategic nuclear warfare, it is a much broader concept. To protect national interests we must deter threats ranging from terrorism to nuclear war. This requires a credible peacetime and wartime capability at the level of conflict we need to deter. Our national interest also requires an extended deterrent capability. Perhaps most importantly, protecting national interests while preventing war requires an ability to control escalation, and naval forces and our peacetime strategy are ideally suited to that purpose.[8]

So far so good, but then readers were taken into the unfamiliar, and to some disturbing, waters of naval 'warfighting'. Phase I referred to 'Deterrence or the Transition to War':

> Through early, worldwide, decisive use of sea power we—along with sister services and allies as appropriate—would seek to win the crisis, to control escalation and, by the global nature of our operations, to make clear our intention to cede no area to the Soviets by default and to deny them the option to engage in hostilities on their terms. While seeking to enhance deterrence at the brink of war, we must also consider that deterrence may fail.[9]

Some thought that the 'early aggressive forward movement' of forces on a global scale called for in succeeding paragraphs might have precisely that unfortunate result, especially so as the next two sections on 'Seizing the Initiative' and 'Carrying the Fight to the Enemy' clearly envisaged an unremitting offensive from the 'battle of the first salvo' to favourable 'war termination'.[10]

The latter would be achieved by:

> firstly, horizontal escalation—'exerting global pressure, indicating that the conflict will be neither short nor localised'[11];
> secondly, threatening and carrying out direct attack against the Soviet homeland using both conventional air and missile strikes and even amphibious landings (In a related chapter General P X Kelly, Commandant of the Marine Corps, held out the beguiling prospect of a final phase in which 'Marine air ground task forces with supporting battleship surface action groups could land on the North Cape of the Eastern Baltic or Black Sea coasts, in the Kuriles or on Sakhalin Island—thereby adding a crucial measure of leverage to the conduct of the maritime campaign...'[12]);
> thirdly, (and most controversially) 'Changing the nuclear correlation and forces.' This would be done by writing down Soviet SSBNs in the anti-submarine warfare offensive and deploying nuclear capable carrier air and cruise missile forces around the Soviet Union.

Watkins took his opponents head on:

> Some argue that such steps will lead to immediate escalation, but escalation solely as a result of actions at sea seems improbable, given the Soviet land orientation. Escalation in response to maritime pressure serves no useful purpose for the Soviets since their reserve forces would be degraded and the United States retaliatory posture would be enhanced. Neither we nor the Soviets can rule out the possibility that escalation will occur, but aggressive use of maritime power can make escalation a less attractive option with the passing of every day.[13]

Watkins argued that the Soviets would find both nuclear escalation and prolonging the war 'unattractive' and they would hence come to terms. He concluded (some would say with some understatement) 'Our strategy is not without risk ... But', he went on, 'the risks exist for both sides, that is the nature of deterrence.' The problem, as John Mearsheimer has pointed out, is that, for a Soviet Union faced with immanent and imminent threat, or when faced with rapid attrition of its SSBN forces, the risks of *not* taking military action might seem to outweigh even the risks of striking first or otherwise escalating. The fundamental objection of the critics is that mounting an intensive and clearly articulated offensive threat to assets the Soviets value greatly, their SSBNs, their base infrastructure and their homeland in general, the Americans (and by extension NATO) have confronted the Soviets with precisely this destabilising dilemma. In a crisis, especially at sea, where the 'battle of the first salvo' is vital, the incentives for the Soviets to strike first might become overwhelming, perhaps even with nuclear weapons, despite Soviet pledges of 'no first use'.

The Soviets are clearly concerned about the 'Maritime Strategy'. The latter's supporters would argue they are meant to be, but concern can be counter-productive if it is based on misperception and results in outcomes that are negative in terms of the interests of those trying to create the concerns in the first place. Soviet colleagues constantly express their worries that the 'Lehman-Watkins Ocean Strategy' poses a pre-emptive threat to vital Soviet assets, not just their SSBNs and naval bases, but also their logistical infrastructure. Nuclear-capable carrier aircraft and missile carriers in relatively close proximity to the Soviet homeland create serious instabilities, they argue, especially as Soviet spokesmen have expressed concern over their inability to distinguish conventional from nuclear delivery systems at the point of launch.

Western naval commentators find it hard to comprehend this Soviet perspective, but it must be addressed if the 'Maritime Strategy' is to live up to the expectations of its authors. No one's interest, least of all the United States Navy's, would be served by rapid Soviet escalation. Indeed, as we have seen, the whole logic of the 'Maritime Strategy' depends on escalation not taking place. The effectiveness of the forward strategy, therefore, depends on the tempering of Superpower and NATO: Warsaw Pact rivalry at sea with a confidence building régime of some kind to allay the worst Soviet fears and demonstrate the strategically and even operationally defensive aspects of the forward strategy, as exercised in practice.

Some American naval spokesmen give a highly misleading impression. Vice Admiral Henry C Mustin is perhaps the best example. This ebullient officer did much to increase the effectiveness of the Second Fleet but his writings demonstrate the intellectual confusion that has led the Navy to score some 'own goals' in the Maritime Strategy debate. He argues for the forward strategy as an alternative to a 'passive convoy escort navy posture' which it is not (neither is convoy escort 'passive') and he confuses the 'offensive' with the 'initiative', something Sir Julian Corbett was warning against in his lectures to British officers before the First World War.[14] Mustin's emphasis on the conventional 'punishment' aspects of the forward strategy is equally counter-productive:

> ... deterrence with conventional forces must contain a credible threat of retaliation with non-nuclear means against targets that the Soviets value enough to give them pause ... If the Striking Fleet is to be an element of conventional deterrence, it must be in a position to deliver convincing retaliation to Soviet adventurism. This retaliation by definition must include strikes into the Kola—the maritime equivalent of the 'Deep Strike' concept for the land battle.[15]

SACEUR would not see 'Deep Strike' as conventional punishment, rather it is defensive or 'denial', helping the land battle by dealing with 'follow-on forces'. The Soviets are concerned enough about SACEUR's definition of Follow On Forces Attack (FOFA). Even more, they see Admiral Mustin's definition of 'deep strike' as a destabilising, offensive threat to their command and control. To add to this misperception seems less than wise, especially as the ability of naval forces to mount early and decisive 'deep strikes' would be very limited. Carriers only carry one squadron of A-6 all weather strike aircraft each: the striking power of TLAM-C Tomahawks is also rather low. No wonder the Soviets see a hidden nuclear agenda behind such claims.

What makes an emphasis on 'conventional punishment' so counter-productive is that the nature of the actual, exercised forward strategy is the use of naval power as a vital adjunct to deterrence by traditional 'conventional denial'. Recent NATO maritime exercises have indeed reasserted the role of the carrier striking fleet but in a way that promises protracted hostilities, not pre-emptive strikes. Since 1985, NATO's Striking Fleet has been experimenting with putting carriers into Norwegian fjords, where they are better able to fight off the expected Soviet submarine and air attacks. The areas where this tactic is exercised, Vestfjord and Andfjord, are forward enough, but not that far forward. Carrier and amphibious forces deployed in these areas are able to give aid to the defence of Northern Norway and create sufficient concerns for the Soviets to hold back forces to deal with them. Their prime role, however, is to act as bait to force the Soviets to attack them in unfavourable circumstances rather than to act as an overwhelming striking force in themselves. True, the latent threat of the Striking Fleet might still tempt a massive pre-emptive strike. Yet, the moderate level of the offensive Western threat deployed (NATO would be lucky to muster a Striking Fleet in the early stages of a crisis of three carriers); the Soviets' perception of the capacity of their own defenses using conventional forces alone to deal with the threat posed by the Striking Fleet and, not least, the Soviet 'no first use' doctrine, should all combine to maintain stability. The Striking Fleet would thus be able to carry out its key roles of demonstrating Alliance solidarity and forcing the Soviets to hold back most of their maritime strike assets in a defensive posture.

The United States Navy is now taking the opportunity of a change in Administration to clarify the real meaning of forward operations. It does not need to retract; just explain that it does not regard pre-emptive strikes from the sea against Soviet targets as being practical. This is particularly the case with the submarine battle. The dynamics of submarine vs. submarine warfare are such that rapid destruction of SSBNs is impossible. At the most, there might be slow attrition in a shooting war, but that need not lead to premature nuclear release by either side. The Soviets fully understand the potential of conventional forces to manipulate the nuclear balance: after all they invented the concept of 'multivariate operations' on land.

Bilateral American-Soviet discussions on naval doctrine would also be helpful. But eventually the United States Navy is soon going to have to face reality and accept the need for some formal régime of confidence and security building measures (CSBM) at sea. Advance warning of large naval exercises might prevent misunderstandings or sudden disturbing deployments of multiple carrier battle groups. Building such a CSBM régime will probably be a necessary accompaniment to progress in the Conventional Forces in Europe (CFE) Talks in Vienna (see Chapter 8). The West can reasonably claim special maritime needs given the asymmetry of its dependence on sea communications. But it can hardly expect the Soviet Union to reduce its offensive threat on land to Western Europe if it retains a self-consciously offensive operational doctrine at sea.

As force levels on land come down, either as a result of unilateral cuts or multilateral arms control, so the importance of maritime forces will clearly rise. Reinforcement capacity, in NATO's case the ability to move ships across the Atlantic, will become much more important. Defending this shipping will still require some forward operations, corresponding to the battlefleet of old, to tie down as many Soviet assets as possible in defence. Moreover, the forces that would be available at the outset of a crisis, notably carrier battle groups and amphibious warfare forces, are likely to be those that lend themselves to power projection rather than defensive sea control. The likely decline in the United States Navy's funding is going to make this even more the case than it is at present. Although the number of carrier battle groups will decline marginally, the main cuts in forces will probably come in numbers of frigates, whose main role is convoy protection. NATO's need for a forward maritime strategy will, therefore, be confirmed but it must be carefully and sensitively re-articulated and adjusted to reflect the changes in the context of East-West relations.

The main future roles of naval forces in underpinning extended deterrence are thus the synergistic projection of conventional power to the flanks and the maintenance of Atlantic sea lines of communication so that conventional hostilities can be continued as long as required. This role is vital on the Southern Flank as well as the Northern. Geography means that Greece and Turkey depend on sea communications in crisis and war and two of the five 'campaigns' in CONMAROPS 'Eastern Mediterranean' and 'Mediterranean Lifelines' are devoted to defending this shipping. The Sixth Fleet carriers have also been important sources of mobile high quality air power since the late 1940s, and amphibious reinforcement would still be vital to the defence of Thrace.

Some argue that maritime forces might also play a larger role in maintaining nuclear uncertainty throughout the European theatre. The decision to dismantle ground-launched cruise missiles (GLCM) and Pershing II has led to suggestions that naval forces might 'substitute' with sea launched cruise missiles (SLCMs). I have a number of reservations about such a policy:

Sea launched systems lack the direct theatre relevance required to fulfil the role of 'linking' events in that theatre to the overall strategic nuclear balance.

The requirement to maintain sea launched systems on station would reduce and constrict the necessary and inherent flexibility of the missile platforms, all of which have more important alternative conventional roles.

Emphasising the theatre nuclear role of maritime forces might encourage the maintenance of pre-emptive doctrines of Soviet naval nuclear use. The pressures on the Soviet Navy to denuclearise their thinking should be enhanced not the opposite.

Rather than emphasise the nuclear role of naval forces it would be better, as Paul Nitze has reportedly suggested, to move towards mutual naval denuclearisation (except Submarine Launched Ballistic Missiles (SLBMs)). This is clearly in the West's interest. In the words of the United States Naval War College's first Strategic Studies Group Director: 'the use of nuclear weapons at sea appears to be to our clear disadvantage'.[16] Given the perceived nuclear threats posed to the Sovet Union from the sea by United States' naval forces, there seems to be scope here for some interesting and constructive trading. The United States Navy might argue that a latent nuclear threat is an essential means of posing sufficient concerns to the Soviets for them to care enough about the forward deployment of maritime forces for them to take the bait. The Soviets, however, also make it clear that they see the problems that might be posed for them by improved means of conventional attack from the sea. Relying on the latter should, therefore, be sufficient to create the significant 'concerns' upon which the logic of a forward strategy rests. These can, and must, be distinguished from dangerous, destabilising 'threats'.

A proposal to denuclearise navies would be firmly within the logic developed in the 'Maritime Strategy'. For, as this chapter has tried to show, it was a pioneering attempt to think through the dynamics of extended deterrence in a post-nuclear age, an age in which nuclear weapons have not gone away but in which they are regarded as having little or no operational utility and in which their overall deterrent effect is, therefore, more subtle and elusive. In a world where the perceived outcome of a conventional war is as important as the prospect of nuclear war, if not more so, concepts of conventional warfighting in general, and maritime warfighting in particular, must play a central part in maintaining the strategic links between the United States and her allies.

Those links are not abstract 'sea lines of communication', to use that most misleading term. They are made up of discrete units, ships, which themselves must be available if the provision of means of defence is not to become pointless. Given the decline in NATO's merchant fleets touched on in the previous chapter, real doubts have arisen over the availability of shipping for maritime purposes. This could significantly undermine deterrence. It is this fundamental maritime question that we must now examine more closely.

CHAPTER 3

The Atlantic Link—NATO's Merchant Fleets and Extended Deterrence

As the last chapter has shown, nuclear weapons will in the future play a *relatively* reduced role in NATO's overall deterrence strategy. The likely results of first use, rapid and uncontrollable escalation to a full scale nuclear exchange significantly diminish the credibility of nuclear deterrence to a purely conventional attack. Credible deterrence must therefore rely primarily upon a robust conventional capability. As the CFE talks reduce current Warsaw Pact preponderance, NATO's land and air commanders will be able to destroy any initial conventional thrust without nuclear escalation. Then what? Hostilities may well continue. Certainly some *capacity* to continue hostilities at a conventional level must underpin the 'counter-blitzkrieg' front line, just as it may be backed up by a capability not to resort to nuclear weapons. This implies the maintenance of the ability to muster, man and operate *ships* to bring in not just military supplies and reinforcements but also economic supplies to maintain a minimum wartime living standard for NATO's peoples and to sustain war production, as required by the course of hostilities. Europe is not self-sufficient and as pointed out in Chapter 1, Western Europe is heavily dependent on seaborne oil for its total energy supplies, 30 per cent, compared to the United States' 16.6 per cent.

Moreover, it is not just a question of a 'long war'. NATO's capacity to respond adequately to the *initial* attack depends crucially on the safe and timely arrival of the maximum number of transatlantic reinforcements. Almost all the men can come by air. Virtually all the equipment, if not pre-positioned, must come by sea, in ships. The current NATO plan calls for 30 American and Canadian combat brigades, 100 air squadrons and 300,000 men to be brought across the Atlantic in the first 30 days after the decision to reinforce is taken ('R'-Day). By R + 180 no less than 1.5 million men, 8.5 million tons of ammunition and stores and 15 million short tons of fuel should have been transported to Europe. Other military forces require a further 7.2 million tons of cargo and 9.6 million short tons of petroleum products over the same timetable, making a total reinforcement and resupply demand of 40.2 million tons. In addition to this, about 100,000 military personnel, 25,000 tons of *materiel* and perhaps 20,000 vehicles have to be transported from the United Kingdom to Europe.[1] Ninety-eight per cent of personnel can be airlifted, but, even with the pre-positioning of significant amounts of heavy equipment in Europe, 90 per cent of equipment and supplies must go by sea. Shortages of aircraft and congestion problems at airfields as well as the limited cargo loads of most transports put significant constraints on reinforcement airlift.

According to EASTLANT's figures, the whole 180 day reinforcement and resupply plan demands 3,045 shiploads.[2] At the SeaLink Conference in Annapolis in 1986 Admiral Baggett, the Supreme Allied Commander Atlantic (SACLANT), gave slightly different figures; 400 shiploads per month for military reinforcement and 400 for resupply. These figures, however, only refer to the early weeks of reinforcement, when the demand is at its highest.[3] One would, therefore, expect military demand to be something in the order of 800 shiploads per month arriving between R and R + 60 and reducing to about 350 shiploads per month for the next 120 days.

It must be emphasised that these are figures for 'shiploads' and not ships. Some cargoes are solid and some liquid: certain items can be carried in some ships without significant modification and not in others; ships vary greatly in size and carrying capacity. Notional shiploads are thus used by planners as a unit of measurement of sealift demand not necessarily a requirement for the same number of hulls. The above figures may also understate future demand. A 'Sealift Study' is currently under way which will probably increase demand further.

SACLANT also stated at the 1986 SeaLink Conference, that 'the United States and the European Allies are each committed to providing 600 ships' for military reinforcement and replenishment ('Re-Re') purposes.[4] These 1,200 vessels are presumably considered able to deal with the 3,045 shiploads *on the required timescale*. It gives therefore a useful standard against which to compare figures of shipping availability published at around the same time.

In relating supply to demand, it must be made clear at the outset precisely which ships are being considered. Not all ships are of the right kind or are likely to be in the right place. Both the United States and European NATO take special measures to ensure the availability of the correct kinds of ships when and where required. It is these vessels that are considered in the paragraphs below. The key is *availability* and type, not total shipping capacity. Indeed it is availability of the right types in the first 60 days that are the critical parameters.

Over the last decade, the United States government has built up both an operational sealift fleet, controlled by its Military Sealift Command, and a Ready Reserve Fleet of rapidly mobilisable vessels. It has approached American shipowners to commit a proportion of their ships to requisitioning in time of emergency, within 60 days of mobilisation. This scheme also includes some American-owned vessels under flags of convenience. Finally some of the old ships of the large 'National Defense Reserve Fleet' are capable of mobilisation within 60-90 days. This provides an available sealift fleet that seems to meet the NATO requirement—but only just.

According to the Joint Chiefs of Staff (JCS) 'Posture Statement' for the Fiscal Year (FY) 1987 the United States had the following funded resources available for military sealift purposes:[5]

TABLE 3.1 *United States Funded Resources Available for Military Sealift*

	Dry Cargo	*Tankers*	*Total*
Military Sealift Command (Directly Controlled)	13	21	34
Military Sealift Command (Reduced Operating Status)	8	—	8
US Flag Merchant Ships	184	112	296
Flags of Convenience Ships (Effective US Control)	27	64	91
Ready Reserve Fleet (5-10 days notice)	70	9	79
National Defence Reserve Fleet (Those remaining in 60-90 days)	137	6	143
	439	212	651

Two points about these figures are noteworthy:

1. There was less than a 10 per cent margin over the NATO requirement for 600 American ships.
2. The above total covered all possible immediate US sealift requirements, including the Pacific and the Middle East as well as NATO.

These considerations would lead to the conclusion that American sealift capabilities are currently at best marginal and at worst inadequate. Certainly the need for NATO Europe to make a significant contribution to its own reinforcement is as great, if not greater, than ever before.

In 1973 the United States entered into an agreement with NATO to increase the availability of Allied shipping in the event of a major reinforcement operation. Hence a list was prepared of suitable NATO flag ships which normally frequented American east coast ports and which were earmarked in peacetime to facilitate acquisition in rising tension or transition to war. The ships were considered available to the United States when the North Atlantic Council requested reinforcements. In the late 1970s, the European Allies agreed to increase their commitment to *400 dry cargo vessels*. In order to ensure the timely availability of the 400, given refit requirements etc, a 50 per cent margin was considered desirable; hence the figure of 600 dry cargo ships, which the United States includes in its current JCS figures and which SACLANT mentioned in 1986.[6]

European NATO's 'Sealift Ship List', as administered by NATO's Planning Board for Ocean Shipping (PBOS), includes bulkers, tankers and passenger ships as well as the vital general dry cargo vessels.[7] In 1987 it comprised the following:

TABLE 3.2 *European NATO's Resources Available for Military Sealift*

Vessel Type	*Number*	*Total Deadweight tonnage (DWT)*	*Percentage of Total Tonnage*
GENERAL DRY CARGO			
Breakbulk			
Freighter	163	2,743,902	28.2
Partial Containership	9	151,262	1.6
Refrigerated Ship	8	93,387	1.0
Barge Carriers	3	65,373	0.7
Total	**183**	**3,053,924**	**31.4**
Container			
Non-self-sustaining	106	3,475,349	35.8
Self-sustaining	86	1,992,305	20.5
Total	**192**	**5,467,654**	**56.3**
Roll-on/Roll-off			
Ro-Ro (standard)	36	739,182	7.6
Container/Ro-Ro	37	458,530	4.7
Total	**73**	**1,197,712**	**12.3**
DRY BULK CARRIERS			
Geared—under 50,000 DWT	6	163,691	
Geared over 50,000 DWT	1	50,299	
Gearless	1	28,078	
	8	242,078	
Total Dry Cargo Ships	**456**	**9,961,368**	
PASSENGER SHIPS (TOTAL)	**11***	**53,421**	
TANKERS			
Product	51	1,739,880	
Chemical	10	270,820	
Liquid Petroleum Gas	1	9,065	
Liquid Natural Gas	2	24,974	
Total	**64**	**2,044,739**	
Grand Total	**531**	**12,059,528**	

Note: * 4 Norwegian, 2 German, 2 Italian, 2 British, 1 Dutch

Over the previous year the number of dry cargo vessels had come down by 50 hulls net, the number of passenger ships by 5 (transferred to the Bahamian register) and the number of tankers by one. Europe is not expected to provide tankers to the main Re-Re task and the limited number of tankers on the list is up to the stated requirement. The passenger ship list is however below the requirement as, most importantly, is the key dry cargo list.

There has been a little improvement in the situation since the 1987 list was produced. Both Norway and Denmark have produced new 'captive registers' with less demanding requirements for inclusion. In its 1987 report, PBOS drew attention to these captive registers and ships flying flags of convenience as possible candidates for inclusion on the Sealift Ship List. Some 50 suitable Norwegian vessels, including 38 formerly on the list were then registered under flags of convenience. The Board noted that non-NATO crews were no bar to adding ships to the Sealift Ship List as preparations could be made to replace non-NATO crews 'to the extent practicable' when the ships were taken up in an emergency. The 1988 PBOS list showed an increase of dry cargo ships to 473 and passenger vessels to 12; tankers were reduced to 62.[8] Nevertheless the central fact remains that the dry cargo tonnage is still well below the desired margin: the safety surplus is only 18 per cent not 50 per cent as intended. The loss of margin is especially serious, given the crucial importance of speed of mobilisation. There is thus no exaggeration in claiming that *a significant shortfall in NATO Europe's military sealift contribution currently exists.* In its 1986 Report PBOS clearly stated its concern that the needs of the Alliance could not be met in all circumstances.

An official study is currently in train on NATO's demand for shipping to maintain wartime economic activity in Europe and North America. Short term economic disruption would be inevitable and probably acceptable but large-scale shipping movement would certainly need to be continued if hostilities were prolonged beyond a week. Demand for luxury goods would disappear but demand for some essentials, for example, oil and gas to replace lost North Sea supplies, might well increase. The 'Study of Supply and Demand for Merchant Shipping in Crisis and War' being carried out under the auspices of NATO's Senior Civil Emergency Planning Committee (SCEPC) will report in 1990. Until this is done estimates of economic shipping demand, either in terms of shiploads or ships, can only be 'guestimated' at best. In 1987 Deputy SACLANT estimated NATO (including United States) monthly economic shipping requirements at 1,500 shiploads carrying between 90 and 110 million tons of cargo.[9] As far as ships are concerned, an unofficial American study published in 1983 assessed the annual economic shipping requirement at 515 for North America and 892 for NATO Europe. These 1,400 vessels seemed to be all bulk carriers bringing in supplies of oil, bauxite, and other non-ferrous ores, iron ore, phosphates, cement, sugar, salt, fertiliser, gypsum, wood products and similar cargoes and for Europe grain and coal. The study contained the following table:[10]

TABLE 3.3 *Annual Economic Shipping Requirements for North America and NATO Europe*

	United States Ships (Million DWT cargo capacity)		*Yearly imports (million metric tonnes)*	*NATO/Europe Ships (Million DWT cargo capacity)*		*Yearly Imports (million metric tonnes)*
Crude Oil	37.4	299	290	63.1	69	570
Bauxite	2.3	95	25	0.7	25	6
Iron Ore	0.7	6	20	12.2	107	120
Phosphate	0.3	15	5	1.5	85	22
Other Bulk	3.0	515	25	10.9	363	110
Grain	—	—	—	3.7	131	45
Coal	—	—	—	7.8	112	75
Total	**43.7**	**930**	**365**	**99.9**	**892**	**948**

The cargo total corresponds with the SACLANT figures, but the shipping total seems to reflect rather more optimistic assumptions about ship utilisation. One might reduce Europe's shipping demands compared to the above figures given the end of dependence on imported grain and reduced oil imports compared to the late 1970s but wartime energy imports are difficult to calculate, given the uncertain fate of North Sea oil supplies in war.

In 1986, SACLANT stated that the pool of ships declared to the NATO Defence Shipping Authority for possible use in war totalled some 5,500 vessels larger than 1,600 DWT, a decrease of 2,000 ships over the previous five years. This figure is often mis-used to over-state the availability of shipping. It pays no regard to rapid availability and is therefore irrelevant to discussions of Re-Re requirements in the early stages of a conflict. All it covers is the ships that it is hoped will eventually be available to the Defense Shipping Agency (DSA) in wartime. It includes Flag of Convenience (FOC) vessels with no legal obligation for them to be made available in an emergency. Indeed there is not even the obligation to make national flag ships available. It is probable that currently there are enough vessels in the DSA Pool to cover economic shipping requirements but one cannot be certain and, given the continued decline of NATO members' fleets, this situation will not continue for long. In its 1986 report, PBOS clearly stated that the trend in world shipping showed a NATO Alliance dependent on shipping not owned by Alliance members to meet critical needs in an emergency, including transatlantic reinforcement and resupply. This is still the situation today.[11]

In future, a steadily higher proportion of Western ships will probably be flying the flags of neutral or non-aligned states, even if they are owned by companies registered in NATO countries, or with majority shareholdings in the West. A high proportion of the merchant ships owned by the United States, United Kingdom, Federal Republic of Germany and Norway fly foreign flags. As noted above, procedures exist for requisitioning such ships but they sometimes raise tricky legal problems. Moreover, a potential enemy is bound to perceive an alliance without its own *national* means of carrying vital reinforcements and supplies as suffering a major weakness; this seriously undermines deterrence. Currently, the Warsaw Treaty Organisation seems to assess NATO's reinforcement capabilities as satisfactory, and its reliance on the sea rather than land communications as a positive advantage. This assessment, however, is explicitly based on an assumption of the availability of shipping that might disappear if NATO flags were no longer seen on the world's oceans.

Manning is also a serious and growing problem as national fleets decline. A serious fall is taking place in the numbers of western seamen. Between 1982 and 1988, for example, the number of qualified UK 'seafarers' fell by over half. The figures are as follows (in 1,000s):

	1975	*1988*
Officers	25.1	9.6
Ratings	25.2	13.6

The decline in officers and officer cadets is especially worrying. In 1982, there were over 4,000 deck and engineer cadets; today there are only just over 400.[12]

Mismatches of ships to tasks also create problems. Containers, for example, can only carry about a third of all military supplies and equipment and container ships require highly specialised port facilities or mobile/self-loading/unloading gear that might not be available. This puts a new emphasis on turn-round times, historically a factor limiting optimal utilisation of available shipping. Many modern merchantmen are large and face port restrictions because of their deep draught. Moreover, the types of ship most suitable for supporting military operations, for example, roll on/roll off vessels, break bulk 'dry cargo' ships and barge carriers are in short supply throughout the world despite the chronic problem of overtonnage.

The current marginal situation, notably in assigned Re-Re shipping, leaves little in reserve to cover attrition, which might well be substantial. Moreover, the use of larger hulls to carry multiple shiploads creates extra vulnerability to single hits.

Military requirements are too often seen solely in terms of ships taken up from trade (STUFT) for direct naval purposes. Ships so utilised cannot be used for their primary transport function and could be a significant drain on vital shipping resources, especially the fast cargo liners vital for reinforcement and resupply. There is no double accounting between the Sealift Shipping List and the naval STUFT plans but, as fleets continue to decline, the pressure on diminished resources will become acute.

The disturbing conclusions of the above are as follows:

In order to fulfil current rapid reinforcement and resupply plans, SACLANT has stated a need for 1,200 ships for the initial stages of a conflict.

On current figures, the Alliance does not have sufficient suitable hulls on its lists of readily available vessels.

There are virtually no American ships on the current sealift list available for global non-NATO military sealift purposes if NATO's full initial demands are fulfilled.

These shortfalls are likely to become more serious as NATO flag merchant fleets continue their precipitate decline.

NATO may soon have to rely, even for reinforcement and resupply, on ships not even owned by NATO nationals.

The demand for economic shipping will probably also outstrip supply, given the above demands for military sealift and the additional requirement for naval auxiliaries. The West's mercantile marines are not a bottomless bran tub from which resources can be plucked without limit.

The Warsaw Pact cannot but notice the disappearance of NATO flags from the world oceans and draw appropriate strategic conclusions.

Even if ships are available, reliable personnel to man them may not be.

Modern Western merchant ships, even if available, may not be of the right type to fulfil the tasks required.

There is little or no margin for attrition in NATO's current merchant shipping assets. Tempting vulnerabilities are being created for hostile naval action.

Although it is unrealistic and, indeed, undesirable to try to reverse the growing internationalisation of maritime activities, shipping can never be an entirely free market activity, if for no other reason than that non-capitalist economies are substantial participants in it. Merchant fleets are important 'defence resources' for NATO that might completely wither away if abandoned to the vagaries of a complex set of distorted 'market forces'. Adam Smith himself clearly recognised that the national security requirement made shipping a special case in his free market economy. He expressed approval of the contemporary British Government's navigation acts sustaining the national mercantile marine. Various forms of government support need to be considered, as appropriate, on both a national and multilateral basis. These measures need not undermine merchant shipping's status as a commercial activity: tax incentives and/or 'pump priming' investment in research and development would avoid the potentially negative effects of simple subsidy. Other possibilities are help on crew costs and the relief of the social overhead attached.

Reduced American (and Canadian) force levels on the European Continent will result from future CFE agreements. Such cuts need to be managed to minimise the need for increased transatlantic supply, for example, by leaving behind equipment stockpiles under suitable maintenance and verification arrangements. Nevertheless, even forces reduced in numbers would have such improvements in their firepower that demands for munitions and other expendable supplies would be maintained at relatively high levels. Changes in force posture and improvements in capability might well increase the demand for shipping rather than the opposite.

In their FY 1987 'Posture Statement' the United States Joint Chiefs of Staff suggested that NATO might consider setting up a reserve of merchant ships on the lines of the United States Ready Reserve Fleet. This might be a pool of privately owned vessels or a reserve owned by member states, either individually or collectively. The question of funding, for acquisition and maintenance of ships and infrastructure and long-term availability of crews needs careful study. Special care would have to be taken to give such a fleet proper maintenance and the relative costings of a state owned 'mothball fleet' *vis-à-vis* supporting active commercial shipping in various ways would need careful assessment.

Alternatively, or in addition, NATO members, either nationally or jointly, must set up more organised reserves of ex-seafarers, with suitable measures and inducements for their skills to be maintained. Britain has set up a Merchant Navy Reserve to provide a pool of experienced seafarers in emergency and is making contributions to British seafarers' training and travel costs in order to encourage the retention of British nationals on board British vessels. Again, a balance must be struck between reserves and encouraging commercial seafaring, but a ready reserve of crews would be especially useful in boosting the PBOS Sealift Ship List with beneficially owned flag of convenience vessels.

Naval authorities in NATO are understandably reluctant to espouse heavy expenditure on merchant shipping as they fear a loss of funds from 'military' fleets. The latter, however, exist in large part to maintain the ability of ships to carry cargoes of various kinds over the sea. The correct balance must therefore be maintained, for without merchant ships the military navies would lose a large part of their *raison d'être* as well as a useful ready reserve of both combatant and support vessels in emergency.

It is essential that what shipping stock is available to the Alliance should be properly exploited. Ships used to convey military cargoes should be used, if possible, to convey economic cargoes on other legs of their voyages. Ballast voyages must be avoided as far as practicable. This implies an effective and integrated NATO control of shipping organisation, fully exploiting modern techniques of control and communication.

Available shipping must be made more suitable for the Re-Re task. As the 1986 PBOS report put it, 'One critical requirement is to make the best use of modern container ships by the provision of flat racks, sea sheds, self-gearing, mobile cranes and temporary staging areas.' It announced a PBOS survey 'of the present availability of such equipment and the likely future needs'. This might lead to a NATO-funded programme aimed at ensuring the availability at suitable locations of appropriate equipment. PBOS also recommended that:

> where they have not already done so, military and civil authorities in NATO maritime countries should develop sufficient and economical procedures for carrying non-containerisable military unit equipment in cellular container ships. Similarly, the authorities should vigorously pursue systematic planning for the wartime employment of alternative systems and procedures for off-loading containers where container port facilities are absent or inoperable.[13]

Ways should also be studied of using bulk carriers for military supply. Such vessels can be used to carry general cargo both in the holds on top of the bulk cargo and on the large deck/hatch areas. Temporary wooden spar decks can be built in the holds and/or substantial amounts of dunnage used. Skilful cargo planning and stevedoring can overcome the problems posed by the basic lack of suitability of these vessels; these might require special training.

Legal measures to allow the return of flags of convenience ships to the owning states need to be further investigated, improved and standardised, preferably on an Alliance-wide basis. The problem of using foreign-*owned* as well as flagged vessels also needs attention, and, perhaps even more so, the use of non-NATO nationals as crew members.

The current political signal to the potential opponent may not be sent unless sufficient merchant ships wear the national flags of NATO members. This may not entail fulfilling *all* assessed wartime shipping demands with national flag ships but the lack of a substantial core fleet clearly in Alliance hands would cast serious doubts over Alliance resolve. The size of that core fleet and the effort made to sustain it, in comparison with the other aspects of overall security policy, needs careful study. Ships under quasi-national flags (for example, the Isle of Man) should be included by the authorities more clearly as NATO vessels. Governments might make such flags more attractive to national owners than the more usual flags of convenience. The new Norwegian International Ship register is a fruitful new initiative that could provide useful extra ships for the Sealift Ship List. If it proves impracticable to make the national flag sufficiently attractive, other countries might follow Norway's example.

In all these measures, the correct balance between sustaining the campaign and winning the initial defensive battles must always be maintained. Nevertheless, just as effective conventional forward defence makes maritime reinforcement relevant, maritime reinforcement makes conventional forward defence possible and worthwhile. And without a robust conventional forward defence, NATO's overall deterrent will cease to deter.

A global war would put an enormous strain on merchant shipping resources to sustain the various campaigns as well as the Allied national war efforts. Wartime shipping requirements are always greatly underestimated in peacetime. This was clearly the case in World War II, when serious difficulties and shortages were faced, despite the cushion of easy access to the world's largest fleets. As Captain Roskill succinctly put it:

> Every strategic purpose conceived by the Allies, and every operation which they planned and executed was conditioned and controlled—and too often restricted—by the difficulty of providing the necessary shipping...[14]

Those who forget the lessons of history are condemned to repeat them.

CHAPTER 4

Europe's Premier Navy: Problems and Prospects

The United Kingdom's current naval position is rather more a result of her past position of naval supremacy at the centre of the greatest of the maritime empires of the 'Age of Vasco da Gama' than it is of current strategic priorities as defined by Defence Secretary Nott in 1981 in the infamous *Command 8288.* The first three of these priorities, which still form the 'pillars' of Mrs Thatcher's defence policy are: strategic nuclear deterrence; home defence; a contribution to the defence of Continental Europe. All three have a naval component: ballistic missile submarines; mine countermeasures vessels; the amphibious reinforcement of NATO's Northern Flank. Nevertheless, the 'real' navy is primarily concerned with the defence of Atlantic communications, the fourth and least important perceived priority.

It is clear from Sir John Nott's more recent writings that the Royal Navy's leaders were completely unsuccessful in 1981 in arguing a convincing enough case for their overall posture in the Eastern Atlantic. This is perhaps partly understandable. In 1981 the NATO concept of Maritime Operations was only just appearing and the American Maritime Strategy was not yet in place to provide a new strategic and operational coherence to Alliance naval thought. Nowadays, official British Ministry of Defence spokesmen are only too ready to emphasise the Royal Navy's commitment to the 'forward strategy'. In 1989, Britain's impressive force of nuclear-powered attack submarines (SSNs) is only one boat short of the 1981 reduced planning total of 17 with the delivery of HMS *Trenchant.* Indeed, it seems that the latter figure has been increased to 18 boats. These assets are available to join the American SSNs in forward operations. HMS *Talent* will join the fleet in 1990 and one more boat, HMS *Triumph* is on order. Design work has already begun on a new SSN 20 class boat to continue replacement of the old 1960s vintage Valiants and Churchills in the 1990s but, because of the Trident 'cuckoo in the nest', it now seems that construction of these new attack submarines will be delayed. Some long term reduction of the British SSN total cannot therefore be ruled out.

Britain has begun the construction of a new class of conventional submarines, the Upholder class, for Continental Shelf operations and is refitting nine of the quarter century old Oberons. Whether this is the best use of scarce assets is a moot point. It is true that conventional boats are required for training and useful for special forces insertion, but given the ever quieter trend in Soviet submarine performance, the types of passive sonar anti-submarine warfare (ASW) operation for which conventional submarines are currently most useful seem to be of diminishing utility. If there ever was a case for NATO role specialisation it is in the submarine area.

This is especially important given the continued vital importance of the Royal Navy's surface fleet to NATO's maritime strategy and therefore the need to continue relatively heavy investment in it. One problem in justifying such heavy expenditure is the lack of clearly defined force goals.

Beyond a commitment to 'about 50' frigates and destroyers there is little more specific guidance. This reflects an understandable requirement for flexibility in actual operational allocation of units, but it does not provide a firm basis for maintaining force size. All that 'about 50' means is that this is the currently affordable contribution to whatever NATO roles happen to be required in a crisis. Logically, therefore, if other more specific defence priorities seem more pressing, there is nothing to stop Britain being satisfied with bringing her total of frigates and destroyers down to 40, 30, 20 or even less.

If the case for the surface fleet is to be properly defined and made, we need to be much more specific. Ships need to be related to specific groups, deployments and tasks whose importance can then be judged against other priorities, both within the overall naval force posture and the whole defence budget. This does *not* necessarily mean that one is tied to specific scenarios. It is an inherent and very attractive feature of naval forces—surface ships in particular—that they are so flexible. Nevertheless, it is stated in Ministry of Defence statements that NATO roles and tasks drive current force sizing and planning. A coherent official exposition of how assets would in all probability be related to those roles and tasks in crisis and in war would thus help to create an informed debate about the adequacy or otherwise of the United Kingdom's naval force provision. It might also provide a basis for firmer and more secure in-house planning.

One marked feature of recent British history has been the absence of discussion of maritime strategy and operational doctrine. This is now changing, thanks to the all-pervading influence of the new forward 'Maritime Strategy' both within the planning process and in public debate (see Chapter 2). Ideas of forward carrier and submarine operations that go back to the earliest days of the Alliance are now being articulated in a new and coherent form. It is now easier to pose questions about the relative utility of certain naval deployments and activities compared to others.

In the past, matters concerning surface naval forces have too often been discussed in a primarily 'East of Suez/Out of Area' context. This has made the surface navy seem something of a throw-back to the past, an area of defence provision especially vulnerable to cuts: exercises like *Command 8288* have been the result. 'East of Suez' was a response to a real need, that of securing peaceful decolonisation, as well as being a brilliant exercise in force preservation for the decade 1957-67.[1] Nevertheless, it had had its day as soon as the fundamental decision to withdraw from East of Suez was announced on 16 January 1968. This is *not* to say that a capacity to intervene 'out of area' does not remain important. Indeed, recent events in the Gulf (see Chapter 6) have more than vindicated the use of maritime forces for this role. Nevertheless, as has been made clear in successive White Papers, out-of-area capability is an 'add-on' maintained by forces procured to do something else somewhere else. It remains an *additional* reason for maintaining a surface fleet but cannot be the main one. The NATO role is paramount, at least in current circumstances.

Within this overall NATO Atlantic role, there are a number of missions. These can be broadly divided into three:

(i) forward deployment in the Norwegian sea and beyond;
(ii) barrier operations at the Greenland-Iceland-UK 'Gaps' (de-emphasised nowadays as a major role for surface forces);
(iii) direct protection of shipping sailing both in convoy and independently.

Part of (i) also includes Britain's contribution to the land defence of the European mainland in Norway. The relative priority given to each of these missions is a matter of legitimate parliamentary and public concern. The willingness to discuss strategic matters displayed by Ministry spokesmen before the House of Commons Defence Committee was both novel and most laudable.[2] Yet it remains hard to obtain a picture of the full implications of the new emphasis on forward strategy for force sizing, or the relative allocation of forces to various tasks, without some harder numerical basis.

During the debate over the Nott defence review in 1981, the following indication was published of the 'planned disposition of British naval forces in war'. Paraphrasing slightly these were:[3]

Striking Fleet—1 carrier and 14 escorts.
Protection of Atlantic Shipping—1 carrier and up to 10 escorts.
ASW in the Channel—up to 12 escorts.
Protection of the reinforcement of Norway—7 escorts.

This makes a total operational requirement of 43 destroyers and frigates, a realistic figure, given an available operational fleet that stood at that time at exactly 50 ships, not counting those listed in the White Paper as being in long refit or reserve.

Since then the overall situation has changed significantly. On the supply side, the number of operational ships has come down. Although 48 destroyers and frigates were listed in the 1987-8 White Paper, Mr Richard Mottram, Assistant Under-Secretary of State (Programmes) confirmed to the Defence Committee on 2 March 1988 that this meant only 36 fully operational units. The 1989 White Paper, perhaps in response to the controversy over frigate numbers, lists only 34 destroyers and frigates operational or preparing for service, with seven on trials and training duties and seven more undergoing refit or on standby.

On the demand side, official statements have made it clear that the United Kingdom has shifted towards a greater emphasis on forward operations. This has altered the balance of asset allocations towards operations in the North. Moreover, Britain's Striking Fleet role has received a new emphasis with the formal constitution of the 'Anti-Submarine Striking Force Atlantic' as a NATO command in 1985. One might therefore postulate an approximate reallocation of forces thus:

> Anti-Submarine Striking Force Atlantic deployed to insert the Striking Fleet through the GIUK 'gap'—1 ASW carrier (CVSA) and 9 escorts.
> Cover for the amphibious reinforcement of Norway, precursor operations of Norway, and subsequent forward operations under ASW Striking Force Command—1 CVSA and 9 escorts.
> ASW in the Channel—9 escorts.
> Protection of Atlantic Shipping—9 escorts.

The Channel escorts might expect the support of the Royal Fleet Auxiliary (RFA) *Argus*. The third Invincible class ASW carrier, normally in refit or reserve but mobilised in crisis with an *ad hoc* air group composed of aircraft currently based ashore, would seem the obvious candidate for shipping defence in the Atlantic. However, at least until the new Aviation Support Ship eventually appears, one or both of those valuable assets might be allocated to the Northern reinforcement role (assuming there is time to mobilise the third CVSA and its air group in time). The basic shape of the surface fleet thus seems therefore to be a large ASW striking force made up of two individually deployable ASW carrier task groups and two escort groups that might eventually expect carrier support.

The current Royal Navy could probably meet these force goals, but only just. Further cuts might imply that the lesser commitments, to the Channel and the Atlantic shipping, would be inadequately serviced, or would rely on vessels that were not readily available at sufficiently short notice. The question might be asked, however, whether the allocation to the latter two tasks is even now sufficient, given the importance of sea communications in both the Atlantic and the Channel to military reinforcement and the arrival of vital necessities to maintain a minimum standard of life for the population. A single group of warships in the South Western Approaches based (eventually) around a carrier can be at best only a support group or the escort for a single convoy. The dilemma is only too clear. If the Royal Navy wishes to participate in the forward maritime strategy, then its contribution in more traditional terms to the campaign in the South Western Approaches might be limited to a surprising extent. It is these issues that a more closely defined force structure would help eludicate.

This is not to decry or undermine the forward strategy or the United Kingdom contribution to it. A contribution to forward operations remains important for two main reasons. First, Norway's security is vital, both as an Alliance member, an attack on whom we must treat as an attack on ourselves, and as a potential forward base for Soviet forces that would be more favourably placed both to threaten Atlantic shipping and the United Kingdom itself.

A second, and equally vital factor is the not inconsiderable British influence that the ASW Striking Force gives over the operations of the NATO Striking Fleet as a whole. It must be remembered that the Striking Fleet is not subordinate to EASTLANT but yet is the single major NATO naval asset in the whole Atlantic battle. Abandoning all European influence over its operations would be unwise, especially given doubts, held in certain quarters, over American tendencies to use carrier battle groups in an overly aggressive manner. Critics have exaggerated these problems but a British contribution to Striking Fleet operations, especially in the crucial ASW area, effectively subjects the operations of the Striking Fleet to joint Alliance control in a way that could not be achieved otherwise. The undoubted expertise of the ASW Striking Force also enhances the security of the Striking Fleet in its twin roles of holding down Soviet assets in a defensive posture and helping to hold Norway.

Forward operations, however, especially if two groups are required, are going to take up a large number of valuable assets. It was clear from the discussion before the Defence Committee that NATO's naval commanders might face a number of most uncomfortable dilemmas. As noted above, the contribution to the direct protection of shipping might be seriously neglected. Alternatively, a shipping defence crisis in the South Western Approaches or mid-Atlantic might draw away ships required in the Norwegian Sea. More assets would, of course, ease this problem but ships are expensive items, especially if they all must be capable of main fleet operations in areas of maximum threat. One conclusion that might emerge from a redefinition of force goals along more specific lines is that not all the escort force need be capable of these demanding roles. If, say, only 18 or so operational ships are needed to operate in the forward battle (and Britain's European Allies can help make up ASW Striking Force numbers—see Chapter 5), the ships left for Atlantic and Channel operations might be of lower capability, given the reduced threat, especially from the air. Indeed more ships of this more austere level of capability might be affordable, especially if they could be operated by ships' companies still further reduced below the Type 23 manning level. It is even possible that more could be spent on the 'high' Striking Force ships to make them more capable in the demanding environment of forward operations in *advance* of the main carrier forces. In effect, we have this situation today with a limited number of towed array frigates, the key weapon in ASW Striking Fleet operations, but the principle could be extended to anti-air and anti-surface capabilities.

A high/low mix would also make sense in the out-of-area context. It must be stressed that the nature of the threat in such situations is now often such that only first rate 'battle' forces can be deployed. In the Gulf, Royal Navy warships had to be fitted with more sophisticated equipment than they normally carry for NATO deployment. Nevertheless, there are less demanding out-of-area roles, for example, the West Indies guardship and South American anti-drug patrols for which 'second rate' vessels are perfectly adequate.

It is currently impossible to argue a credible case either for more austere surface combatants or more capable ASW Striking Force assets if every vessel is expected to take part in highly demanding 'battlefleet' operations either in or out of area. This inevitably has a serious effect on the ability to maintain numbers. Traditionally navies have got round this problem by the basic division of ships into a number of powerful and capable units intended to fight for command of the sea and a large number of cheaper units intended to protect directly the exercise of that command. What has happened since 1945 is the development of the escort with its origins in the latter role into a kind of 'battlecruiser' used for the former. The United Kingdom has produced perhaps the most cost effective vessels of this type in the Type 23 (once they receive their delayed action information systems) but even so will probably not be able to afford enough of these units to meet all its surface requirements in the future. This is demonstrated by the increasing problems in maintaining the 'about 50' total. If the surface fleet force goal was redefined in terms similar to those above, two CVSA groups composed of first rate battle force ships for forward operations and out-of-area deployment, and escort groups of less capable vessels for use in the Channel and South Western Approaches (currently two, but evolving perhaps to a more flexible force structure) Britain would have the basis for the development of a secure, coherent and affordable surface fleet for the twenty-first century, one that makes a great deal of sense in the overall scheme of United Kingdom defence priorities.

Although the Minister of Defence has announced that Britain will continue to deploy 'an amphibious capability in the longer term', the exact shape of that force is still not clear. Money has been put aside in the long term costings to rebuild or replace the two assault ships (LPDs) *Fearless* and *Intrepid* but, as was made clear to the Defence Committee, the two ships have insufficient helicopter operating 'spots' for the required level of lift, two companies. This requires 12 'spots' of which the two LPDs can provide only four. As it was put to the Defence Committee: 'In providing amphibious capability in the longer term, we shall either provide replacement ships for *Fearless* or *Intrepid* or, if appropriate, we might engage in the modernisation of one of these ships, but the question of the operating spots comes down to the concept of an aviation support ship and on that we have made no decision.'[4]

Without such a vessel, possibly mercantile based, Britain's amphibious capabilities would be significantly diminished as the other assets, for example, a CVSA or RFA *Argus*, would either have to be taken from equally vital tasks or would not be available on mobilisation. The doubts over the procurement of such a support ship, however, demonstrate the problems of shortages of resources that pervade the British naval programme from top to bottom. The quieter commitment to 50 mine countermeasures (MCM) vessels that was a positive result of the *8288* trauma has been quietly laid aside, despite noble attempts by the last CINCEASTLANT to re-emphasise it. This is a pity as MCM shortages affect both forward fjord operations as well as the clearing of ports and passages closer to home for which John Nott intended the projected forces.

There is also no doubt that the Royal Navy is currently feeling the strains of overstretch. Extra operational demands, like keeping the Armilla patrol in the Gulf, are combined with shortages of manpower to reduce the number of destroyers and frigates available for operational contingencies to little more than a dozen. Britain is not able to contribute to NATO exercises in her usual strength. In the Norwegian Sea Campaign Exercise 'Teamwork' in 1988, only two RN frigates accompanied HMS *Illustrious* in the ASW Striking Force (ASWSTRIKFOR), while two destroyers and two frigates escorted the UK-Netherlands amphibious force. HMS *Boxer* had to detach from ASWSTRIKFOR to replace HMS *Southampton*, following the latter's unfortunate collision. Shortages of MCM vessels caused by the Gulf deployment could only be made good by a shuffling of the pack that saw the Royal Naval Reserve deprived of two of its River class sweepers to maintain the Fishery Protection Squadron. The Royal Navy's traditional 'can do' attitude is squeezing the maximum value out of its limited resources but something must give in the longer term. That the price to be paid may be in less tangible aspects of capability, such as the loss of experienced personnel and in the training standards of those who remain, makes it all the more potentially serious.

These dangers are, perhaps, the inevitable result of the policies of marginal cost cutting that have been the essence of post-Nott defence planning. This has avoided hard political choices but it does not necessarily create a healthy environment for the Royal Navy, especially as the budgetary allocation to defence begins to decline in real terms, as is now intended. Naval shipbuilding is a long term business and, by its nature, vulnerable to delays in ordering of which the effects will only become apparent some years down the line. The post Falkland commitment to 50 frigates and destroyers has already been eroded to 'about 50', a definition that seems to be disturbingly flexible, especially when ships about to be taken out of service, ships running trials and ships converted to training vessels are included to boost the declared totals. What is needed in the United Kingdom is some clearer thinking on the roles and missions of the surface fleet in order to assess a correct level of strength that it would then be a clear defence priority to maintain. A British version of 'The Maritime Strategy' is long overdue, one that, rather more than its American precursor, would pay due regard to European perspectives on stability and common security as well as the vital component part that naval power will continue to play in deterrence and defence. Moreover, as confrontation in Europe winds down, and the CFE Agreement is signed the case for a *higher* proportion on the UK defence budget going on maritime forces that can cope both with European and wider world contingencies becomes ever stronger.

CHAPTER 5

NATO's Continental Navies

First among the navies of the Continental Signatories of the Atlantic Alliance is that of France which clearly suffers from the national nuclear emphasis of French defence policy. Six nuclear powered ballistic missile armed submarines allow three submarines to be on patrol compared to Britain's one SSBN always on patrol out of four. Yet France's fleet for more conventional operations clearly lacks the overall capability of the Royal Navy. The French, to be sure, are always skilful at publicising their future programmes to put on the best possible show of apparent naval power but substance usually lags behind ambition. France now deploys some nuclear powered attack submarines, with four in service, two more under construction and two more on order. The French SNAs are small, slow and too noisy to be of much use for ASW operations. The emphasis in the design of the first four Rubis class boats was on the anti-surface ship role with torpedoes and Exocet missiles but the new Amethyste boats will be quieter, in order to improve their ASW potential. (Amethyste stands for *Amélioration Tactique Transmission Écoute*; in other words, improved silencing.) The earlier boats may undergo modifications to bring them up to the same standard. The first SNAs are based at Toulon with most of the conventional submarines, including all four 1970s vintage Agostas, at the old U-boat base at Lorient. A second SNA squadron will probably eventually be formed in the Atlantic also.

Centrepiece of the French surface navy is the operational carrier, either *Foch* or *Clemenceau* whichever is in full commission. She carries an air group of up to 15 nuclear capable Super Étendard attack aircraft, a flight of ten old American Crusader fighters, seven Breguet Alize ASW aircraft and at least two helicopters. The latter can be increased at the expense of other aircraft depending on the mission, for example, off Lebanon in 1983, *Foch* carried 15 Super Étendards, 6 Crusaders, 5 Alizes, 3 Étendard IVPs, 6 large Super Frelon helicopters and 3 small Alouette III helicopters. There is only one complete air group but the other carrier, if not in refit, can be used as a partial helicopter carrier if required: for example, 10 Pumas and 4 Gazelles for landing operations together with 10 Super Étendards, 4 Étendards and 3 Super Frelons. France's carriers are useful assets in Third World situations but are not really instruments with which to take on a first class opponent. Especially serious, even against second or third rate opposition, is the lack of organic airborne early warning aircraft; the British CVSAs are much better off, even with their AEW Sea Kings.

The assumption of a relatively benign air environment is continued in the air defences of France's escorts. Only now is the Crotale system of the big C-70 corvettes being modified for anti-missile engagements and the first two anti-air variants of the C-70 have hand-me-down American Standard systems from older ships. The intended construction of more vessels of this type has been prevented by the non-availability of old Standard missiles no longer in production in the United States! This evidence of a shortage of resources is also demonstrated by the problems and delays that have beset the new 3,000 ton frigate project. About half of France's current escort force is made up of small *avisos* of only the most limited ASW potential. They are useful tokens of French presence in distant waters but only capable of escort duties in areas of the most limited threat. Indeed, the new 2,600 ton *Floreal* class *fregattes de surveillance* for procurement in the 1990s to replace the oldest *avisos* are specifically designed for presence and surveillance missions only and have no ASW capability.

Despite all these operational defects, however, the French Navy is not badly designed for its main roles. France owns a string of overseas territories across the globe whose sovereignty must be protected from essentially small scale threats. The possession of a widely deployed base structure makes the demand for mobile 'reach' somewhat less than that required by the British. The ASW potential of the larger fleet units is improving which makes them useful in the direct protection of shipping, as shown in recent NATO exercises. This greater commitment to the Atlantic Alliance being shown by the French is noteworthy. There were more French ships in Exercise 'Ocean Safari 87' than British and as towed array sonars and improved AAW systems become available a contribution to forward operations cannot be ruled out—perhaps below the surface as well as above. The French Navy welcomes these opportunities to show solidarity with its allies, although, currently, internal political realities rule out any more formal NATO integration.

France's national power projection capabilities will also improve. The 34,000 ton nuclear powered carrier *Charles de Gaulle* is finally taking shape at Brest. She will replace the *Clemenceau* around 1996-7 and a second 'PAN' is due to be ordered to replace the *Foch* in the next century. These ships, like the current carriers, will have a *pre-strategique* nuclear role, firing warning shots to threaten wider nuclear escalation. Such valuable Soviet assets as the *Kirov* or similar are seen as suitable targets for the ASMP missiles being fitted to the Super Étendards, although this implies a rather more forward deployment posture than is normally considered for France's carriers. The new ship is eventually due to operate the new Rafael-M combat aircraft although she is expected to commission with Super Étendards and F-18s. The whole PAN programme is a very expensive one and there must be serious question marks over the second ship. Nevertheless, *Charles de Gaulle*, and her 40 aircraft air group, will be one of Western Europe's most powerful surface warships if and when she finally makes it into service in the late 1990s and a contribution to forward operations in the north ought to be considered to give maximum return on investment. Lack of organic AEW, however, remains a fundamental weakness.

The French Navy is also facing the travails of trying to modernise its amphibious capabilities. The two Ouragan class dock landing ships or TCDs are due for disposal in the early 1990s and three new and larger Foudre class were planned. *Foudre* was launched in 1987 but the other two have been deferred. The training cruiser *Jeanne D'Arc* remains a potential helicopter landing platform (LPH) in a crisis.

France accepts that the defence of the approaches to her ports is a national responsibility. She is modernising her force of Atlantique land based patrol aircraft and is investing in mine countermeasures forces, including the projected advanced BEMO ocean going mine countermeasures (MCM) catamarans with DUBM 42 variable depth sonar. These are planned to enter service from 1992. France has also co-operated with The Netherlands and Belgium in the Tripartite coastal minehunter programme (see below) but her order was cut and much of her MCM capability dates back to the 1950s.

Spain, like France is not fully integrated into the military structure of NATO but plans a more overtly integrated maritime posture. It has one ASW carrier group based around the brand new American type 'sea control ship' *Principe de Asturias.* The 16,200 ton carrier carries Sea King anti-submarine warfare (ASW) helicopters and AV-8 Harrier fighters and will be the core of *Grupo Aeronaval Alfa* together with the new American type frigates of the Santa Maria class fitted with towed arrays. The five older Baleares class frigates would also be useful assets with the Group, especially those modified with improved communications and combat data systems. The lack of satellite communications for these frigates presents a problem for dispersed ASW group operations and their acquisition should be given high priority. The Spaniards recognise the limitations and the utility of their new force: they do not regard it as suitable for operations close to hostile shores, including the Mediterranean coasts or the approaches to the Straits of Gibraltar. The control of the Straits in war would, in the view of the Spanish Navy, be a task primarily for land based aircraft and submarines. Admiral Nardiz Vial put it thus in an interview: 'Therefore we are aiming to use the *Principe de Asturias* and its group of escorts on the Atlantic high seas, as far north as the

Greenland-Iceland-UK gap working in close co-operation with the UK Royal Navy and other allied nations.'[1]

Spain hopes to have up to 18 frigate-type ships available by the end of the 1990s, with one new ship being laid down every two years.

For the time being the Spanish Navy may have to flesh out Group Alfa with Descubierta class corvettes and old ex-American destroyers. These are ships of only limited capability but could be useful as active sonar convoy escorts if the Group was deployed in this role. The older ships are also useful for surveillance. Spain also has large exclusive economic zone responsibilities which require relatively simple vessels for patrol and policing duties. Four new patrol vessels are planned. Other new constructions include a vital replenishment tanker and a dozen minehunters. Spain's eight boat submarine force has been modernised and the Spanish Navy hopes for a co-operative European submarine programme to produce a new design in the 1990s. Spain generally places great emphasis on international co-operation to increase the credibility of its naval modernisation programme.

The Spanish Descubierta corvette design is derived from the best 'frigates' in Portugal's Navy. The latter also has a navy more suited to offshore policing than anything else. The construction in West Germany, with German financial support, of the three new Vasco da Gama class frigates will, however, transform the capabilities of Portugal's surface forces by the early 1990s. As important as hardware, however, is the whole question of the optimal naval organisation in the Iberlant area, bedevilled as it is by historical and political factors. A high priority for the 1990s ought to be a new, more integrated arrangement which more accurately reflects Spain's position as the dominant local naval actor.

Carriers are becoming increasingly fashionable in European navies. Italy, after a considerable bureaucratic struggle and a long adolescence with helicopter cruisers, has finally obtained legal sanction to operate Harrier type STOVL aircraft from the 10,000 ton *Guiseppe Garibaldi.* A sister ship is planned to replace the helicopter cruiser *Vittorio Veneto*, now almost twenty years old. The two ships are each seen as the core of task groups (*Gruppi d'Altura*) to contribute to sea control in a NATO war, one in the Central/Western Mediterranean protecting traffic through the Straits of Gibraltar, the other to help control the Eastern Mediterranean and passage through the Suez Canal. In addition, each force would be composed of 2 destroyers (plus, for the time being, the smaller cruiser *Andrea Doria*), 6-7 frigates, and a logistical support ship. Some in the Italian Navy, however, see the main role of Italian major surface units as 'out-of-area', both in the Mediterranean and beyond. In this regard, the Italian decision to deploy a significant task force of modern 'Maestrale' and 'Lupo' class frigates in the Gulf, was a notable new departure (see Chapter 6). If the Italian Navy wishes to continue with this kind of deployment, the large replenishment tanker *Etna* is a pressing priority. To improve further their force projection capabilities, the Italians are also completing two new LPDs that have both been the beneficiaries of a naval version of constructive accounting. One, the *San Giorgio*, is replacing *Andrea Doria's* sister ship *Caio Duilio* which is to be scrapped.

The *San Giorgio* has been built with civilian funds for disaster relief. The need for such creative accounting is pressing. Ordering the two 5,000 ton 'Animoso' class large guided missile destroyers projected in the Legge Navale of 1975 was delayed until 1986 due to shortage of funds. They were finally laid down in 1989-90 and planned to come into service in 1992 replacing the *Andrea Doria*. The replacement of the oldest pair of Italian anti-air missile destroyers of the 'Impavido' class is not yet clear. Two more 'Animosos' were projected in 1988 but their construction now seems unlikely and the number of Italian destroyers will probably remain at 4 with the two 'Animosos' replacing both *Andrea Doria* and the 'Impavidos'. The Italian Navy would like to build up to 28-32 modern escorts, a high/low mix of air defence destroyers (4-6), general purpose frigates (14-16), and small 1,000 ton corvettes (8-12), but attaining this total is problematical, especially with Italy's withdrawal from the NFR 90 programme that promised to upgrade at least two of the frigates to destroyer standard. The pair of 1960s vintage 'Alpino' class frigates now looks like being replaced by two modified 'Maestrale' class vessels. As for submarines, the force goal is 12 boats, two more than currently in service. Two 1,580 ton improved 'Sauro' class boats should achieve this aim by 1993. Four large 2,500 tonners of the 'S 90' type may replace the little 'toti' class coastal submarines later in the 1990s, but the programme may well be delayed as new revolutionary designs of air independent propulsion, using gaseous storage in toroidal hulls, are evaluated.

At the eastern end of the Mediterranean, the Greeks and Turks eye each other suspiciously. Greece can concentrate on the Aegean and Eastern Mediterranean while Turkey has a long Black Sea coastline that must be defended. Both have numbers of fast attack craft and old American destroyers, as well as a mixed submarine force of modern small German and older American built boats. Turkey also has the duty of mining the passage from the Black Sea to the Mediterranean. Both nations are modernising their surface forces. The Greek modernisation process got off to a false start in the early 1980s with none of the expected Greek-built examples following the pair of Dutch built Kortanaers. Finally, in 1988, after evaluating various designs, the Greeks ordered four German Meko-200 ships, one to be built at Hamburg, the others in Greece. Modernisation of some of Greece's old destroyers complements the frigates with their more three dimensional capabilities. Turkish policy is similar but with the West Germans providing the ships, both new and second hand, and the financial aid to pay for them. This aid to poorer European allies is an aspect of the Federal Republic's defence effort that is often forgotten when burden sharing is being discussed.

Although the American Sixth Fleet remains the core of NATO naval capabilities in the Mediterranean, the European contribution both in terms of naval platforms and shore based air cover is highly significant. It is arguable that greater investment in maritime capabilities would be a sensible policy for Italy at least, given her lack of a direct border with the Warsaw Pact and her extensive maritime interest both in and out of area. The pressure of out of area business on Italy's limited number of naval assets caused Western Germany to step into the breach and deploy a destroyer/frigate force to the area, relieving it with another when the first squadron returned home. This kind of 'out-of-regular-area' activity is the most extended in reach that the Federal Republic feels she can currently undertake, given the self-imposed limitations on her strategic reach. It adds to the German desire to integrate more fully into the forward strategy in the Norwegian Sea to provide a continued imperative to the modernisation of the major surface units of the Bundesmarine. Despite the construction of the Bremen class frigates in the 1980s, much of the German fleet is old. It has therefore been necessary to plan an interim Type 123 frigate for the early 1990s to replace the Hamburg class destroyers whose basic anti-surface warfare fit limits their utility. Four will be constructed to be followed by perhaps by four more. Even so, however, the Federal Republic will probably only have 16 modern frigates in the year 2000 against a current NATO force goal of 18.

This may not be too serious as the main preoccupation of the *Bundesmarine* must remain the North Sea and Baltic. This puts an emphasis on the powerful naval air arm with its missile equipped Tornados, the Exocet armed fast attack craft, mine warfare assets, both offensive and defensive, and small quiet submarines. The fast mine warfare vessels currently under construction are noteworthy new units with the capability both to lay mines and sweep them. The Troika remote controlled minesweeping system which can be used with these vessels and others is a noteworthy German innovation. The U-boat arm also remains capable both in quality and quantity with its 24 quiet little boats. It has been decided not to build the bigger Type 211 class but instead to upgrade a dozen of the 1970s vintage Type 206s. A new towed array fitted 1,200 ton Type 212 will appear eventually in the mid-nineties and the *Bundesmarine* will deploy these larger 'SSKs' forward in the Norwegian Sea and perhaps further afield in the Atlantic. An air-independent fuel cell propulsion system is under development for the Type 212 and running trials in U-1. The refurbished 206A 'SSCs' will continue to be operated in the North Sea and Baltic. The price for extra capability might, however, be a reduction of the U-boat force to 18 units.

It is sometimes suggested that the Federal Republic should reduce its number of larger combatants and concentrate even more fully on coastal and shallow sea operations. Certainly, if hard choices are to be made as to the Federal Republic's contribution to NATO, this is the logical direction in which to go, with informal inter-alliance role specialisation emphasising Germany's contribution in the land-air battle and other more maritime nations putting in proportionately more effort at sea. This is especially the case as long as the Federal Republic limits the reach of its forces. If greater European integration reduced those inhibitions then the arguments for a German contribution to Europe's 'blue water' forces would be stronger.

Denmark has already put both of her frigates into reserve. The Danish Navy has thus become wholly coastal as far as high level operations are concerned. Denmark, has, however, slightly increased her small submarine force, with three second hand boats of German design bought from Norway replacing the two old Delfinen class. Three modern corvettes provide back-up to a light flotilla that includes Harpoon-equipped fast attack craft of Swedish design. The older fast attack craft are to be replaced by the new Flex 300 general purpose vessels that can carry out almost any task from minelaying and countermeasures to missile attack, depending on the plug-in weapons fit. Denmark has had to make some hard choices and the price of modernisation of the coastal flotilla has been the reduction of the longer range capability fleet to that of an offshore coastguard like Ireland's or Iceland's. Possibly this has gone too far: a couple of frigates allow a contribution to be made to Standing Naval Force Atlantic (SNFL) an important symbolic act in peace and deterrent act in crisis.

A NATO nation with a rather more finely balanced policy of strong defence and common security is Norway which has followed a subtle and successful policy of full membership of NATO combined with a series of common security restraints close to the Soviet border. There are some fears that the new emphasis on forward operations in United States and NATO maritime doctrine might overturn this compromise but these are mitigated to a considerable extent by the new assurance of full Alliance support in crisis. The Norwegian Navy thus sees itself as both a first line of defence and a 'socket' into which Allied support and reinforcements can be plugged. It feels it must retain as full a spectrum of capabilities as possible. Coast defences are clearly crucial, with a strong submarine flotilla of about a dozen German built boats (to be maintained partly by new construction and partly by modernisation), fast attack craft armed with both torpedoes and Norway's own Penguin missile, mine warfare forces, and shore batteries. Norwegian MCM forces are being modernised in innovative ways with a new class of surface effect vessels. This is especially important, given the vital need to clear the fjords if the option of inserting carriers into them is to be exercised. Nevertheless, it has also been decided to retain the squadron of small frigates to help defend the vital sea communications up the Norwegian coast. Forward operations have put a new emphasis on convoys up the Norwegian leads to bring in supplies vital for all aspects of maritime warfare in the North. These require close escort by small general purpose escorts like the current Oslo class. The current ships are being modernised to allow them to last into the 1990s when they will be replaced. In Norway the vital tasks of fishery protection and oil rig patrol are carried out by a separate civilian coast-guard. This has some advantages, given certain sensitivities and treaty limitations, notably in the Svalbard area. Coastguard vessels are also useful in coastal convoy operations. Also vital are Norway's land based air assets, both maritime patrol aircraft and F-16 fighters. The interaction and synergy of naval, air and land forces in the whole forward Norwegian sea battle cannot be over-estimated.

The other European allied country that has a key role in crisis management and forward defence in the Norwegian Sea is The Netherlands, which still deploys a navy of considerable quality. The force goal is three escort groups each led by an area defence AAW ship accompanied by about half a dozen ASW frigates. The current building programme with eight towed array frigates of the Karel Doorman class either under construction or on order will bring the total of modern ASW ships to 18. Together with the four AAW frigates, one of which is destined for the reserve, this will allow the aim to be met, just. Dutch towed array frigates can make a contribution to ASW Striking Force operations. They are also fully capable of providing a substantial part of close ASW escort and for American carrier battle groups. The Dutch have also invested heavily in submarines—a little too heavily it seems, given the serious cost overruns on the latest boats. The disastrous fire in *Walrus*, the original name boat of the class, has made the situation even worse: the fifth and sixth boats have been cancelled in favour of two smaller submarines. The Netherlands will eventually be able to contribute a most useful force of advanced quiet towed array submarines to the NATO pool of underwater assets. However, given technological trends, the money would have been better spent on frigates, or the projected amphibious transport vessel. The latter would be a most useful and timely contribution to the Anglo-Dutch amphibious force and Europe's general out-of-area capability. Given the continued doubts over the extent of controversial British investment in amphibious shipping, this would be an excellent means of intra-European burden sharing.

Both The Netherlands and Belgium play a key role in mine countermeasures in the shallow waters of the North Sea and the Channel, although the latter also has four small frigates that supplement Dutch ships in shallow water ASW and contribute to SNFL. As mentioned above, both nations have also joined with France in the development and deployment of a common 'tripartite minehunter', a success story for joint European procurement. The Netherlands has taken 15 of these vessels and Belgium ten with an option on five more. France cut her order to ten. The programme is administered in Paris and all three countries build hulls to a common design; The Netherlands provides the power plants, the Belgians the electrical equipment and the French the minehunting gear and some of the electronics. Given the high cost of new MCM vessels, this allows costs to be spread and the more complete replacement of the large number of older minesweepers, some since converted to hunters, which were procured in the 1950s, many from the United States. This is especially crucial as MCM capability remains the most vital way in which European naval capabilities complement those of the United States, both in the NATO context and out-of-area.

This informal role specialisation may extend to frigates also when the Americans are forced by budget cuts to prune the size of their fleet. This will no doubt hit the lower end of the mix of surface forces, a process which will re-emphasise the European role in shipping escort tasks. The planned 'NATO Frigate Replacement', NFR 90, seemed until recently the main opportunity for a joint project in this field. It turned, however, into a fleet destroyer rather than a frigate 'proper'. The British indeed saw it as the replacement for the current Type 42 area air defence ships, a kind of mini Aegis-cruiser to help give cover to forward operations into the next century. They planned to buy 12 ships, the largest European batch (only the USA, who said they would build 18, will have had more). The Germans wished to use four NFR 90s to replace the three DDGs as well as the last of the older frigates. The Dutch saw the ship as a replacement for their older air defence frigates, but there were only two of these and the Dutch were to limit their buy to two. Italy planned to buy eight to maintain and increase her strength in more powerful guided missile armed destroyer-type ships, and Spain was reliant on NFR 90 to provide herself, from the late 1990s, with eight powerful ships to up-grade her current surface combatant capabilities. The NFR 90 was, however, grossly over-designed to replace the little French 'Avisos' that are due for replacement about the time the ship is expected. France therefore limited her buy to four. With Canada purchasing a further six the total planned programme was 59 vessels. Joint procurement was to cost 2-3 times national development but these costs were to be divided by eight which provided significant savings. It was argued that only by such joint development could such sophisticated vessels be afforded by Europe's navies.

At the end of September 1989 the British suddenly announced that they were leaving the programme, having failed to reach agreement on either timescale or design with the other partners. France and Italy announced their withdrawal shortly afterwards. These bombshells must

PLATE 1

One of the keys to NATO's forward maritime strategy is the deployment of American carrier battle groups (CVBGs) in the Norwegian fjords. This was pioneered in Ocean Safari '85 by the USS *America* seen here close to the protective wall of the Lofoten Islands in Vestfjord. Early insertion of the Striking Fleet into these waters greatly complicates the attacker's problems of target acquisition and forces the enemy to engage the Alliance's battlefleet on the most unfavourable terms. In classical strategic theory the fjord option exploits the advantages both of the initiative and the defensive form of war. It also ensures the forward defence of Norway. The concept of using fjord conditions as cover originated in British LPD operation in Norway in early 1982 and was combat proved in the Falklands shortly afterwards. (SACLANT)

PLATE 2

As vital to the operations of the Striking Fleet in NATO's overall maritime strategy, although too often given insufficient emphasis in official and unofficial comment, is the direct defence of shipping. Specially intended for this role were the FFG 7 class frigates, delivery of which is now complete to the US Navy with 54 units built. This is one of the earlier members; the USS *Samuel Elliot Morison*. Like other ships of the class she is now operated by the Naval Reserve Force. As the US Naval budget is squeezed shipping defence vessels are best consigned to the reserve, leaving the power projection main fleet forces available to cope with peacetime contingencies. Allies find vessels such as these useful for general naval purposes that include wartime 'sea control'/shipping defence operations in areas of more limited threat covered by the forward deployed Striking Fleet. Spain has five of these frigates currently being delivered as the 'Santa Maria' class. (H M Steele/Naval Forces)

PLATE 3

A major European contribution to NATO's Striking Fleet is the command of the Anti-Submarine Striking Force and the provision to it of towed array ASW vessels to provide deep field protection to the carriers and amphibious ships. The oldest but still some of the best such assets are the four British towed array Leander class frigates one of which, HMS *Phoebe* is seen here. The 2031(I) long range towed array passive sonar is clearly seen on the quarter deck. The new British frigates of Types 22 and 23 and Dutch 'Karel Doorman' class ships will provide this kind of capability into the next century, although the increasing quietness of Soviet submarines is casting doubts on the current salience of longe-range passive detection. (Naval Forces)

PLATE 4

Britain is currently the only European contributor to NATO's threatened forward submarine offensive designed (if deterrence fails), to tie down the bulk of the Soviet Navy in defensive missions. The boats of the 'T' class like HMS *Turbulent* seen here are as good as any nuclear powered attack submarine in the world. The European interest and influence asserted by these vessels makes it more likely that Europe's interests will be taken into account in any necessary re-articulation of Western maritime strategy to make it more fully congruent with the strategic changes promised in the 1990s. (G Arra/US Naval Institute)

PLATE 5

The new era of reduced deployment ashore through arms control and generally reduced tension in Europe puts even greater stress than before on amphibious forces. These are key instruments of crisis management both within and without the NATO area and can be used around the world for such duties as evacuation of European nationals in a crisis and for disaster relief. Italy, France and The Netherlands are investing in impressive new capabilities for amphibious warfare while, ironically, the United Kingdom delayed its decision on the replacement or refurbishing of its battle hardened forces such as the assault ship HMS *Intrepid* seen arriving at Portsmouth. (W Sartori)

PLATE 6

Although the continued relevance of larger conventionally powered hunter killer ASW submarines (SSKs) can be questioned with the diminishing utility of passive sonar, small conventional coastal submarines (SSCs) still remain indispensable weapons for those continental European navies with a coast defence problem. Quiet and virtually undetectable, they make hostile marine movement a most hazardous business. Norway has operated these little German built Type 207 boats since the 1960s and is currently transferring three, including *Kya* seen here, to Denmark. Six will be retained by Norway to operate alongside six new larger Type 210 boats currently entering service. (Van Ginderen/US Naval Institute)

PLATE 7

As well as submarines and land based aircraft, coast defence involves missile armed fast attack craft. The Federal German Navy has considerable forces of all three types for use primarily in the Baltic, although the aircraft and the submarines have important, potentially wider roles. The Bundesmarine is also well equipped with auxiliaries that give even the smaller craft a reach more limited by political sensibilities than physical problems. Here visiting the United Kingdom is a flotilla of the Exocet missile armed Type 148 boats being supported by the armed tender *Main* and the underway replenishment ship *Saarburg*. (H M Steele/Naval Forces)

PLATE 8

Crucial to the success of NATO's Shallow Seas campaign is the performance of the Alliance's mine countermeasures forces. Here the British *Cattistock* operates with the Dutch *Naaldwijk* and *Abcoude* and the Belgian *De Brouwer*. This kind of close European co-operation is as relevant to the out of area context as NATO's coastal waters. MCM forces from these European nations operated under the cover of British frigates and destroyers as an integrated force code-named 'Calendar' in the Gulf in 1988. (Ian Allan Library)

PLATE 9
European co-operation is twice symbolised by the Dutch minehunter *Hellevoetsluis* seen at Ostend in November 1988. She is a member of the Dutch-Belgian-French 'Tripartite' programme of which the Netherlands has purchased fifteen examples, Belgium ten and France ten. She was also a member of the first Benelux 'Octopus' deployment to the Gulf in 1987, along with her sister *Maasluis* and two older Belgian minehunters. (M Louage/USNI)

PLATE 10
Portugal supplies the only in-place maritime forces to NATO's IBERLANT area in the Central Atlantic. Currently these are made up of corvettes of limited capability like the *Alfonso Cerqueira* seen in the foreground and the French built frigates of the 'Joao Belo' type seen in the background. The latter are being modernised and supplemented by three much larger and more modern 'Vasco Da Gama' class frigates built in Germany with Alliance aid. This will allow Portugal to deploy two escort groups to help safeguard convoys, one force around the Azores and Madeira, the other closer to the Iberian coast. (Naval Forces)

PLATE 11

The French Navy is intended to put on shows of force outside the NATO area. This is Task Force 623 in the Indian Ocean in 1987. Close examination reveals only three escorts for the carrier, an air defence and an ASW destroyer and a small frigate. The other ships include two mine countermeasures vessels and most of France's naval auxiliaries, plus one of the three chartered tankers then being used by the French Navy. This kind of infrastructure is as essential as the provision of actual warships to give maritime forces the necessary reach for world wide deployment. (Marine Nationale/Naval Forces)

PLATE 12

The Italian Navy is currently designed to operate two task groups ('Forze D'Altura'), one on each basin of the Mediterranean, eastern and western. The main units of these groups would be ships like the helicopter cruiser *Vittorio Veneto* and the guided missile destroyer *Audace* seen here refuelling from the fleet auxiliary *Stromboli*. Italy currently has only two such tankers which limits her Navy's reach. (Naval Forces)

PLATE 13

During the 1980s Italy has adopted a more forward naval policy, not only with its Gulf deployments in 1987-8 but in 1984 sending the mine countermeasures vessels *Bambu*, *Palma*, and *Mogano* through the Suez Canal to help clear the Red Sea of mines. Two years before Italy had sent patrol vessels to Sharm el Shaikh to participate in the multinational force observing the Sinai peace settlement, a commitment that still remains. (Naval Forces)

PLATE 14

The Greek Navy has an anti-surface warfare orientation with Exocet armed fast attack craft backed up by modified ex-US World War Two type destroyers like the *Apostolils* and *Sachtouris* seen here operating with the smaller craft. (Naval Forces)

PLATE 15

Both the Greek and Turkish navies have German built Type 209 submarines that are most suitable for shallow water sea denial operations. This is the Greek *Poseidon* that entered service in 1979. In the background is part of the massive Greek stockpile of merchant shipping that is perhaps an even more important maritime contribution to both the Alliance and European security. (USNI)

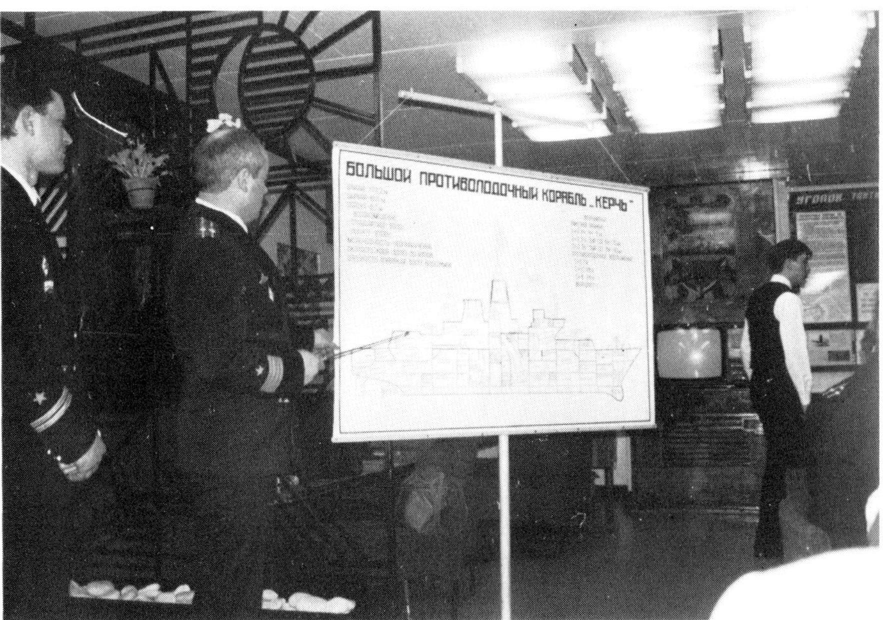

PLATE 16
Captain Alexander Pavlov of the Large Anti-Submarine Ship *Kerch*, in the cruiser's wardroom, giving a briefing on his ship's layout and characteristics to the Foundation for International Security visitors on 21st February 1989. (Author)

PLATE 17
The ratings' accommodation was cramped with much wood in evidence. (Author)

PLATE 18
The ratings' recreation space appeared to be shared by senior and junior ratings.
(Author)

PLATE 19
On the forecastle were the standard Soviet twin-tubed chaff rocket launchers.
(Author)

cast doubts upon the whole project, especially as the Americans remain ambivalent about the programme. The US Navy does not feel it needs more smaller frigates of this kind, preferring much larger destroyers proper. There are, however, strong industrial pressures to install an American-based weapon system. West Germany also seems to be wavering and there are reports of an Anglo-German air defence ship to meet their joint needs in the early years of the next century. Whether such a ship, or more national solutions to the air defence problem, will ever appear cannot at present be assessed. Certainly the travails of NFR 90 must cast doubts over both the quality and the quantity of Europe's naval forces in the twenty-first century.

Whatever the future of NFR 90, two related questions will still have to be addressed, the sophistication of the anti-air warfare capability to be fitted to Europe's warships and the degree of American technical domination. The USA is the only country with current technology of sufficient class in the shape of the Aegis system. The latter, as it stands, is too bulky for European purposes, and too expensive given the extensive software rewriting necessary for application in European ships not previously tied either to American hardware or computer language. The development of a new anti-air warfare missile system for Europe's navies is, however, a central issue for their development into the next century, especially if they wish to play in the big league directly confronting the Soviet Navy in northern waters. Such an expensive and sophisticated requirement is exactly the kind of major project that can only be done by Europeans in a collaborative framework, with or without the input of the United States. Bets are being hedged in a manner that demonstrates only too well both the current European difficulty in defining the correct degree of 'Atlanticity' in their moves towards greater co-operation and the differing requirements of different navies. The NATO Anti-Air Warfare System (NAAWS) sees the United Kingdom, The Netherlands, Spain and Germany tied up with the United States and Canada, and the Family of Anti-Air Missile Systems (FAMS) sees the United Kingdom, Italy and Spain teamed up with France, with Germany and The Netherlands as observers. FAMS, the front runner for UK procurement, covers three missiles, a point defence system for France and Italy, a 'Local-Area Missile System' for the UK and Spain and an area defence missile for France. 'Local-Area' means an extended range point defence system (10 kilometres against sea skimmers; about twice that against less demanding targets) rather than area coverage proper. This makes sense in pure cost-benefit terms as it responds to the accurate perception that against an increasingly stealthy threat, close-in detection engagement is more certain and profitable than longer range fighting. Nevertheless this approach does cast some doubt on whether the full implications of forward operations have been thought through. Missile equipped surface combatants are there to inflict attrition on enemy air forces as well as defend themselves from air and missile attack and Europe's navies will never have the organic capacity to engage in the wider air battle provided by super carriers. This might not matter while land based air cover is available, but in out-of-area situations of increasing potential danger the problem might be serious. It would be a pity if future Europeans could see air threats on their sensors and not be able to engage them.

In all circumstances assets must be optimised through co-operation at the operational level as well as in procurement. NATO's navies already operate in a closely integrated way: when combined into single operation groups, the ships fit together well with common communications and procedures. Within NATO, the greater degree of flexibility that has been shown in sending forces far from what have previously been their normal operating areas should continue. The despatch of a Norwegian vessel to join a Standing Naval Force Channel (STANAV FORCHAN) potentially depleted by Gulf commitments was another useful step in this direction. Whether more NATO standing naval forces are required in normal times is doubtful, given the extra operational burdens and inflexibilities they would force on participating navies. However, the Alliance's contingency plans 'in area' pay due regard to the naval potential of NATO Europe as a whole and the flexibility of maritime forces for distant deployment.

It has been suggested that to supplement these NATO plans, arrangements should be concluded between European countries for example, a United Kingdom-Netherlands-Norway agreement to cover the early deployment of the UK-NL amphibious force. According to published reports of conceptual planning now being carried out by NATO's European members, doubts over the early deployment of US forces are leading to the exploration of early forward deployment options based upon European forces only. NATO governments will be reluctant to emphasise such plans publicly lest they become self-fulfilling but they demonstrate what might be done to further Europe's naval potential as the United States comes under increasing budgetary pressure.[2] The welcome tendency of continental European navies to play a larger role in NATO naval exercises must be consolidated and extended, especially with French and Spanish units. This should not, however, be at the cost of a reduced British presence. No other navy is as authoritative in terms of Atlantic relationships: loss of British influence over NATO's, and hence America's, operations, plans and doctrine would be a loss that Europe as a whole could not repair.*

* The end of the NFR 90 project was confirmed in January 1990.

CHAPTER 6

The Gulf Precedent—Birth of a Western European Navy?

Something of major significance happened in 1987-8 in the Gulf. The navies of five Western European states made the first very tentative steps towards concerted European naval action in an area outside Europe of common interest and concern. Additionally, three of those European navies were operating in close co-operation, with an assurance of support by one nation to two others, something that would have seemed out of the question only a few months earlier. Important precedents were set for future naval co-operation and collaboration.

Before August 1987, only two European navies were operational in the Gulf. France had a destroyer and three small frigates of its Indian Ocean Squadron and, because of its confrontation with Iran over the Gordji affair, was sending out its operational carrier and two escorting destroyers. The British had deployed their 'Armilla Patrol' of a frigate and a destroyer in defence of British shipping since 1980: with the increase in intensity of the tanker war, and the requirement to 'accompany' British merchantmen, the Patrol had been quietly reinforced with an extra frigate since the beginning of 1987. On 24 June, one of the Kuwaiti tankers re-flagged by the United States, the *Bridgeton*, hit a mine 20 miles west of Farsi island. This led to requests from the United States to her European NATO allies to send mine countermeasures vessels to the Gulf to operate under American command as a kind of NATO out-of-area operation. The Europeans were not at this stage willing to associate themselves so closely with American policy in the Gulf. Belgium, The Netherlands and Italy all, at this stage, believed that shipping should be protected in the Gulf in a United Nations framework and even Britain, while sceptical of the United Nations idea, was reluctant to send MCM vessels until clearly required for national purposes.

The event which led to a wider European presence was the Iranian decision in August to move its mining offensive 500 miles south east-wards beyond the Straits of Hormuz to the busy waters off Al Fujairah in the United Arab Emirates. On 11 August, after the tanker *Texaco Caribbean* had been hit and holed and more mines had been spotted, the United Kingdom decided to send a force of four Brecon class mine countermeasures vessels to support the Armilla Patrol. France also decided to add three MCM vessels to its forces in the area, to give support to its national squadron.

Britain, it was reported, hoped that other European countries, more dependent on Gulf oil than she, would also send MCM forces. Discussions were reported with The Netherlands, Belgium, Italy and the German Federal Republic. The most obvious candidate was The Netherlands, dependent on the Gulf for almost two-thirds of her oil supplies, compared to Britain's dependency of a mere 6 per cent or so. The other most obvious contributor was Europe's specialist MCM navy, Belgium. Opinion in The Netherlands was split. Growing public support for sending minehunters was expressed in certain quarters, but this was balanced by the views of those worried about over-identification with a forward American policy in the area. There were, in addition, genuine operational doubts about sending weakly defended MCM vessels into such dangerous waters. It was thus doubly important to place any Dutch action in an international framework and, moreover, a European one. The Dutch, who held the Chairmanship of the Council of Ministers of the Western European Union (WEU), therefore convened a special meeting of WEU foreign ministry and defence officials in The Hague on 20 August to discuss the situation in the Gulf.

In October 1984, as part of the reactivation of the WEU, the member states had announced that they would meet whenever appropriate to consider the European implications of crises in other areas of the globe. The August 1987 meeting was the first time such consultations had taken place and it was significant that one of the aspects specifically covered was freedom of navigation. The meeting was seen at the time as a precedent of the highest significance. The Dutch Chairman issued his invitations on the 13 August, but it took a week for other nations to obtain approval at the highest level for the meeting of senior officials from the defence and foreign affairs ministries of member states to take place on 20 August. The consultations in The Hague were seen by some as having laid the foundations for the deployment decisions of the other European states. The officials 'agreed to consult each other on national measures taken, and decided to exchange information to develop further co-operation'.[1] It was on the basis of the August conversations that the Dutch, Belgians and even the Italians, took their national decisions to send naval forces to the Gulf. Certainly without some multilateral framework it is unlikely that the Dutch and later the Belgians, would have sent their minehunters. The WEU contact politically neutralised much of the opposition. In addition, the operational problem of vulnerability was solved by Britain's making bilateral commitments to their Dutch and Belgian allies that their MCM vessels would operate in close tactical co-operation with the Royal

Navy Armilla Patrol. This included support of a technical and logistical nature as well as the key promise of surface warship cover against air and surface threats.

On 7 September, after a meeting between Dutch defence minister Willem van Eekelen and British junior defence minister Ian Stewart, the Dutch government announced its decision to send two minehunters, *Hellevoetsluis* and *Maasluis*, to work in co-ordination with the British MCM flotilla. A week later, stimulated by their Dutch neighbours, the Belgians decided to send two minehunters, *Breydel* and *F. Bovesse*, together with their command and logistic support ship *Zinnia*. The Dutch and Belgians decided on a fully integrated joint operation codenamed 'Octopus', under the command of a Belgian officer flying his flag in the *Zinnia*, but under the operational control of the Dutch maritime headquarters at Den Helder.

Even before the Dutch and Belgians decided to set up their integrated flotilla to work in association with the British, the Italians had decided to appear in the Gulf and in considerable strength. The decision was made on 4 September after an attack on the Italian freighter *Jolly Rubino*. The force decided upon was a substantial one including three frigates, a similar number of MCM vessels and two support ships. The aim was to protect Italian merchant shipping all the way up to Kuwait, much further north than Britain's Armilla Patrol had ever ventured. It was particularly important to emphasise the national nature of this decision as some in Italy felt that she had considerable potential for a special political and economic role in the region that might be compromised by too great a degree of association with other Western powers. Nevertheless, the potential presence of the forces of five of the seven WEU members in the Gulf meant that the second Hague meeting of officials on 15 September could 'note' the various national deployment decisions and re-emphasise all the members' united commitment to the principle of freedom of navigation. Significantly, the participants 'reiterated their decision to continue the process of concertation' of their Gulf activities.[2] A new international activity had spawned new terminology. The dictionary defines 'concerted' as an adjective meaning 'mutually planned' and 'arranged in parts'. Converting this adjective into a noun seemed to describe the WEU activities rather well.

A further meeting of senior WEU officials on the Gulf question was held on 14 October. This discussed how to improve contacts between the five member navies active in the region to improve co-ordination at the practical and technical levels. It was also agreed to continue consultations. Less than two weeks later WEU defence ministers also discussed the Gulf question at their meeting in The Hague. This dimension of the meeting was overshadowed by the publication on 27 October of the important 'Platform on European Security Interests', but naval co-operation in the Gulf was nevertheless a significant agenda item.

What was being developed was a three level process of WEU 'concertation'. On the spot, in the Gulf itself, the local commanders concerted operations as required. A notable example of this occurred in November 1987 when the mines laid by the ill-fated *Iran Ajr* off Ra's Rakan, in the approaches to Bahrain, were successfully dealt with by British, Dutch and Belgian minehunters in a joint European operation, the first major example of its kind. A British frigate covered the operation but there was no overall commander. Instead it was a classic example of 'concertation', the Belgian commander interpreting his British counterpart's informing him of his intention to hunt for mines as a request for assistance.

At a middle level were 'representatives of naval staffs in the five capitals, the so-called points of contact (POC) functioning as a *plaque tournante*, and designating which matters were to be dealt with by the political level or the commanders at sea'. At the highest level, senior officials, representing ministers, met to agree on the general framework of co-operation and its limits.

At the first meeting of the captains who were the respective POC in November 1987, it was agreed that they would inform their respective forces of the desirability of co-operation and mutual assistance and that they would also explain to each other the missions of their respective forces. Lessons were drawn from an earlier MCM operation near Fujeirah, when there had been neither co-operation nor exchange of information. As one participant put it:

> Not only was this operation a waste of effort from a military point of view, but it gave rise to many questions in the Arab world about Europe's military efficiency. The naval staffs therefore agreed that operational control authorities should provide each other with advanced information of ships movements, mine countermeasure operations and port visits.[3]

The naval POC saw the operational sense in trying to formulate a more closely integrated MCM force which would economise efficiently on assets. They also wanted a system whereby a warship from one of the WEU countries would give support to any other WEU ship close by. Despite its operational logic, this latter idea did not find support at the meeting of senior officials held at the beginning of December 1987. The larger countries, for their various reasons, insisted that the European naval contingents in the Gulf should remain national forces under national command. It was to be made clear that in no sense were any of the European forces there to be seen as a WEU flotilla with a WEU flag or commander. The only international commander in any sense was the Belgian officer commanding the Benelux force. The latter term is not inappropriate given Luxembourg's decision to give financial support to the joint operation, an initiative that was encouraged by the WEU discussions.

At this time, only the Benelux minehunters were there explicitly for an international purpose to help shipping generally to cope with the mining threat. The lack of more combatant Dutch and Belgian vessels prevented there being any awkward questions of whose ships were to be defended directly, but it did leave a protection gap to be filled by the British within the Armilla Patrol's limited means. The British also helped solve support problems by allowing use of the support vessels HMS *Abdiel* and later HMS *Herald* and the repair ship *Diligence.* Beyond that, however, there were, at this stage, no other specific co-operative arrangements. The French, always anxious to maintain freedom of action, remained formally uncommitted to any other European navy's support, despite their possession of the most powerful forces in the area. Equally the Italians operated completely on their own, their domestic political difficulties having prevented any more definite co-operative arrangement, even if closer association had been desired. The fact, however, that formal discussions had taken place between all WEU governments provided a basis for concerted action on a wider basis. Most notably, WEU officials could take the initiative in calling together the POC if it was felt circumstances warranted it: if the problem could not be settled at that level then it went to senior officials.

It was not just the desire for freedom of national action which constrained both the profile of the WEU and the integration of the individual Gulf squadrons into a multilateral European framework. Britain, especially in the person of Mrs Thatcher, was anxious lest the European naval operations be interpreted in any sense as Europe 'ganging up' on the United States. The nature of this particular tightrope was made plain by the initial British decision to send its minehunters. The United Kingdom had at first refused to provide *carte blanche* British support for an American presence, about which many in the British foreign policy and defence establishment had reservations. Nevertheless, the United Kingdom would have preferred not to have been put into the position of having to give the Americans a direct refusal. Prime Minister Thatcher and others with similar attitudes to Anglo-American relations cannot have been displeased that the situation very soon changed and a European MCM operation proved desirable on its own merits. For not only did an enhanced European Allied presence in the Gulf please the Americans, but it also gave some European influence over American actions, for example, in choosing the appropriate response to attacks on United States merchantmen in October 1987. Mrs Thatcher was also anxious not to go too far along the path of European integration, given her well-known reservations about the whole process of European construction. She personally 'handbagged' proposals to set up a more integrated Benelux-United Kingdom force under joint command. The Benelux countries who were enthusiastic about the proposal, were frustrated that the joint command idea, that had been the crucial striking point, had not originated from them! Despite this setback, it was decided in early 1988 to halve the number of MCM vessels given the reduced mining threat.

Especially interesting in the context of balancing Atlantic and European relationships was the Federal German decision, announced in October 1987, to deploy Bundesmarine surface combatants to the Mediterranean. The destroyer *Molders*, frigate *Niedersachsen* and support ship *Freiburg* were sent to operate, first as part of NAVOCFORMED: when it returned home, the squadron was replaced by a second German force. The emphasis on the Atlantic Alliance and 'supporting' the Americans seemed to reflect real German concerns about a negative American response to too independent a European line in the Gulf. Nevertheless, it is hard to imagine that the unprecedented German action had not been discussed in The Hague. The Federal Republic thus was able, within its self-imposed limits of permissible action, to fill in for a depleted Italian Mediterranean presence. The Italian Gulf Squadron, three frigates plus reliefs, required six ships, no less than 50 per cent of Italy's modern Maestrale and Lupo class ships. It was thus a significant drain on NATO Europe's Mediterranean naval resources.

On 16 April 1988, the mining threat returned dramatically. The frigate USS *Samuel B Roberts* hit a mine in an area previously declared secure and began a major escalation of the maritime conflict in the Gulf. The Benelux force was in the area and began a mine hunting and clearing operation, later aided by the British and the Italians. This major operation around Rostam and the Shah Allum Shoal led to a meeting on board a United States warship between the European and American naval commanders. At this meeting 'it was agreed that MCM squadron commanders should meet at least once a month and that they should inform each other about a range of different operational issues such as, for example, the standardisation of MCM reporting procedures.'[4]

This was an excellent example of the subtle, low key integration of the various 'European' and American activities when common interests were affected.

At the next POC concertation meeting in Rome, the possibility of designating informal areas of interest for the various European national forces was discussed along with harmonisation of movement, turnovers, maintenance periods and leaves. The aim was to have at least one command unit and three MCM vessels available for action at any one time in each of the three areas of interest stretching from Qatar to the Straits of Hormuz. In June 1988, in a parallel process, the delayed integration of the British Armilla Patrol and the Benelux Octopus flotilla took place, Operation 'Calendar' being born, named after joint MCM operations at the end of World War Two. To placate Downing Street's sensitivities, Calendar Force was commanded from Northwood via the Senior British

Naval Officer Middle East and the British MCM Task Unit Commander. If the Gulf War had continued, it is likely that a Dutch frigate would have been sent out to replace a British Armilla vessel and help provide cover for the Calendar operation.

After the cease fire, there was a high level concertation meeting in London on 6 September. This laid the foundations for a decision by the POC to begin joint mine clearance operations along the principal shipping routes in the southern Gulf. It was declared that 'the task should be conducted by individual MCM forces operating under existing national command but that local MCM commanders should be authorised to adjust boundaries to suit operational conditions and force capabilities.'[5] Thus was Operation 'Clean Sweep' born that demonstrated yet again what had been achieved in the Gulf and what had not. The naval commanders on the spot got on well on the whole, despite continued problems of higher political concertation. Nevertheless, French unilateral instincts proved especially strong once more and there was a negative operational impact that was frustrating, especially to the integrated Calendar force and its commanders.

There is no doubt that significantly more could have been achieved in the Gulf given fewer political inhibitions on all sides. The Dutch, who were the key players in fostering concertation at all levels, estimate that only seven MCMVs and one or two support vessels would have been required rather than the maximum European total of fourteen MCMVs and five support ships. At most, they argue, two frigates would have provided sufficient cover rather than the three usually deployed in MCM covering operations, and this, coupled with better co-ordination, would have allowed MCM cover operations to have had less impact on accompanying merchantmen. As the Dutch POC concluded, 'the Gulf operations could not be classified as an example of satisfactory performances. In fact it (*sic*) only produced limited co-operation'.[6]

It is easy to share these frustrations. It all seems very messy, but such is the nature of the organic growth of European construction, a process usually much stronger in its results than attempts to impose a neat and tidy artificial framework on a complex reality would allow. The seven members of the WEU were individually faced with a situation where their vital interests, notably their maritime oil supplies, had been put seriously at risk. The situation was complicated by their perceptions being not identical with those of their Superpower ally. The various European states, moreover, had wished to maintain their own national policy nuances, both towards the Gulf states and the United States. Nevertheless, the Europeans had a sufficiently common purpose for a framework to be established for consultation, co-ordination and even 'concertation' of naval activities. If the WEU did not exist for this purpose something very like it would have had to be invented.

As its members stated in their 27 October Platform, 'we see the revitalisation of WEU as an important contribution to the broader process of European unification.'[7] That unification process is *sui generis*, the gradual coming together of historic, sovereign states, not the creation of a grand federal framework from scratch. So it might be that the Gulf crisis of 1987-8 might have been the catalyst for the beginnings of a European Navy, not some grandiose bureaucratic structure, but a flexible framework of co-operation between separate national forces. European political solidarity against a common threat was demonstrated by the WEU meetings and their announcement of a continuing framework of co-operation. There may be options for greater 'concertation' in the future. As Gulf deployments became more burdensome, information exchanged within the WEU did indeed allow an adequate level of European naval presence while minimising the burden on the individual fleets. The process only proceeded step by step, but each step was a significant one and a foundation for further progress.

The WEU has thus emerged as the appropriate framework for a Europe 'unashamed to assert itself discretely'[8] in the defence and security field in general and the naval field in particular. Never before had there been this kind of multilateral European co-operation 'out of area'. This may have wider implications still. Up until recently, those who presented 'out of area' arguments in support of European naval capabilities looked as if they were looking backwards on past imperial glories and their case looked somewhat fragile when compared to the competitive requirements of the pressing realities of national and European defence. Now, however, we see a new phenomenon. The Gulf has shown that Europe does indeed have requirements for naval defence outside the NATO area that are as novel as they are necessary. It may well need to defend these interests in its own way and by its own means and it may only be able to do this in a multilateral and concerted framework. 'Concertation' ought, not only to make that defence more sustainable from a naval point of view, but also to make such activities much more palatable to domestic public opinion. In this way, Europe's Navy could well emerge, not in the 'wiring diagrams' of management theory, but at sea, where it may increasingly be required. For the pressures in the direction of a more unified European naval approach are probably too strong for the countervailing fears and inhibitions to hold them back. The world is getting more multipolar; the authority and power of the United States and the Soviet Union are in relative decline. In these circumstances, Western Europe will have little option but to do more to look after its own naval requirements—especially if it is still requiring a security guarantee from a United States that will expect greater European efforts rather than opposite. Once certain instincts and inhibitions are overcome it might all prove much easier than expected.

CHAPTER 7

Soviet Naval Policy in the Gorbachev Era

Like so much else in the Soviet Union today, naval policy is in a state of flux and uncertainty. There are no authoritative statements of Soviet naval policy any more and the latest product of the team that produced the late Admiral Gorshkov's major works, the book *The Navy*, is denounced as 'bullshit' and 'Gorshkovshina' by the other side in the debate that is clearly in full swing. Like other aspects of *perestroika*, 'reconstructing' the Soviet Navy, and even more so its industrial infrastructure, is far from easy. Personal contact with Soviet naval experts can provide a certain 'feel' for the dynamics of this crucial debate (see Appendices 1 and 2), but readers are warned that this can only be a vague and impressionistic one. The remarks made below must be regarded as tentative. By the time they appear, more evidence may be available as to what is actually happening.

One fundamental problem in getting to grips with what is going on in the contemporary Soviet Union is the inadequacy of traditional methodology in the era of *glasnost*. There is still a tendency to regard what appears in print as the 'party line' to be analysed with all the rigorous textual exigesis traditionally applied to Soviet publications. To some extent this has happened with *The Navy*, which is a great mistake. Equally, however, it is an error to accept everything one is told in informal contacts. It may reflect only one person's opinion; what things seemed like at a particular moment in a dynamic debate to one interested party in it.

A good example of how one can be misled is over the Soviet carrier programme. In 1988, every impression was given that the two Tblisi-type carriers would indeed just be large aircraft carrying cruisers like the *Kiev, Minsk, Novorossiysk* and *Baku*. Moreover, they would probably be the last of such vessels. They would carry a mix of missiles and advanced Forger II type STOVL aircraft (the YAK-41). Other evidence seemed to bear this out but, in 1989, American sources announced that a third large carrier-type ship, even larger than the Tblisis had been laid down. Experiments continued with conventional aircraft using ski-jumps and these clearly bore fruit for *Tblisi* went to sea in 1989 operating Su-27 and

MiG-29 fighters. Controversy continues in the Soviet Union over the correct designation of these ships but their supporters seem to have won.

The continued development of carriers is especially disappointing the Soviet Navy for, despite their relatively subordinate position in Soviet naval strategy, big ships like carriers have important symbolic status. It is quite possible to integrate carriers like the new Soviet vessels into the new concepts of defensive sufficiency: they are primarily fighter carriers designed to throw out an outer air defence barrier around Soviet coasts and SSBN bastions. They may even have a legitimate role as a Soviet contribution to international peacekeeping. Nevertheless, they also provide evidence to the other side of latent Soviet power projection capabilities that can be seized upon by those who say nothing has changed in the Soviet Union.

Big ships like the carriers, aircraft carrying cruisers and the huge 24,000 ton, nuclear powered Kirovs, a fourth example of which is still taking shape in Leningrad, had their conception in the Brezhnev era. Gorshkov was able to argue a case that seemed powerful to Brezhnev, with his passion for spectacular motor cars, that the USSR needed such huge status symbols to counter the American Navy's carriers and the projected strike cruisers that never appeared. *Kirov* was a Soviet strike cruiser, grotesquely large in comparison with its 12,000 ton American counterpart (that was never built), a reflection of space intensive technology. The advent of the huge *Kirov* may, however, have affected the United States Navy's decision to reactivate the Iowa class battleships. It is not to be wondered at that Soviet arms controllers worry about the arms race momentum of large naval combatants.

The momentum of the current naval programme is visible further down the scale. In his 1988 testimony to the House Armed Services Committee, Admiral William O Studeman, then director of Naval Intelligence, was able to point to a Slava class cruiser, six Sovremennyy class anti-surface warfare destroyers and three more Udaloy class anti-submarine destroyers on the stocks.[1] A new class of frigate seemed to be under construction at Kaliningrad as did a new amphibious assault ship.[2]

As for submarines, the rate of construction continues, at the oft quoted rate of one boat every six weeks or so: eight boats were launched in 1988. What those who parrot this cry often fail to recognise, however, is that not all the boats end up in the Soviet Navy. There may well be clues here to general Soviet Naval policy and the problems of managing and ratifying shipbuilders. What has clearly happened recently is that conventional submarines have been syphoned off into the export market. In 1988 the Soviets launched two SSNs, an Akula and a Victor III, an Oscar II class anti-carrier guided missile submarine and a Delta IV SSBN. All were for the Soviet Navy as was one Kilo class conventional submarine but the three other Kilos went for export. The Soviet Union has supplied Kilos to Algeria, India, Poland, and even Romania. These relatively quiet, small diesel boats would be admirable counters to the NATO Striking Fleet fjord options but instead they are being sold to allies and friends.

This fits snugly with the preferred manner of recent naval reductions. The building rate has been kept up, the most expensive and sophisticated platforms taken into service, other new vessels built for export have been sold off, old units have been scrapped and the fleet operated at a generally reduced tempo. As the American Director of Naval Intelligence (DNI), Admiral Brooks, reported to Congress in early 1989:

> OPTEMPO is the number of days that an operational Soviet ship is at sea, either in local training or operations, involved in an exercise or deployed out of area ... Overall Soviet Navy OPTEMPO remained at reduced levels last year, continuing the trend begun in 1986. In 1988 Soviet naval units spent more time in port and at anchor and less time at sea than in previous years; they also reduced the extent of distant deployments and exercise activity, especially out-of-area exercises. OPTEMPO for Soviet general purpose naval forces since 1986 has been lower than in previous years. Additionally, although overall SNA (Soviet Naval Aviation) strength continues to grow, SNA sortie rates have declined since 1986. Such reduced OPTEMPO has an immediate impact on reducing costs for major consumables such as fuel, and may also reduce the burden on shipyards, since required repairs can be scheduled at longer intervals.[3]

Admiral Brooks went on to argue that the reduced OPTEMPO and the conducting of major exercises close to the Soviet Union also allowed the development of a more responsive potential counter to the forward strategy as large numbers of assets were in port ready to meet an enemy attack. He did concede, however, that this had been at a cost in operational expertise.

The new operational patterns show a Soviet Navy trying to fit in with the new defensive strategy dictated from the Kremlin, while maintaining its strength as much as possible. There is considerable latitude for more cuts in Soviet naval forces in all fleets given the retention of many old ships and submarines of dubious fighting value. It is likely that the Soviet leadership will take full political advantage of these reductions which will have little effect on the real fighting capacity of the Soviet fleets.

Only a third of the Soviet SSN force, 29 or so Akulas, Sierras and Victor IIIs are quiet enough to be combatworthy in the ASW role, the quiet Mike class trials submarine has been lost in an accident and there are less than half a dozen operational Oscars. The rest of the Soviet submarine force is noisy and relatively easy meat for Western ASW forces. Yet the modern submarines could still cause enormous problems to Western maritime forces and communications if not pinned down by forward deployment and the availability of significant force levels in defence of the Atlantic link. The scope for mutual arms control of a structural nature is thus limited.

One area where arms control might help, however, is that of naval nuclear weapons. The Soviet Navy clearly still regards these as usable equalisers against superior Western conventional forces, a kind of answer to the forward strategy. Soviet submarines carry nuclear headed torpedoes as a matter of course. Soviet anti-carrier warfare missiles, air, surface and submarine launched, rely for complete effectiveness on nuclear warheads. Soviet large anti-submarine ships (BPKs) carry a very limited number of nuclear capable ASW missiles. This all sits very uneasily with the Soviet Government's clearly articulated 'no first use' policy. Soviet naval spokesmen will pay lip service to this; they will also make even more sensible statements about the instabilities that result from uncertainties over whether missiles fired towards one are nuclear or conventional before they actually explode (a clear problem for them posed by the Tomahawk land attack cruise missile). Yet the nuclear emphasis in Soviet thinking clearly remains.

It is in the West's interest to make common cause with the Soviet Government and force strategic sanity upon the Soviet Navy. The Americans have realised that they will never obtain release for their old nuclear armed ASROC and SUBROC anti-submarine missiles or their nuclear Terrier surface to air missiles; they are therefore scrapping them unilaterally as they sensibly did with the ASTOR nuclear capable torpedo many years ago. The Soviets ought to be encouraged to do the same with the panoply of nuclear weapons they currently deploy, either in a reciprocal unilateral move or in return for further cuts in carrier based bombs, or even nuclear armed cruise missiles (if the latter problem proves unamenable in the Strategic Arms Reduction Talks (START)).

It is in no one's wider interest to start unleashing tactical nuclear weapons at sea. The West does not need to, because of its conventional advantages. Even in the unlikely event of its conventional weapons proving ineffective against strong double hulled Soviet submarines, the possibility of blurring the most vital political signal available to NATO—i.e. nuclear first use—will preclude premature operational use at sea, especially to solve ASW problems that should have been solved conventionally long since. Western politicians will have little sympathy with their naval leaders if the latter request the use of nuclear depth bombs.

Even more so do the Soviet naval commanders need to get out of their nuclear fixation. Even in the bad old days of an overtly offensive Soviet operational doctrine on land, the aim was to win beneath the nuclear threshold. Even less nowadays will a Soviet leadership take kindly to requests for nuclear release to deal with operational problems for which the Soviet Navy will be expected to have conventional solutions.

With this congruence of interest in naval denuclearisation, the way should be clear for some co-operative or interactive reductions. Perhaps mutual unilateralism now makes more sense given the unilateral American initiative and Western political instincts against formal denuclearisation. On the other hand, a grand trade-off of United States nuclear submarine-launched cruise missiles (SLCMs) and sea-based bombs against all Soviet naval non-SSBN nuclear systems, including those deployed by shore-based naval aircraft, has a clear logic. As for the other Soviet concerns about Western maritime strategy and the potentially offensive threats it poses, these must be addressed as part of the general process of conventional arms control and confidence building. It is to this most crucial issue that we finally turn.

Note: Since writing the above further discussions with Soviet experts have produced revealing new insights into current Soviet thinking on maritime strategy. See Appendix III.

CHAPTER 8

Conventional Arms Control in Europe—The Naval Dimension

In his Guildhall speech of 7 April 1989, President Gorbachev called for naval arms control negotiations between the United States and the Soviet Union and between NATO and the Warsaw Pact. This is but the latest and most direct of a series of proposals by Soviet spokesmen, at various levels, for dialogue in the naval arena. The most specific Eastern naval agenda that has been officially produced has been the Warsaw Pact Proposal tabled at Talks of Confidence and Security Building (CSBMs) at Vienna on 9 March 1989. This proposed the following:

1. Notification of naval exercises involving over 20 combat ships of more than 1,500 tons each, or over 5 ships with at least one over 5,000 tons and equipped with cruise missiles or aircraft, or over 80 combat aircraft.
2. Notification of transfers into or within the zone of naval groups of over 10 ships of more than 1,500 tons each, or over 5 ships of which at least one is over 5,000 tons and equipped with cruise missiles or aircraft.
3. Notification of marine force transfers involved over 3,000 men to the territory of another state.
4. Notification of transfers to the territory of another state of over 30 naval combat aircraft.
5. Observation of exercises involving over 25 combat ships of more than 1,500 tons each or over 100 combat aircraft.
6. Limitation of exercises of over 50 combat ships.
7. Naval exercises to be limited to 10-14 days.
8. No more than 6-8 naval exercises by each side annually.
9. Prohibition of notifiable exercises in areas of intense civil activity or areas of international significance.
10. Inclusion of naval activities in annual calendars.
11. Conclusion of an agreement on prevention of incidents in sea areas and airspace adjoining Europe.

These will be considered later in the chapter, but, first, we must examine why the Soviet Union says it is interested in naval arms control and confidence building, why it may well be really interested in such a process, why the West has been reluctant to engage in naval dialogue, and the relationship of naval dialogue to the CFE process.

Soviet spokesmen argue that naval forces are an inescapable component of the balance of forces, both global and European. They emphasise the capability of Western navies to operate against the shore with amphibious forces and, more especially, long range aircraft and missiles, a capability that has been emphasised by current robustly stated strategic and operational doctrines of forward deployment and offensive action. The nuclear cruise missile has converted many American destroyers into strategic missile platforms. This self-consciously 'offensive' doctrine, the Soviets say, is incompatible with Soviet moves to a more 'defensive' orientation and force structure. Traditional Soviet fears of forces that can strike in depth at their logistical and C^3I infrastructure seem to apply, perhaps with special force, to naval strike forces, possibly because the Soviets feel they might be used with less restraint than land based forces.

The Soviets also argue that naval forces are inherently destabilising. A situation where a relatively few vulnerable platforms of great striking power operate in close physical proximity to each other is, they say, a recipe for pre-emptive pressures and first strikes. The nuclear element compounds this instability problem especially, given the lack of a clear dividing line between conventional and nuclear systems or between tactical and strategic weapons.

Finally, the Soviets argue that naval forces create arms race problems. They are expensive and last a long time, affecting the strategic situation, positively or adversely, well into the future. Thus, problems of arms race stability add to those of crisis stability to be addressed co-operatively through arms control.

The above concerns are all probably real, especially among the Soviet diplomatic and academic arms control community. It seems to have been difficult for the latter to argue the case for progress towards stability on land when the West seems to wish to keep unaffected and untrammelled the self-consciously offensive threats posed by its naval forces. Assuming, because of its wider *perestroika* objectives, that the Soviet government really does wish to make progress in arms control on land (and in the air) the West's traditional view is indeed an obstacle to selling 'arms control' to its own hardliners.

Also detectable, however, is a desire to use naval dialogue to help in the internal debate over the Soviet Navy and its new construction programme. There is every indication of powerful rearguard actions:

> by the Soviet Navy against the official nuclear 'no first use' policy,

grounded on a Soviet naval requirement for nuclear weapons as a counter to the forward maritime strategy.

by the naval shipbuilding ministries against major cuts in building programmes. There are indications that this is having some success, for example, in the carrier programme, which last year seemed almost certain to be stopped.

There could, of course, be more cynical and negative objectives mixed in with the above. If naval cuts have been decided upon, it makes sense to try to maintain the naval balance, and perhaps even enhance the Soviet Union's position by trying to use arms control to cut Western forces. At a more political level, exploiting the naval arms control issue might cause splits within NATO between those states with more 'continental' and those with more 'maritime' perspectives. It could also be used to turn Western publics and legislatures against expenditure on vital core maritime components of the West's overall strategic posture.

So far, although more or less willing to include relevant naval forces in strategic forces negotiations, the West has opposed the inclusion of independent naval operations on the European arms control and confidence building agenda. There is a unilateralist school of thought in the United States Navy that wishes to be left out of the current trend in East-West relations and disagrees with the basic principles behind underlying current Western policy towards negotiations with the East. As a recent article by a serving officer puts it:

> conventional stability..., is not in the best interests of the West. Deterrence is... If the Soviets can achieve conventional stability, they can be expected to mount a far more aggressive and opportunistic foreign policy offensive using all 'peaceful means' short of armed conflict. If, to achieve that stability the United States has agreed to limit naval operations and cannot block those initiatives, either by naval presence and reaction in the Third World or by presenting a deterrent threat to the Soviet homeland and raising in the Soviet mind the possibility of an accidental war, Gorbachev's naval arms control propaganda will have paid off for the mid-term.[1]

Such 'old thinking' must be music to the ears of certain Soviet naval officers. Yet these views, important though they are in demonstrating the prejudices that must be overcome, should not be seen as typical in the Western naval establishment. Neither do they detract from the real problems naval arms control poses both in general and for the west in particular.

These can be summarised as follows:

Naval forces are global in 'reach', scope and relevance. It is difficult if not impossible, therefore, to isolate particular balances in specific theatres, for example, Europe.

The complexity of today's maritime warfare means that naval balances are often highly asymmetrical in terms of platforms and weapons: like no longer fights like. Stable balances cannot therefore be conveniently defined on the basis of parity in particular platforms.

The size of a nation's or an Alliance's naval forces has much more to do with its stake in the use of the sea than the size of the threat it faces. Historically, sea-dependent defenders have had to deploy vastly superior forces against non-sea dependent attackers. It is difficult, therefore, to define apparently equitable balances.

The freedom of the seas is an important principle in itself in that it is undesirable to curtail by accepting constraints on the well established uses warships make of international waters.

Navies are not in themselves capable of destabilising offensive action, the 'seizing and holding of territory'. Indeed, navies more often act as stabilising factors in international crises than the opposite. Unduly curtailing activities might therefore prove destabilising and therefore undesirable.

In addition to the above general arguments, the West has more specific difficulties with the concept of naval arms control.

The NATO Alliance relies on an ability to use the seas for military reinforcement and resupply as and when required. Many of its members are also highly sea-dependent economically.

Geopolitical realities give the United States little choice but to use the seas to exert legitimate influence in support of its interests, friends and allies in the rest of the world. This maritime power, which is often stabilising, is a necessary counter to the high levels of continental land power inevitably deployed by the Soviet Union.

The strength that results from the above demands gives the West much more to lose than the Soviet Union from agreed limitations in force sizing and operational flexibility. NATO may be able to define a positive balance of advantage in negotiating about land forces relatively easily. Many, however, find it hard to see any similar advantage in negotiating about the balance at sea, especially as the Soviet Navy has more recently, unilaterally and on its own initiative, taken up a much less threatening operational posture.

All these are powerful points and must be taken into consideration. Yet the Soviets are likely to see overriding factors. Much of the same logic, turned on its head, could be used to deny the utility of conventional arms control on land to the Soviet Union. It is not unreasonable therefore for a Soviet Union that seems to be willing both to define its security interests in a new way and to negotiate away many of its traditional strategic advantages to expect the West, where *it* has the perceived advantage, to make progress in the same direction in the interests of overall stability. Although it might be argued that an effective defensive posture should be able to cope with the other side's offensive capacity, in practice military leaders are going to be very reluctant to restructure their forces in a 'defensive' direction if they can point to overt and overbearing offensive capabilities on the other side.

This does not mean that the Soviet Union is going to demand the inclusion of naval forces in the Conventional Forces Europe talks (CFE). The Soviets repeatedly insist that they have accepted that there is no direct linkage between CFE and naval dialogue. The CFE negotiations have a self-sufficient internal logic that both sides accept and the only way sea-based forces have come in is via aircraft. Drawing the boundary line between the maritime and land dimensions of air power is very difficult indeed: certainly the land-based/sea-based division is too operationally and strategically simplistic. Land based naval air forces are an integral part of the naval balance, more even for the Soviets than for the West, and there is little or no intellectual justification in expecting to include them in CFE if one absolutely insists in keeping sea-based naval air forces out.

Apart from this matter, however, all the Soviets ask for is that from the overall political point of view, progress in CFE be correlated to progress on naval forces and activities. Moreover, they seem to accept that the only likely areas of progress in the short to medium term are in confidence building measures. Such measures may still seem to some to be 'placebo arms control' or even the 'junk food of arms control'. But placebos can be very effective psychologically, especially when, as Johan Holst has reminded us, an important aim is 'generally enhancing assurance of mind and belief in the trustworthiness of the other side'.[2] Even 'junk food' can satiate hunger and make a parallel healthier diet more acceptable. And some food, sometimes dismissed as 'junk' can be proved to be surprisingly nourishing when analysed scientifically and dispassionately.

Some confidence building measures might be purely unilateral and declaratory. Nevertheless, they might be effective. When for example, as discussed in Chapter 2, the United States Navy makes it clearer that its forward maritime strategy does not imply a sudden surprise, pre-emptive (and impractical) descent either upon Soviet SSBNs (PLARBs) or Soviet base areas in the Kola Peninsula, this should have a most constructive effect both on Soviet and popular Western perceptions of current US maritime strategy. It need not imply abandonment by NATO of forward operations as a vital part of its overall defensive doctrine, i.e. a means of tying down the bulk of the Soviet navy in a defensive posture; indeed it will make such operations much less controversial.

Similarly if the Soviet Union issued detailed official data, for example, on submarine class names and numbers to help the compilers of the standard naval reference works and brought out issues of *Morskoi Sbornik* with as much information on Soviet naval activities as are regularly published on American (and indeed Soviet) activities in issues of United States Naval Institute *Proceedings*, this would have a constructive effect. Sir Geoffrey Howe said in Vienna in March, 'the key to confidence is information'. Giving precise information about vessels scrapped and the precise level of residual holdings is of real and particular importance in a context of unilateral reductions to prevent threat inflation by interested Western parties.

Another area where unilateral Soviet CBMs with a maritime dimension are called for is along the border with Norway. The Norwegians have for some time restricted Allied activities east of 24 degrees East and given warning of exercises significantly below the Stockholm threshold. The Soviets have not so far reciprocated as much as the Norwegians would have liked. The time has come for them to do so with a reciprocal unilateral régime limiting exercises. The 'Kirkenes' amphibious brigade should also be put into some kind of reduced readiness category like the Army formations deployed in the Kola Peninsula.

Discussing matters of mutual concern is a confidence building measure in itself. This should be expanded at an official level. The bilateral United States-Soviet, United Kingdom-Soviet, West German-Soviet, and Franco-Soviet Incidents at Sea agreements, as well as providing 'rules of engagement' for the East-West confrontation, already provide a context for such bilateral meetings. It is a matter of debate whether a clearly successful mechanism such as Incidents at Sea agreements should be over-burdened with an additional agenda but the Franco-Soviet agreement with its wider agenda, which includes personnel exchanges, is an interesting precedent. There might be advantages if the official teams that meet to discuss Incidents at Sea contain officers representing, say, the Plans divisions of both naval staffs, to help clear the air, to discuss each side's naval plans and programmes, and to prevent misunderstandings about each side's naval forces. Alternatively, such meetings might occur independently; regular meetings of Chiefs of Naval Staffs might also prove fruitful.

It might prove difficult to achieve internal alliance agreement on a NATO-Warsaw Pact 'Incidents at Sea' agreement. A 35 nation 'agreement on prevention of incidents in sea areas and airspace adjoining Europe' called for by the Warsaw Treaty Organisation (WTO) in Vienna in March might be even more difficult to obtain and would be subordinate to the existing bilateral arrangements between the relevant signatories. A better and more practical option is to widen the existing series of bilateral 'Incidents' agreements between NATO's major naval operating nations and the Soviet Union. This is being done by both Norway and Canada.

The only major contributor to NATO's forward strategy now left out is The Netherlands. This omission should be rectified rapidly. If a self-consciously 'small country' like Norway can sign a bilateral agreement with the Soviet Union, there could be no problem for the Dutch to do so, despite their natural preference for multilateral frameworks. Perhaps some joint Dutch-Belgian arrangement would satisfy Dutch sensitivity and reflect the close operational relationship of the Dutch and Belgian navies.

As for extensions to the provisions of 'Incidents' agreements themselves, it is hard to go much beyond the suggestion made by Admiral Hill in his seminal book *Arms Control at Sea*, that the parties to the Incidents agreement agree in principle 'that submarines of both sides will refrain from deliberate close approaches and mock attacks on vessels of the other party, both surface and submarine; and that if they believe a dangerous situation is developing they will transmit (on active sonar) in order to reveal themselves'.[3] Until recently, Western submarines had a well publicised sonar advantage that gave them an interest in such close encounters. The erosion of that advantage makes close manoeuvring less attractive. Technical progress thus reinforces the political imperative to damp down the intensity of the sub-surface confrontation and thus bring it into line with the improved climate of East-West relations.

As for multilateral agreements on confidence and security building measures (CSBMs), the classic paradigm is the Stockholm agreement of 1986. The CSBM Talks in Vienna are seeking to build on this agreement whose main aspects are:

- notification of 'significant' military activities over a certain threshold.
- observation of such activities over a certain threshold.
- an annual calendar of notifiable activities.
- a requirement to give warning of very large exercises up to two years in advance.
- on-site inspection to verify compliance.

Can these provisions be extended to the oceans and, if so, how and where?

The Warsaw Pact, which tried to include independent naval activities at Stockholm has, as we have seen, returned to the charge at Vienna with a set of naval proposals. These raise some basic problems that must be solved in the construction of a CSBM régime that would be in any way acceptable to the West. The latter began the Vienna CSBM negotiations by attempting to exclude independent naval activities from the Talks but, by the middle of 1989, official NATO spokesmen were revealing a new flexibility on the possibility of some kind of CSBM/'Transparency' régime at sea.[4]

Much work, however, needs to be done to develop the details of such maritime CSBMs. The fundamental problem that must be addressed first is the definition of the kinds of naval activities that are significant in the context of naval confidence building. The key here is which activities can be construed by the other side as 'threatening'? This question may be discussed by reference to the *nature* of the activities, the *area* in which they take place and the *time* they take: all three factors are interactive.

1 **Nature:** the characteristics of an activity that, if occurring unexpectedly, may diminish confidence are:
   Unusual concentration of naval forces;
   Unusually high activity levels (manoeuvres, flying operations, firing of weapons);
   Shift from normal peacetime command and control arrangements;
   Presence of forces with potential against the shore, notably carriers with long range dual capable strike aircraft, units carrying long range nuclear and conventionally armed land attack cruise missiles and large amphibious forces.
2 **Area:** the areas most sensitive to the participants are:
   On the Soviet side, the Northern Norwegian Sea, the Barents Sea, the Eastern Mediterranean, the Black Sea, the Baltic Sea, the Sea of Japan and Sea of Okhotsk;
   On the Western side, the entire Norwegian Sea and western Barents Sea, the Atlantic Sea Lines of Communication, the English Channel and North Sea, the Baltic, the Mediterranean, the Sea of Japan, the North Pacific, the Caribbean.
3 **Time:** Certain activities in certain areas might be seen as threatening even if they lasted for only a brief period of time. More sustained activities a few days steaming distance away from the sensitive areas might also seem threatening because of the potential for surprise forward movement by the whole or part of the force.

The basis of any multilateral confidence building arrangement must be 'notification', giving warning of manoeuvres that might otherwise take the other side by surprise and create a perception of threat. A lot of notification already takes place for safety reasons. Notices to mariners (NOTAMs) warn in advance of activities that might otherwise be dangerous, the principle of notification therefore is thus fully accepted already. It only remains to put it in a political framework. It is also important that *notification* be reported conceptually from *observation* and even more so from *constraint*. A lot of observation takes place at sea anyway as the oceans are free for all, unlike land areas. Notification, as well as creating confidence would make it a little easier for normal peacetime surveillance platforms to be properly placed to monitor events if other states wish to do so. The criterion for *official* observation, however, ought to be very different from those for mere notification. Only very large exercises that might create special concerns ought to qualify for such formal observation. It is important to emphasise this distinction as it is not so much the principle of notification that causes problems but the fear that all naval activities might have to be formally observed.

Naval professionals fear even more that notified activities might be 'constrained' in some way. It must be emphasised therefore in any notification régime that a warship's *right* to move in international waters is not being affected in any way. Moreover, routine low level activities such as trials and training must be allowed to take place freely. They usually threaten no one. CBMs, even notification measures, ought to acknowledge this and exclude normal day-to-day activities, or they will be rightly unacceptable to the naval establishments of either side. This leads to two interim conclusions:

> ***The first*** is that the areas initially to be covered by maritime CSBMs should be relatively limited. The majority of the areas of special concern mentioned above are 'ocean areas adjoining Europe' as included in the Madrid mandate, but even this area might be too large. It might seem appropriate for example to split the Eastern Atlantic/Norwegian Sea area from the Mediterranean. Naval operations in the former area (except 'out of area' transits) are wholly concerned with European security, or at least, the NATO-WTO confrontation. In the Mediterranean, naval forces are relevant to a wide range of situations, North African and Middle Eastern as well as European. Somehow, therefore, the Mediterranean naval problem should be addressed separately, although certain members of the 35 CSCE nations would undoubtedly disagree!
>
> It might also be necessary to draw up a set of different sub-zones in which different notification criteria applied. The latter would be most stringent for areas within missile range of the shore or across vital sea lines of communication.
>
> ***The second*** conclusion is that notifiable activities should be limited to clearly defined concentrations of naval power under a single overall operational commander. This is close in its wording to the Stockholm accords. Moreover, every professional knows what a naval operation, or naval exercise, is and in what way it differs from routine training conducted by ships or groups of ships at sea.

The Warsaw Pact March proposal contained a series of provisions concerning 'transfers' of naval forces into or within the zone of application. This again potentially interferes with normal non-threatening activities, probably to an unacceptable degree. It is only legitimate to expect notification of activities that are potentially threatening in terms of nature, area and time. This brings us back to clearly defined concentrations of naval power in certain areas and time frames under a single operational commander. In any case the 'transfers' might also be subject to a notification régime but the threshold would have to be much higher than those in the proposal and the 'single overall operational commands' criterion would also be relevant. The transfers of marines or shore-based aircraft detailed in the WTO proposal are more appropriately addressed by 'land' or 'air' CSBM régimes, just as amphibious landings are covered in the existing Stockholm accords.

Notification would not only benefit the Soviets. Obtaining prior warning of WTO naval exercises would be a significant asset for NATO naval commanders who have been taken by surprise by sudden Soviet naval activities in the past. Forward NATO areas, Norway in particular, might benefit from notification of major movements of Soviet surface ships and amphibious forces. This must, however, be balanced against any attempt to constrain legitimate and non-threatening Western naval activities, and the need to reassure allies, again such as Norway, of the certainty of maritime reinforcement in crisis.

Turning now to the main issues in notification, the Stockholm figure of 42 days, i.e. six weeks, should not pose too many problems at sea. Naval operations do, however, have an inherent flexibility that needs to be reflected in a more flexible notification régime. Although 42 days could be the norm, emergency naval movements 'out of area' that might otherwise be notifiable could be allowed at, say, 48 hours notice, as long as the cause was clearly stated and explained to the other signatories to the agreement. This exclusion would be a broadened variant of the 'alert' exception in the Stockholm accord.

Drawing up detailed notification criteria poses difficult problems. The WTO Vienna proposal seemed totally unrealistic to Western Naval officers. Indeed, some otherwise well disposed to the idea of a maritime CSBM régime, felt this played into the hands of those who argue that the main Soviet aim is propaganda. To notify all movements of five ships, including a single cruise missile armed ship of over 5,000 tons, would effectively make virtually every activity of the United States Navy subject to notification. As long as such vessels remain nuclear launching pads some relatively low notification threshold *in certain areas* might be appropriate, but nothing so general as implied by the Soviet suggestion.

As emphasised above, the key notification issue is threat. A pair of carriers exercising off the Virginia Capes is totally non-threatening; the same carriers within A6 range of the Soviet Union pose a considerable conventional and nuclear strike threat; the same carriers cruising just below the Greenland-Iceland-UK Gap might be a serious *potential* threat. Even small numbers of Tomahawk missile equipped surface combatants are quite threatening if deployed within missile range of Soviet targets.

The numbers of ships that would trigger notification is thus a function of their capability, location and the time they spend in the designated area. Defining such thresholds therefore could be a complex exercise. One possibility might be a set of sub-zones in which something like the WTO 'five' ships might be notifiable in all circumstances in certain very limited areas close to 'non allied' shores. Relatively large carrier or amphibious shipping movements would be notifiable in more distant areas defined again in terms of proximity to 'non allied' territory and especially if they intended to loiter or exercise there for more than a few days. If areas were important for other reasons, for example, the main sea lines of communication for a set of allies, they would be the subject of more stringent notification provisions for the forces of others. Areas close to one's own shore would normally be free of notification requirements, although if such areas were close to 'non allied' territory, the stringent notification criteria would take precedence and apply.

Notification criteria should cover major surface combatants only. Auxiliaries such as replenishment and depot ships, intelligence gatherers or even, perhaps, amphibious ships not operationally loaded should be excluded. The Soviet proposal of ships over 1,500 tons looks self-serving, given the large number of small surface combatants of about 1,000 tons in the WTO navies. A more appropriate criterion would be ships over 900 tons plus smaller craft if fitted with dual capable weapon systems.

Reluctantly, it will have to be accepted that submarines must be left out of notification. Including submarines creates insuperable verification difficulties. Those must of course be balanced carefully against the fact that large-scale movements of submarines into the Atlantic are the most disturbing naval activities from the Western point of view. It might be hard to hide a large scale submarine movement from 'national technical means', but the submarine community would resist notification of normal activities even more so than the surface sailors. There would also be inevitable arguments about the exact numbers of submarines engaged in any notifiable activity. Submarines are probably most stabilising when they are most covert and it is conceivable that more openness might actually increase threat perception rather than vice versa. The submarine threat problem is better addressed by the mutual denuclearisation measures (excluding SSBNs) discussed in the last chapter rather than attempting an impractical, unverifiable and therefore inherently disputed underwater régime that erodes rather than builds confidence. The only real solution to this awkward problem is a solution to the denuclearisation issue. Submarines equipped with limited numbers of conventional cruise missiles are much less threatening than submarines armed with nuclear cruise missiles or surface ships with larger missile magazines.

Aircraft, like submarines, create special problems. It is to be noted that the aircraft sortie provision in Stockholm Accord 31.1.2. is not a criterion for notification *per se*; it simply generates a need for supplementary notification in an already notifiable activity. The Soviets have proposed a rather different naval exercise notification figure of '80 aircraft' which would again cover all normal US carrier activities. Higher levels might be negotiable, or 'sorties' used as notification trigger on their own, linked to the 'single operational command' overall criterion which is the keystone of all definition of notifiable maritime activities. On the whole, however, making aircraft sorties a primary generator for notification does introduce complications and the Stockholm 'supplemental' model is preferred. Air sorties, of course, must include land-based aircraft as well as sea-based.

All the above refers only to *notification*. As for *observation*, as was made clear above, close surveillance of other nations' activities on the high seas is a well-established national maritime activity, and in the case of certain major states is governed by agreements designed to 'Prevent Incidents at Sea'. It is not proposed that these arrangements should be disturbed. They may well be enough to cope with normal activities, even with a notification régime. However, it is possible that if there were notification and no linked provisions for observation by agreement, unilateral surveillance might increase to a level so high as to *increase* the risk of incidents. This would be particularly the case in very large exercises.

On balance, therefore, the most promising way forward might be to make very large 'set piece' exercises observable on an agreed basis.

> Briefings could be given ashore prior to the observable activity to attachés, accredited observers and authorised officers who would be observing from surveillance units. These briefings would enable such observers to 'follow the flow' of the exercise and satisfy themselves that it was 'non-threatening in character'.
>
> Facilities in one non-combatant vessel of the nation carrying out the activity for a limited number of observers to accompany the main flow of activity, with update briefings and situation reports, to enable them to confirm that the activity is non-threatening and carried out in accordance with the provisions of the notification.
>
> Maximum numbers of allowed surveillance platforms might have to be limited in some way, for example, by allowing each bloc (NATO/WTO/NNA) to send two vessels. Each signatory might be allowed to send only two officers to the briefing and one observer to the assigned observation.

The observation criteria proposed by the Warsaw Pact, 25 combat ships of more than 1,500 tons or over 100 combat aircraft, are too low. About 40 vessels over 900 tons would seem about right for observation. Again NATO and NNA naval commanders might well find they had at least as much to gain from formally observing Soviet naval exercises as the Soviets had from observing theirs, although the Soviet Union very rarely has fleet exercises of more than 15 units. This once more reflects the fundamental East-West maritime strategic asymmetries; the West *needs* large-scale maritime exercises while the WTO does not.

The Stockholm 'constraints' *requiring* warning of one year for exercises of more than 40,000 men, and further constraints for those of more than 75,000 men, might also find a maritime echo. Maritime exercises of this scale, for example, Teamwork '88, involving 45,000 personnel, are always planned well in advance. The WTO proposal speaks of limiting exercises by size (50 combat ships), time (10-14 days) and number (6-8 annually). The acceptability of the principle of constraints should be separated from the figures which are once more far too low. The proposed ban on notifiable exercises in 'areas of intense activity or areas of international significance' would also need drastic watering down. Limitations on exercises in certain areas, where traffic separation schemes are in operation, are however included in current 'Incidents at Sea' agreements, and this could provide a basis for more general agreement. No constraint other than those imposed by International Law or prudent seaman-like practice could be entertained by the West.

As already emphasised, surveillance akin to on-site inspection already takes place frequently at sea, and the high seas are free for all. However, some supplemental, more intrusive 'inspection' measures might be considered appropriate. A naval agreement might therefore lay down certain procedures, for example, a right to ship visits by helicopter, no interference with sensors, the right to expect informative answers to certain questions if there was any doubt that the agreement was being broken. To prevent abuse, such requests could only be part of a full 'inspection', subject to all the Stockholm-type restrictions.

The Soviet Union has proposed that naval measures should be a subject of discussion at the Vienna CSBM Talks. As stated above, the Western position on this issue seems to be softening significantly. NATO can build constructively on its existing Vienna CSBM position which proposes comprehensive information exchanges on what Sir Geoffrey Howe broadly described as 'the size, location and equipment of participating states *armed forces*'[5] (author's emphasis); the West has also accepted the principles of discussing doctrine. It might well thus seem appropriate and even necessary for the West to concede the inclusion of naval matters in discussions of this kind. It would also seem discriminating to exclude naval personnel from the 'improved access by accredited diplomatic and military personnel to government authorities, and greater freedom for them to travel'[6] also proposed by the British Foreign Secretary as a legitimate subject for discussion at Vienna. The stage would thus be set for acceptable CSBMs covering independent naval activities. The whole pace of progress must be subject to the general dynamics of the parallel negotiations. The Western priority is steady movement in CFE: although the West might gain significantly from a notification régime at sea, the main aim in creating it would be to lubricate the negotiations of substantial reductions in the Warsaw Pact threat ashore.

CHAPTER 9

Maritime Forces and European Security—The Future

Maritime forces and general maritime capabilities must play a considerable role in the future of European security. If American ground and air forces are to continue to be deployed in Europe, especially in reduced numbers, maritime reinforcement will become more rather than less important. This will require both a credible maritime strategy and sufficient shipping to sustain initial conventional resistance and maintain 'long war uncertainty'.

European navies will play a relatively larger role in this process both as precursor forces and in contributions to joint operations with the Americans. Before the carriers arrive, European forces (plus Standing Naval Force Atlantic) can demonstrate crisis commitment without creating too many Soviet concerns. Equally, they can prepare the way for American carrier and amphibious forces to enter their fjord bastions by neutralising both the submarine and mine threats. Moreover, in order to be in a position to enter the fjord bastions, the NATO Striking Fleet must enter through waters swept by a European-based and commanded ASW Striking Force, clearing a path through the GIUK gap and into the Norwegian Sea. Once the Striking Fleet is safely ensconced, then the ASW Striking Force must keep at bay the enemy submarines which are trying to penetrate the carrier operating areas. During this phase, European assets can help screen the carriers and amphibious vessels and escort the vital convoys bringing up supplies. They can also contribute to and help influence the forward submarine offensive. Making the forward strategy work, as a kind of maritime fortress constructed at the right time and which the enemy ignores and by-passes only at his peril, is a co-operative Alliance venture.

There is nothing inherently offensive about the forward strategy, despite what some of its supporters say. Indeed, the fjord option makes this very clear. Putting the striking fleet into the fjords puts the ball firmly into the Soviet court; it is they who must then make the decision to attack. If they do, they go in with all the Clausewitzian disadvantages of the attacker. Hence, prudently, they might keep their forces back, especially if there is a Western submarine offensive to worry about in the

Barents Sea. One can quite easily imagine two great fleets maintaining themselves as 'fleets in being' in their northern fastnesses while a slow-motion submarine war goes on both in the Barents Sea and under the ice pack and, perhaps, a few Soviet submarines get out to do battle with the convoy escorts of the Atlantic lifelines campaign.

The probability of an early surge by Soviet submarines must, of course, be considered but, equally, a prudent Soviet naval commander would find it difficult to send too many assets far away as long as the Americans and their NATO allies had the option to bring forces close to Soviet base areas. The only thing keeping the Western enemy at bay in these circumstances are the Soviet submarines and aircraft: they have to be retained for this primary duty as long as the risk of carrier and cruise missile attack remains.

A few forward deployed Soviet submarines in the Atlantic could cause chaos, however, especially if they were of the newest and quietest types. The forward strategy is thus not an alternative to direct shipping defence but a way of containing the threat and reducing it to a level where NATO shipping defence forces can cope. European navies, notably NATO's southern and less integrated navies, have a major role to play here. Using classical terms, they will exercise the command of the sea gained by the main fleet in its forward operations.

It is not just a question, however, of defending the reinforcement and resupply ships. That sealift itself must be found. Europe is going to have to join the United States in considering direct ways of maintaining some core fleet of vessels for defence purposes. The principle of successful state intervention to maintain the health of private shipping for defence purposes is older than military navies and fully consonant with free market principles. Unless something is done to maintain the means of sea use, spending money on its defence will be wasted, as will all other aspects of national security expenditure.

Investment will also be required in Europe's own naval forces. This means much more explicit strategic thinking in order to make the required 'naval case'. This goes against the instincts of Europe's navies who know the value and importance of flexibility. Flexibility, however, is a vital *additional* benefit obtained by possessing forces designed to do specific things that are vital to the security concerns of the owning governments, rather than a powerful argument for expensive naval forces in itself. 'Flexibility' is, moreover, a two-edged sword: it can allow reduction in capability as well as its maintenance; maritime forces can become just a useful 'nice to have' adjunct to give a little 'flexibility' to an air-land defence budget shaped and costed to meet more specific and pressing threats. The 1981 British defence review was an example of such an exercise. With NATO strategy firmly directed in a more conventional direction, the importance of reinforcement ever greater and a coherent and credible strategy to defend NATO's vital shipping and project power where required, there is no excuse for naval staffs to concede to their air and land colleagues the bureaucratic initiative.

A wholehearted espousal of a confidence and security building régime at sea would greatly help this process. The West's navies must not be seen as Cold War dinosaurs clinging to outdated threats and offensive strategic rhetoric in order to maintain bloated force postures. Navies have a long tradition of acting as stabilising forces in international politics. They lend themslves much more than land and air forces to measures of 'ritualisation' and restraint. They have nothing therefore to fear from limited measures of co-operative security. Indeed, legitimised and formalised, their strategies and force postures might well command more universal consensus.

Navies have less to fear from the new world of reduced East-West tension than any other forces. The Soviet 'threat' has indeed only ever driven Western naval policy to a limited extent, hence the problems we have just discussed. Even Mr Nott, in 1982, was willing, reluctantly, to grant some naval expenditure to cope with 'out of area' contingencies and it is here, outside Europe, that the primary potential applications of force will emerge in the future. The East-West confrontation may have stimulated and sustained some Third World conflicts but it also set bounds to them for fear of provoking a major crisis. Third World nations will therefore in future be freer in taking action against foreigners with whom their interests conflict. Those foreigners will often be Europeans. Nationals will be threatened; ships carrying vital cargoes will be subject to attack. Limited naval force will be the opposite response and Europe may have to look after itself rather more than it has been used to doing. The cry will then be, 'Where is Europe's navy?'.

Appendices

Important landmarks in this research project were two pioneering meetings between British, American and Soviet naval experts, the first in Adderbury in Oxfordshire, England in July 1988 and the second in Moscow in February 1989. The latter was combined with a visit to the large anti-submarine ship **Kerch** *at Sevastopol. With the permission of the participants we are publishing the official record of the discussions. This gives a first-hand impression of the concerns and perspectives of both sides and the possibilities for progress in constructing a common security régime at sea. No names are mentioned to preserve anonymity.*

An extra appendix has been added to give readers the benefit of the third round of unofficial East West naval discussions, a dialogue on maritime strategy, that took place at Adderbury between distinguished experts from the USA, United Kingdom and USSR in November 1989 shortly after the main part of the book went to press. After the meetings the Soviet party was taken to Devonport to visit the frigate HMS **Avenger.**

APPENDIX I

Adderbury Conversations on Naval Strategy and Arms Control 30-31 July 1988

A. United States Maritime Strategy

1. The Americans explained their maritime strategy in terms of the nature of Western forces, the nature of adversary forces and national strategic culture. United States maritime strategy (a) was a defensive deterrent against a threatening land power, and (b) emphasises coalition warfare. Forward positioning of forces was required by both these factors. It reduced misperception and contributed to stability as well as economising on forces. Alternative strategies like direct defence of shipping were more force intensive. Once war begins, the American participants argued, maritime forces must be used offensively to be effective: the offensive was the stronger form of war at sea. The distinction was also drawn between Soviet power on land, which is both superior and 'inherent' given the Soviet Union's demography, location and system, and American sea power which was superior but not inherent given the unwillingness of the United States government and people to understand its strategic benefits, which are often long term and indirect. Sea power allowed the West to conceive of conventional maritime conflicts perhaps of a prolonged nature. Nuclear weapons were of little operational relevance to naval conflict: they cancelled each other out but they also reduced the objectives of each side. It was also pointed out that in prolonged conflicts in the past, powers confined to land strategies have usually lost.
2. In discussion, the Soviet participants saw a contradiction between the concept of a defensive deterrent and the traditional notion found in Mahan that those who owned the sea also owned the world. Moreover, naval forces tended to be the first to start conflicts. There was, however, consensus between the Superpower

participants that the fundamental role of navies affected what went on ashore: the land was the place where the decision was obtained. European participants said that their perspectives might be different: coalitions or states might be dependent on the use of the sea for their survival. Indeed, as the United States became more dependent on maritime trade its own vulnerability might increase. One Soviet participant doubted whether a large-scale war in Europe could remain conventional. With rapid escalation naval battles for lines of communication would rapidly become irrelevant. The Americans, however, felt the nuclear threshold was relatively high: indeed nuclear forces' main role in such a war would be to absorb conventional forces both for their attack and defence (e.g. SSBNs).

B. Soviet Maritime Strategy

1. A Soviet participant explained their naval strategy in terms of the technological revolution wrought by submarines, aircraft and long-range missiles. The influence of navies on the land battle had thus become more important. The Soviet Navy had a defensive orientation, being directed at protecting the Soviet Union and its allies from seaborne attacks. Most of its weapons were aimed at naval targets not targets ashore: its amphibious forces were too small to play a decisive role. The Soviet Union was not going to land troops from the sea on the American continent. The Soviets relied primarily on conventional means at sea. If nuclear weapons were used at sea their use would spread to the land and it might be worthwhile to pursue Paul Nitze's idea of a tactical denuclearisation of navies. Another Soviet participant expressed concern about naval forces having great momentum from an arms race point of view, given their long lead times and service lives and their relatively vague and broad operational context. Destabilising trends had to be managed rationally and intelligently. Multilateral dialogue in which assumptions and strategies were explained could help, especially as the first unilateral moves towards stabilisation might look destabilising to the other side. Sea-based systems, previously considered stabilising, were now acquiring destabilising features; counter force SLBMs, accurate hard-to-detect cruise missiles. In its emphasis on attacks on SSBNs and forward crisis deployment, United States maritime strategy seemed destabilising and escalatory. Naval warfare could indeed be inherently destabilising given the concentration of enormous firepower on a small number of platforms. The most important thing to discuss, however, was not only limiting or cutting hardware, but strategies, planning

and mutual restructuring and reductions of the navies in a defensive direction.

2. In discussion, Western participants expressed doubts about the possibility of devising a wholly defensive force structure for naval forces. Forces attacking ships could be sinking merchantmen: navies attacking shore targets could be defending Europe. The 'battle of the first salvo' emphasised by Gorshkov could look offensive or defensive depending on one's point of view. At this point a Soviet participant emphasised that Gorshkov's theories need not be Soviet state policy and could indeed be wrong. The Soviets again emphasised the asymmetry of the American naval threat to land targets with carriers and cruise missiles and the relatively small proportion of Soviet naval strength allocated to land targets. Operations against sea communications in the Atlantic, they argued, were a secondary task for the Soviet Navy, although the targets were important—960 cargo ships loaded with troops and weapons in the first month. Soviet participants acknowledged the complexities of reducing Eastern and Western navies, given the differences in operational tasks. The best way forward was to start with peripheral, modest but useful means of increasing predictability and confidence building.
3. American participants emphasised that the United States fleet had to be able to participate in the land battle if it was to deter. If the Warsaw Pact attacked first then all naval operations were defensive, except anti-SSBN operations. In response, the Soviet experts emphasised that if, on the contrary, the East was on the defensive then operations against carriers and convoys were defensive. If both sides reduced and restructured land forces and tactical air so that neither side was capable of attack, naval problems would become clearer and then United States and NATO maritime strategy would become unjustifiably offensive: restraints to match those on land would then be required. If significant movement was taking place at Vienna, then it would be the right time to do something significant navally. The United States, however, opposed direct linkage between naval matters and the Vienna talks. There was also the Third World dimension. The United States would continue to value its capacity to intervene in local actions. The Soviet Union might find such capability useful also. To this the Soviets expressed their disagreement.

C. American Concerns with Soviet Maritime Strategy

1. American participants stressed the importance of Atlantic communications to the defence of Europe. If forces on land were

reduced, reinforcements, and hence the Atlantic, might become even more important. Soviet submarines and bombers posed a threat to Atlantic reinforcements, and to the flow of manufactured goods and raw materials across the Pacific. The new Soviet bomber posed a particular threat to Atlantic communications. The United States was forced to adopt a forward strategy to tie down these forces or draw them out to be destroyed. Moreover, Soviet amphibious forces posed threats to America's allies within Soviet 'bastions'. Soviet 'wing-in-ground' machines (WIGs), air cushion landing craft and merchant ships were a potent amphibious threat: most forces landed would be army troops not marines.

2. Discussion then focused on SSBNs. The Westerners argued that quieting was the best solution to the problem of vulnerability. 'Trailing' might become cost effective if numbers came down to very small figures (5-8), but decoy submarines with identical characteristics might be used to prevent this. The Soviet participants claimed there was a blocking mechanism, to prevent unauthorised missile launch: American participants doubted if the electronic blocking was total. For both sides firing of ballistic missiles was impossible while the SSBNs were under attack. One could see from an SSBN's movements if it was preparing to fire. An American participant insisted that the idea of SSBNs being on some kind of 'hair trigger' was grossly over-played and that it was as difficult to launch an American missile under current procedures as it would be with any formalized electronic locking system.
3. According to the Americans, the most threatening Soviet nuclear weapons at sea were long-range air-to-surface missiles. The United States, it was agreed, would rather not use nuclear weapons at sea, but they were difficult to dispose of. One needed nuclear weapons to deter their use by the other side, weapons that threatened to spread the nuclear war to the land. A no-first-use option at sea would be in the United States' interest but the West still needed the option of striking with nuclear weapons from the sea against targets ashore because of the need to utilise the Navy to affect the land battle as much as possible. There was no direct symmetry between naval forces vs. naval forces and land forces vs. land forces. The United States, it was stated, had given up most nuclear anti-submarine weapons: nuclear depth bombs were not being modernised. Operationally their use created great problems and political approval for their use would be impossible. Banning them, however, would be very difficult to verify: it was better to allow them to pass out of the inventory. It was suggested nevertheless, not only by the Soviets but also by the Western participants,

that the common interest expressed by both sides in removing tactical nuclear weapons at sea might be exploited in some way.

4. Reciprocal cuts were suggested by a Soviet participant, on the Soviet side in forces orientated against Atlantic shipping, i.e. submarines and land-based aviation in return for reductions in land attack and strategic ASW forces by the West. The problem, Western participants replied, was that Western forces were not sized in relation to the threat but in relation to the assets being defended, for example, the number of escorts depended on the number of convoys, the number of maritime aircraft on the number of patrol areas. Quieter submarines required more ASW forces. Balanced reductions would therefore not work. One American participant stated that reductions by both sides on the ground might actually increase the need for offensive naval forces.

   The Soviets suggested that regardless of the assets being defended, which is relevant also for the Soviet Union in defending its shores and SSBNs, limitations and reductions on offensive capabilities of both sides would, other things being equal, improve their respective defences for which the forces would not be limited.

D. Soviet Concerns with United States Maritime Strategy

1. Soviet participants expressed general concern with the 'aggressive' nature of United States naval doctrine as perceived by them, the growth of the cruise missile threat, the large size of the United States Marine Corps and the growth planned for amphibious forces. Particular concern was expressed with the major NATO maritime manoeuvres that take place close to Soviet territory, within range of NATO strike systems. These exercises seem provocative to the Soviet Union, for example, three carriers operating simultaneously in the Sea of Japan.
2. One Soviet participant made the point that it was 3,500 kilometres from the inter-German border to the Urals. Taken the opposite way, that distance reached out 2,000 kilometres into the Atlantic. There was therefore symmetry in limitation measures of some kind affecting both areas. He argued the time required for Soviet troops to advance from the Urals to the line of division was the same as for United States troops to move from the United States to Europe. Reducing forces in Europe to a minimum level and giving them a defensive character would, he argued, reduce the need for naval communications.
3. Much discussion centred on sea-launched cruise missiles (SLCMs). One Soviet participant suggested a ban on long range SLCMs. The Soviet Union did not need them and the only way they could be used was to approach within 2,000 kilometres of the coast of

the United States. This was difficult, given the strong ASW defences in these areas. Another Soviet participant, however, argued that SLCMs might be more useful to the Soviet Union than the United States. The Soviet Union had smaller submarine launched ballistic missile forces than the United States. Eight hundred SLCMs would therefore be a proportionately greater increase in nuclear naval striking power for the Soviet Union. Cruise missile submarines can be deployed forward freely in peacetime and a higher proportion of United States targets are close to the coast. Long range cruise missiles could be fired from SSBN bastions to hit European targets. Soviet participants insisted that current 'cruise missiles' like the SS-N-3 had always been anti-ship, not land attack systems.

4. One Soviet participant suggested a SLCM verification system based on functionally related observable differences (FRODs), counting rules and inspections. It might be necessary, he argued, to change the operational characteristics of a system to make limitations on it verifiable. This was being done with mobile ICBMs: information on technical capabilities, counting rules and inspections were allowing mobile ICBMs to be included in a START agreement. These might make mobile ICBMs less effective but they were necessary to make 50 per cent reductions possible. A similar principle should be applied to SLCMs. Counting rules could confine cruise missiles to certain submarines: other submarines could be inspected very infrequently. Certain types of submarines could be designated as cruise missile carriers. Different launchers could be used for nuclear and conventional missiles. Missiles could be tagged and checked at the assembly plant to check overall numbers. A number of different kinds of synergistic measures, all individually acceptable, could provide a workable SLCM verification system.
5. Very considerable emphasis was placed by Western participants on the need for more Soviet data. Soviet participants supported this and stated they were trying to achieve a more open approach. This process of military *glasnost* is under way and arms control progress will greatly accelerate it.
6. Western participants in this session and others experienced doubts about the existence of a real naval arms race. There had not been any build up in Western naval forces, indeed numbers of carriers, for example, had come down. In terms of quality, many naval weapons were old and had been around for some time. The Soviet experts pointed out that military shipbuilding competition, and introduction of successive generations of more effective naval weapons continuing at high tempo, makes the naval balance less stable, the first salvo more tempting, and expenditure more burdensome.

E. Soviet Ideas on Naval Co-operative Security

1. A Soviet participant set out a series of areas where one might begin to include naval forces in the arms control process. When progress was being made on land many people asked whether dialogue on naval matters would follow. One had to start at the easiest measures and then move to more substantial ones. The best measures to develop would be:

   (a) ***Incidents at Sea agreement:*** The existing pair of bilateral agreements were helpful but they were not specific. Perhaps one ought to insert data on distances of approach etc. Such agreements might also evolve into a framework that involved other countries regionally or globally.
   (b) ***Trust building measures:*** Notification of manoeuvres is helpful in itself and creates a mechanism of communication. Invitations of observers to exercises also create an atmosphere of trust. The implementation of the Stockholm I provision is going smoothly.
   (c) ***Restrictions on activities:*** To limit the scope of manoeuvres, the number allowed in a certain period of time, in certain regions and areas.

2. A British participant said that there would probably be general agreement that the best way to go was gradually to build confidence. He expressed doubts about specific distances as this would tend to define an acceptable distance of approach laid down by treaty that might be inadvisable in certain circumstances. He also raised the possibility of measures to avoid submarine incidents, for example, mutual unilateral declarations of intent by all SSN operators to avoid submarine incidents. Submarines knowing other submarines were in the vicinity would act with restraint and if they thought a dangerous situation was developing would transmit on active sonar. As for confidence building measures, establishing the size of exercises to be affected might be difficult. Routine training ought not to be affected, only heavily pre-programmed exercises. Observers might best be accommodated in auxiliaries equipped with remotely communicated plots. This would allow a similar view of the flow of the exercise to that obtained by observers of exercises on land. The main purpose of observers is to ensure that the exercise is not a threat: their purpose is not to gather intelligence. A number of measures, for example, inspections, briefings, agreed approaches of the other side's warships to the area of manoeuvres, would all add up to increased confidence.

3. Discussion ensued on the practicability of inspection of naval exercises. Soviet tactics, it was argued by an American participant, tended not to put auxiliaries with the combatants. Their forces were more dispersed and emphasised submarines and aircraft that were more difficult to observe. It was argued, however, that exercise briefings plus some air observation would give a good impression of what was happening. Soviet participants also disputed that their exercises were more dispersed than the Americans'.
4. It was pointed out that dialogue was already beginning at Chiefs of General Staff level between the United States and the Soviet Union. More discussion of tactics, operations and doctrines would have an enormous confidence building effect.
5. A Soviet participant emphasised the question of fixing minimum limits between ships, and between submarines and ships. There are difficulties in establishing distance limits between submarines but submarines can track surface ships with a great deal of precision. Given incidents between submarines and surface ships, for example, in the Mediterranean, it was desirable to put more precise and detailed parameters into the agreement. There might be other parameters other than distances of approach. The problem might be resolved at expert level.
6. An American participant expressed doubts about altering an agreement that had worked well for the previous sixteen years. Set approach distances might make it work less well. As Admiral Gorshkov said, 'the better is the enemy of the good enough'. The best way of restricting the approach of submarines to surface ships is for them to be ordered not to. As for CBMs, one should define closely where confidence was being built and about what. Surprise attack from naval axes was unlikely. One should not uncritically apply to naval matters measures which work on land, but there is little dispute about their value in Europe. In reply, a Soviet participant said that many of the criticisms of naval CBMs apply in principle to those on land also. However, he agreed it was indeed necessary to know where one was going: there was an old Russian naval saying 'if you do not know where you are going then any course will take you there'.

F. Western Ideas on Naval Co-operative Security

1. A British participant led the discussion by emphasising the need to build the right kind of confidence on both sides. Unannounced exercises can cause alarm. More dialogue, properly conducted, would build confidence. Given the dispersal inherent on both sides' exercises, observation would have to be supported by good

briefing. Many constraint measures supported in the past by the Soviet Union—nuclear-free zones, zones of peace, etc., were not in the forefront of any worthwhile agenda as they were non-negotiable. Anti-submarine warfare sanctuaries to safeguard SSBNs pose serious difficulties for the West due to asymmetries in SSBN operations. They also have inherent problems: if too small they are subject to blanket attack, if too large they are difficult to police and possible violations raise the temperature considerably. They safeguard Soviet operations while doing nothing for US SSBN operations. They are therefore non-negotiable.

2. On the question of tactical nuclear weapons at sea, there was rather considerable vagueness on both sides as to doctrines of use. No one seems sure when these weapons should be used, what for or with what likely result. Why not therefore keep SLCMs and scrap the rest? One significant problem was doubts over the effectiveness of conventional ASW weapons, especially the effectiveness of torpedoes. Many Western naval officers would like to keep the option to use nuclear ASW weapons in desperation. In the above water field, nuclear weapons were less necessary: they were some kind of last ditch reserve. One acceptable proposal might therefore be a 50 per cent reduction in TNW for use at sea.
3. A Soviet participant suggested extending the ban in the Incidents at Sea agreements on naval exercises in busy straits to a ban on unexpected exercises in areas close to such channels, for example, the Gulf of Mexico, the Straits of Gibraltar, the Baltic and the Channel; American battleships in the Baltic and Soviet warships in the Gulf of Mexico had both created political storms. Western participants were quick to deny the Soviets any potential *droit de regard* over the Baltic. No one in the West, it was argued, wanted large scale 'spheres of influence' at sea. The only legitimate question was rights of passage in territorial waters: these excluded intelligence gathering and surveillance.
4. Some Western participants strongly expressed the view that even nuclear depth charges were operationally and politically unusable. Soviet participants agreed there might be scope for discussion to remove tactical nuclear weapons from naval forces. The West would have an interest in an agreement because nuclear weapons were as essential to the Soviets at sea as they were to NATO on land. The problem of land-based aviation being an important maritime nuclear strike arm could, however, be addressed by not allowing anti-ship missiles to be deployed in nuclear versions. Soviet strategic aviation was replacing its currently outwardly similar nuclear missiles by new ALCM and new bombs. If conventional weapons could deal with carriers the need for nuclear weapons would diminish.

5. An American participant emphasised that the American maritime strategy was not a nuclear strategy. US naval strategy was primarily conventional. Soviet participants, however, emphasised that denuclearisation of naval forces was not so attractive unless it was done elsewhere. Conventional and nuclear warfare were closely connected. One had to be careful not to increase the likelihood of conventional warfare. The aim was to raise the nuclear threshold and deal with the risk of inadvertent escalation. Defensive restructuring was the main priority, reduction was secondary. One could never solve the problem by just deploying 'defensive' systems. One had to concentrate on the operational level: where possible one ought to try to reduce the comparative advantage of offensive operations. One could not totally eliminate the threat to sea lines of communication or naval threats to the shore. What one might be able to do was to reduce relatively Soviet forces and capabilities against Atlantic communications in return for Western reductions in strategic ASW and the capability to use strike carrier forces to attack bases.
6. Western participants were very sceptical about this. Navies had inherent flexibility and reach that it was hard to limit and which were necessary for a capacity to deal with still important Third World countries. Naval forces were not specialised into offensive and defensive components. The threat to Atlantic shipping is much more conditioned by the capability of submarines than the numbers: a reduction of 50 per cent in numbers of submarines would not change the threat. Better submarines, even in smaller numbers, require more escorts as one reverts to convoy, a strategy driven by numbers of ships, not the numerical strength of the threat.
7. These difficulties seemed to emphasise CBMs and perhaps a reduction in tactical nuclear weapons. As to the areas to be covered by measures, there was agreement that the Mediterranean posed special problems. A Soviet participant suggested it might be better to concentrate on the Atlantic north of the Tropic of Cancer. After that other areas might be considered.
8. Western participants felt that more Soviet naval visits to Western ports would be helpful. It was pointed out by one participant that it had indeed already been agreed that the heads of the United States Navy and the Soviet Navy would meet and that a few more port visits were being arranged and exchange of personnel encouraged on a bilateral United States-Soviet basis. Such small steps should be built upon and extended to other Western countries.

G. The Way Forward

1. First the connection between naval co-operative security measures and the wider arms control agenda—especially the conventional stability negotiations—was explored. A Soviet participant said that the processes were *not* linked, just as there was no direct linkage between conventional and nuclear arms control. Attempts directly to link progress at sea with the start of the conventional arms control talks would drown the whole thing. Nevertheless the Soviet Union wanted both progress at sea and on land. The best way was for progress to be made in some kind of parallel way, with processes that were not linked officially or formally. There might, however, be an understanding that maybe, at some time ahead, a more formal connection might be made. Speed of progress in one area might well be faster than in another. In no way would Soviet maritime concerns hold up initial progress in conventional arms control but if long-term progress in these talks was to be expected, then Soviet maritime concerns would have to be addressed in some way or other.
2. As for naval negotiations, CDE II was suggested although there were serious problems given the 35 nation format. The Soviet Union hoped to include independent naval operations in the second round of CDE but it did not seem likely that they would succeed. Alternatives were direct negotiations, for example, meetings of NATO and Warsaw Pact experts, bilateral contacts between experts, visits of chiefs of services, exchanges of naval personnel. The Soviet participants gave the impression of wanting something, however small.
3. There was general support for meetings of experts either official or unofficial. Much might be achieved by bringing together people who really understood operations. It was very important to the Soviets that Western misperceptions be corrected. Both sides needed to convince the other that they were less threatening than their adversaries thought.

Commentary

A. The Problem

(i) The July consultation clearly demonstrated that there was a form of symmetry between the Western threat perception created by an offensively orientated Eastern force posture in Europe and the perceptions created in the East by an offensively orientated Western maritime force posture at sea. The Soviets seemed to be saying:

(a) we recognise your valid concerns with our forces on land;
(b) we are therefore willing to make major asymmetrical cuts and engage in major defensive restructuring to create a more stable situation;
(c) it is, however, difficult to justify this if you continue to insist on a blanket ban on any consideration of independent naval operations.

(ii) It is, however, hard for the West to make any kind of concession at sea. The high seas are free to all; it would be an unacceptable political concession to have them divided up into spheres of influence where legitimate movement was constrained. Moreover, the West is crucially dependent on maritime supplies in peace and war. That dependence will not necessarily be affected by conventional force reductions in Europe, indeed it might well be increased. Neither is the West that strong at sea that it can dispense with an offensive operational doctrine. Moving to 'defensive restructuring' might well increase the demand for forces, given the nature of maritime operations. The foward maritime strategy is a result of a perception of inadequate resources for alternative strategies; it is not a rationale for an unnecessarily bloated United States Navy. It is interesting that the initial cuts in United States naval forces have come in convoy escorts not power projection forces. The latter are also most useful in peacetime contingencies as well as wartime.

(iii) The Soviet Union clearly feels unconfident at sea. It was interesting how Western fears of premature denuclearisation in Europe got more than an echo in Soviet attitudes to denuclearisation at sea. Exploiting this perceived Soviet vulnerability at sea made a great deal of deterrent sense when Europe was threatened by apparently overwhelming conventional military power. It still makes sense—as long as the Soviet Union fails to show the effects of its changes in doctrine in its overall force posture. It will progressively fail to make sense, however, when and if the first significant moves are made to dismantle that land threat. The West's offensive posture—fully admitted by the American analysts—will have to be amended in some way to correspond, while still keeping as strong an overall defence posture at sea as possible, as mandated by Western interests both in and out of area.

(iv) Certain fundamental differences of perspective kept emerging. Not least was the very different approach taken by Soviet and Western participants towards the very nature of navies and the sea. The former saw patterns of maritime strategy in very military terms; areas of sea, spheres of control or constraint, sea power very much as an extension of conventional land power in the peripheral sea areas. Although there were differences of perspective between the Americans and the Europeans, the former emphasising the sea as a medium for power projection ashore, the latter as a medium by which the wherewithal to survive economically and militarily arrived, both had a much clearer idea of the inherent flexibility and reach of navies and the difficulties those features posed to any arms control trade-off.

B. The Requirement

(i) Nevertheless, the Western view that maritime operations are permanently 'off limits' cannot be sustained, especially if progress is to be made elsewhere, and even more so if it is being made elsewhere. The aim is to:

(a) show that we recognise Soviet concerns;
(b) demonstrate some willingness to address these concerns both formally and informally;
(c) in no way commit ourselves to reducing Western naval forces in the short to medium term.

(ii) This last point is crucial. Many in Western defence and naval bureaucracies see the beginning of a maritime dialogue as 'the thin end of the wedge'. This perception is increased by official Soviet statements that seem to call for rapid and major cuts in Western naval forces. Possibly these calls reflect the 'hardline' ideas and mind-set hinted at by our Soviet colleagues. They do not help. The consultation demonstrated that there was real scope for progress *if the agenda was left limited to practical measures* such as confidence building measures and perhaps limitations on tactical nuclear weapons. It was encouraging to see the consensus that could be obtained in these issues between Soviet and Western participants.

(iii) It must, however, be recognised that formal negotiations on even these limited matters can only be a medium not a short term objective. What is needed is a thin end of a wedge whose wider end is made up of these limited practical measures, nothing more, at least until CST has made such substantial progress that each side clearly perceives that we are in a qualitatively different security situation. What is needed now therefore is to continue talking unofficially and, before not too long, to begin to make more contacts at an expert level. Official bilaterals might lead on to wider consultations. However, the Soviet Union is going to have to be a good deal more forthcoming in all such discussions in reaching the standards set by the Americans in terms of the quality and quantity of the data that is produced on operational and technical matters. Similarly the Americans are going to have to become more open-minded in their approach to the nature of the East-West security problem and perceptions of common security. One, however, will probably lead to the other.

APPENDIX II

Moscow Conversations on the Limitation of Naval Activities and Confidence Building Measures at Sea, February 1989

1. Soviet Proposals

First, Soviet participants expressed their satisfaction that the naval dialogue was continuing. Naval forces, they argued, were an inseparable component of the global balance of forces and had to be taken into account in the efforts to avert armed conflict, strengthen stability, facilitate reductions in force levels and reduce the expenditure on huge military infrastructures. A basic premise on the Soviet side was that the naval balance is highly unstable. Fleets are not confined to national borders, they maintain contact and they possess huge destructive power. The limited number of naval platforms facilitates a first strike, and as a rule such a strike ensures victory. As a consequence, in crisis the greatest threat of first strike occurs at sea. Moreover, at sea there is no sharp line between conventional and nuclear weapons. All ships and submarines are potential carriers of tactical nuclear weapons and there is no clear cut border between these and strategic nuclear weapons. Naval forces were also more expensive than others and had huge arms race inertia behind them; ships take a long time to construct and last a long time, current ships and submarines will serve into the twenty-first century and will influence the future strategic situation. The elimination of naval arms from the arms control agenda was thus a major problem.

The Soviet participants pointed out that up to now naval forces have not been included in negotiations. The West's answer was that the main problems lay elsewhere. Therefore, until negotiations on land and air forces began, naval discussions were inappropriate. Negotiations were now starting in the correlation of forces and armaments from the Atlantic to the Urals. There was no *linkage* between these latter talks and naval matters, but from the *political* point of view, progress on the problems of Europe had to be *correlated* with negotiations on naval forces and activities. The latter were an inseparable part of the correlation of forces. At some point, both sides would have to start negotiations on naval matters, and informal exchanges of opinions such as this were useful as preparation for official contacts. One had to know the positions and arguments of others. It was hoped, however, that these discussions would lead on to practical deeds.

Another Soviet participant then went on to remind the group of the intensive and positive developments in world affairs since its last meeting at Adderbury at the end of July. Positive trends in world affairs had developed intensively and strongly: implementation of INF, the Vienna meeting, the unilateral cuts in WTO armed forces, the withdrawal from Afghanistan, progress on Kampuchea and Angola, Gorbachev's speech at the United Nations and his forthcoming visit to the United Kingdom. Constructive trends were developing very fast and it was hoped that limiting the confrontation on the oceans would be discussed in a constructive manner. We had to pass through misunderstanding to bring forward points of understanding. American participants at Adderbury had called upon the Soviet Union to be more frank and concrete in its approach: this had been taken into account in the recently published data on naval forces released to the United Nations and the data released on naval forces in the European region. Three problems were then identified.

(i) Security had to be mutual, based on principles of parity and sufficiency. This principle had to be extended to the naval sphere. It was illusory to think that a one-sided security system would be maintained at sea. Instead, the principle of mutual security and sufficiency should be spread to the naval sphere: it should not lag 'catastrophically behind' other spheres. There should be overall balance in the military-political situation, even though naval forces were not part of the CFE negotiations. The United States argues that its geostrategic position means that it should be a preponderant naval power but the Soviet Union objects to this. The Soviet Union does not argue that its geostrategic position gives it a right to preponderance on land. Sea communications are more or less important to all countries, islands and continental powers alike.

(ii) The Soviet Union feared that Western fleets had a first strike capability in great depth against their own forces. It was logical and understandable that the West should fear the threat to sea lines of communication, but although the West saw forward deployment as an answer to that threat, the Soviets saw the new

'Lehman-Watkins ocean strategy' in a different light. Naval aircraft and cruise missiles could reach deep into the European and Asiatic continents. They were very effective in denying the Soviets *their* rail and road communications. There was thus a very specific and intimate link between naval forces and the problems on land. Both sides would, however, face great difficulty in controlling naval operations, especially the activities of submarines. This would require greater scientific effort.

(iii) It was necessary to create more interest in the naval confrontation. Until recently, naval forces were beyond the horizons of attention, far from the activities of civil populations. The Soviet Union also had not wished to discuss naval matters in the past, partly out of a sense of inferiority. Now all this had changed. The Soviet Union was now ready to talk about naval matters: they would also be subject to more public attention as the danger of the naval confrontation became clearer. The Soviet Union was concerned about the independence of the United States Navy and its great influence in Congress. More effort was needed to start a naval dialogue. The new United States Administration was beginning to develop an agenda in consultation with its allies. The other Western democracies should develop their own positions on this question and dialogue will provide us with the possibility to solve these problems.

A third Soviet participant then listed various Soviet proposals as an invitation to dialogue. He admitted the proposal might contain weak points but the Soviet side would be glad to hear counter-proposals of a constructive character. The common feature of all the Soviet proposals was limitation of arms and organisational structure to the necessities of defence for oneself, friends and allies. The capability for pre-emptive attack should be removed. Parameters and limits were being proposed from the point of view of defensive sufficiency. The Soviet proposals included:

(a) Limiting the possibility of attacking shore targets and the means of capturing territory;
(b) Cuts on a balanced basis in the numbers of warships in different classes and numbers of ships with tactical nuclear weapons on board;
(c) In order to safeguard sea communications, the prohibition of manoeuvres and training in sea routes and in fishing zones;
(d) Measures to prevent piracy;
(e) Terms for withdrawing some nuclear arms from some zones;
(f) Creating in some regions zones of lower armament and zones of

verification: all offensive forces would be withdrawn from these areas;

(g) Limit the number of ships with nuclear weapons on board and prevent them coming close to the shores of the other side;

(h) Limit the deployment of amphibious forces;

(i) Stop the construction of naval bases in certain areas;

(j) Limit naval arms in stages using the United Nations as a forum;

(k) Consider United Nations naval forces;

(l) Naval confidence building measures (CBMs). A system of control and transparency would be created with provisions for inspection. This might be done under the aegis of the United Nations;

(m) Exchange of information on naval activities to improve understanding and predictability. Information could also be exchanged in quantities of ships and aircraft;

(n) Notification of naval manoeuvres and the circulation of observers. The numbers and scale of naval manoeuvres might be limited;

(o) Establish which ships carry nuclear weapons and which do not and be prepared to co-operate to set up appropriate verification procedures.

Of all the above, CBMs offer the greatest immediate potential.

In discussion Western participants made a number of points:

The only way to reinforce areas such as Norway was by sea: in this context amphibious forces were essentially defensive. Indeed, in general, it was difficult to define forces as inherently offensive or defensive. Submarines were another good example; the Soviets viewed them as means of defending their ballistic missile submarines but NATO saw them as a means of attacking lines of communication. These differences of outlook reflected fundamental realities: naval forces were mobile with inherent flexibility.

Naval forces, far from being destabilising had in fact, on the whole, assisted in the maintenance of world stability. In the Gulf, the presence of naval forces was a powerful stabilising influence; Western and Soviet navies had been able to operate in the same waters without conflict.

The United States Navy regarded itself as every bit as much concerned with preventing war as the Soviet Navy. Sailors recognised common interest and shared common understandings. In fact, navies had led the way in East-West dialogue with the Incidents at Sea Agreement of 1972, designed to prevent inadvertent conflict. Other arms control agreements, such as strategic weapons agreements and the ABM Treaty, had an impact on naval forces.

The United States believes that its stake in the sea is greater than that of the Soviet Union and that the advantages for it in Soviet naval proposals are not entirely clear.

The West finds it hard to share Soviet concerns about the threat of surprise attack from the sea.

There was a need to identify the basic conceptions of seapower resulting from the naval histories of the two sides. British experience in the two wars demonstrated the crucial importance of the sea as a transport medium and the need for superiority in numbers to ensure defensive sufficiency at sea. Hence a preponderance at sea was not as threatening as a similar preponderance on land. It was, however, possible to look at the past and come to different conclusions.

There was some discussion of the Incidents at Sea agreement. Some support was given to the idea of expanding such bilateral agreements. It was suggested that the United States was becoming more open-minded about multilateral arrangements if these did not supplant existing working arrangements. It was confirmed that consultations were taking place between the Soviet Union and France on the possibility of an Incidents at Sea agreement. Some discussion had taken place with China but there were no concrete proposals.

In conclusion, a Soviet participant emphasised their view that naval forces were part of the overall strategic balance and that the West was superior to the WTO. The process of deep cuts will soon start and could be very dynamic. Naval forces could capture territory: their task was not just to safeguard communications. An objective evaluation of naval activities was required.

2. Confidence Building Measures

A paper was presented (from which Chapter 8 of this book has been developed).

A Soviet participant stated that discussion in such concrete terms was welcome. The Soviet Union could be equally specific. The West was especially concerned with the Atlantic, the Soviet Union with the Barents Sea, but both sides were concerned with the Norwegian Sea. The latter could thus be singled out as an area for CBMs. Carriers posed special problems as they carried nuclear ammunition: thus they could not but concern the Soviet Union. Two proposals were offered:

(a) any action by fleets should be notifiable if 20 or more ships with a displacement of more than 1,500 tons were involved;

(b) the limit would be lower if one ship had a displacement of 5,000 tons or more: this could be a specific figure, such as five.

(This forms part of the Warsaw Pact proposal at Vienna on 9 March, 1989.)

Operations by Western carrier task forces in the Vestfjord area caused concern on the Soviet side. Attack aircraft could reach from these areas into Soviet territory. The limit of five ships if one was over 5,000 tons was meant to cover concern about the activities of cruise missile equipped warships that could strike at long range against land targets.

As for submarines, the Soviet participant agreed that observation of submarine activities was very difficult. However, he felt that the movement of submarines ought to be notifiable and need pose few special problems if East and West agreed. He also suggested areas into which submarines should not be allowed to enter: if a violation was suspected, recognised channels could be used to get the suspected submarine to emerge. If no submarine was there, then the suspicion would have been proved to be unfounded. He also argued that there should be discussion of each side's thinking on submarine employment and agreement in the defensive nature of submarine operations; otherwise progress on submarine operations could not be made. He also discussed the setting up of areas for the operation of sea-based strategic forces. Surface forces would be prevented from entering such zones: this could be monitored by national technical means. There was also the possibility of controlling submarine activities in such zones also.

He suggested that the threshold for observation should be close to that for notification. In general, the sea should be included in the proven CDE arrangements, adjusted as necessary for the specific features of naval forces. He also seemed reluctant to make Incidents at Sea agreements global or multilateral, although global rules to prevent submarine collisions might be useful.

The question of amphibious forces also needed addressing further. Currently only landing operations were notified, but ships with marines at sea constituted a threat. It did not take long to land a brigade.

A Western participant pointed out that carrier operations were crucially important to Norway's defences. Also asymmetry of forces, for example, submarines and land-based aircraft being the prime counters to Western carrier operations, needed to be taken into consideration. Platforms had to be grouped into packages and proposals should not concentrate on specific platform types.

In reply the Soviet participant said that he was not proposing areas which ships could not enter, but only areas where exercises of certain numbers of ships over some period of time would be subject to notification; submarine exclusion zones, however, might be possible (Western participants made the point that such exclusion zones to protect SSBNs reflected Soviet operational patterns only and were thus highly asymmetrical).

A Western participant doubted whether CBMs were of much utility as naval operations could not be threatening on their own and thus should not pose particular concerns. The Soviets disagreed: they saw the threat posed by ships as being very high: they were capable of strategically independent operations and influencing operations on the ground. A Soviet participant reminded the group that the movement of Soviet ships in exercises off the East Coast of the United States had, if the press was to be believed, caused great concern. Similarly the Soviet Union was concerned by movements in the Baltic. The activities of navies in general were neither offensive nor defensive, but the relationship of the geographical area to the activity established criteria for CBMs to assume that activity's non-threatening nature.

In an extended discussion the following extra items were raised:

> ***data:*** it would help greatly if greater openness was shown in announcing disposals of older units. This would prevent exaggerated notions of a navy's size.
>
> ***nuclear potential:*** a Western participant asked if Soviet perceptions of the pre-emptive dangers posed by navies could be allayed if they did not carry nuclear weapons. In response it was stated that Soviet worries would be significantly less but that modern conventional missiles could be similar in effectiveness to nuclear weapons. Some disturbing factors disappeared with nuclear weapons but the question had to be tackled comprehensively and all weapons, conventional and nuclear, had to be considered together.
>
> ***threatening exercises:*** emphasis was placed on the perceived threat (although some preferred 'concerns' or 'worries') caused by large scale exercises, including independent naval ones. The question of independent naval operations also needed to be addressed as clashes at sea might be the occasion for a side preparing for attack actually starting a conflict. Alternatively, war might break out at sea through misunderstanding.
>
> ***predictability:*** in order to make the forces of each other more predictable, it would be useful to exchange data on naval programmes on a bilateral or multilateral basis.

3. Proposals for Reducing Maritime Nuclear Weapons

A paper was presented by a Western participant recommending that both sides could aim at a co-operative reduction in naval nuclear weapons to ceilings below 50 per cent of their current holdings. The criteria for minimum levels would be the numbers required to engage in 'desperation' strikes on the other side's naval assets and shore complexes.

Various points emerged in the discussion:

> ***Verification:*** portal monitoring, inspection of stores and inspection at the point of embarkation should provide sufficient confidence of compliance for these proposals.

Stability: were some naval tactical nuclear weapons more destabilising than others?

Complete abolition: Soviet participants seemed to agree that complete abolition of naval tactical nuclear weapons was a reasonable idea. The Nitze proposal to abolish all naval nuclear weapons except SLBMs was a reasonable one. Use of nuclear weapons at sea would be a suicidal gesture of despair. The selective use of nuclear weapons anywhere would result in all-out nuclear war and global catastrophe.

Unilateral elimination of certain weapons: Soviet participants pointed to the problems of unilaterally removing one type of weapon as differing levels of technical development might result in advantages. A comprehensive approach to the problem ought to be developed.

Dual capability and stability: Soviet participants pointed out the importance of determining whether a missile was nuclear or conventional. Before it explodes there is considerable uncertainty and the other side may respond unpredictably. It would be better therefore to avoid such situations and use nothing that resembles a nuclear weapon. The elimination of naval arms that could cause such doubts and apprehensions on the other side could have a considerable impact on stability. The abolition of destabilising systems should be a priority.

The relationship of land and sea and nuclear and conventional: a Soviet participant stressed that sea-based systems can be used to hit land targets and vice versa, and on a global scale. The Soviet Union was especially worried about attack from the Norwegian Sea: sudden attacks from the sea would lead to an immediate explosive set of consequences, involving the Pacific as well as the Atlantic. Nuclear weapons counterbalanced disparities in conventional weapons and the deployment of fleets: in this sense they were a counter to the strategy of forward deployment. One needed therefore to think about the problem of sea-based nuclear weapons as a complex whole.

Need for new Soviet thinking: one Soviet participant welcomed the Western paper and suggested it should be matched by new Soviet thinking especially as the Soviet Union was committed to the doctrine of no first use and the elimination of all nuclear weapons. He said he was not altogether clear on the question of sea-based TNW but either a ban or a limitation of numbers might be possible. This might be done unilaterally or by mutual agreement. This would both reduce the intensity of the naval confrontation and help lead to the reduction of all TNWs.

Cruise missiles: various solutions were suggested for the cruise missile problem: numerical limits (400 nuclear: 600 conventional) or overall limits with freedom to mix (but if these were too high they would allow circumvention).

Flexibility: one Western participant said that, although abolition of naval TNW was desirable, naval officers liked to maintain flexibility. The Western proposal would allow them to do so.

4. The Way Forward

Issues raised in this session were:

(a) ***The Soviet perception of a threat from the sea:*** It was clear that the Soviet Union was worried about the threat posed by United States carrier battle groups and amphibious forces to the Soviet Union itself, for example, the Kola Peninsula. Such threats, they argued, were destabilising as they might provoke escalatory Soviet acts in response.

(b) ***The nature of Western maritime strategy:*** Western participants emphasised that, rhetoric aside, the reality of Western (i.e. NATO's) maritime strategy as deployed on exercises was not pre-emptive. It threatened protracted conventional combat if deterrence failed, not massive nuclear pre-emptive attack. Indeed, the idea of holding Soviet nuclear assets at risk was similar to the Soviet concept of 'multivariate operations' on land reducing Western nuclear forces in Europe. Far from there being an imminent threat of nuclear attack, it would be almost impossible to obtain nuclear release to solve operational problems at sea.

(c) ***The requirement for doctrinal symmetry:*** The Soviets made it clear they felt that military doctrines had to be reconstructed on a bilateral basis. A pronounced offensive orientation in Western naval forces was unacceptable if Warsaw Pact forces had a pronounced defensive orientation.

(d) ***A framework for asymmetrical reductions?*** One Soviet participant suggested that existing asymmetries could be taken into account in proposing mutual reductions of combat capabilities. The forces that look most threatening to the other side could be reduced, for example, the capability of the Soviet Navy to disrupt Atlantic communications could be reduced in return for reductions in the American capacity to attack Soviet SSBNs and deliver strikes against Kola. Such might form the basis for arms reductions that might follow the setting up of a CBM régime.

(e) ***Evidence of changes in Soviet naval strategy:*** Another Soviet participant pointed to the reduced level of Soviet naval activities and the reduced number of Soviet visits to Cam Ranh Bay. He agreed, however, that the Soviet Union had not, however, explained their non-offensive strategy satisfactorily.

Commentary

1. The Moscow discussions and the associated visit to BPK-708 *Kerch* in Sevastopol marked a considerable step forward in the process of naval dialogue. They:

   (a) elucidated the nature of the political correlation between progress in naval matters and CFE.
   (b) emphasised Soviet concerns about the destabilising threat of sudden strikes from the sea—however incomprehensible this fear seems to Westerners.
   (c) produced some pioneering specific proposals on naval confidence building measures (CBMs).
   (d) demonstrated consensus that CBMs of various kinds were the most fruitful options for practical exploration.
   (e) provoked new thinking among Soviet colleagues on the question of tactical nuclear weapons at sea.
   (f) clearly demonstrated a Soviet commitment to increased openness in naval affairs for which appropriate Western responses are necessary.

2. As before, we must build further on this progress. Two priorities seem clear:

   (a) Take further the discussion on naval CBMs and examine the issues in further detail, for example, define realistic threshold criteria.
   (b) Engage in detailed East-West dialogue on maritime strategy. Soviet colleagues must be persuaded of the true defensive nature of NATO's forward strategy and the reasons for the West's not thinking that it poses destabilising threats with its naval forces. This requires careful re-articulation of the forward strategy, as well as first-hand historical analysis of the background of its formulation. Similarly, the Soviet Union needs to explain its strategic thought more clearly.

APPENDIX III

Introduction

After completing the main body of the book, in November 1989, the author chaired an important meeting of naval experts, the third in the series begun in July 1988. This proved to be a significant gathering in making clearer to both sides mutual concerns and the very different way East and West viewed basic concepts of maritime strategy. The problem of misplaced threat perception caused by the other side's exercises was clearly revealed. The Soviets elucidated in some detail the recent developments in their strategic thinking, notably their concept of 'lines of alert' in the Norwegian Sea, Mediterranean, Indian Ocean and North Pacific. They also made clear the reduced role of the distant deployed 'combat patrols' begun by Gorshkov. Their function seems now to be primarily reconnaissance and reporting. The very limited Soviet agenda for their proposed official naval dialogue on measures of predictability and transparency was also noteworthy. Westerners were able to reassure Soviet colleagues about the nature of both NATO and US Maritime Strategy, especially as the latter was currently evolving. Perhaps the most important result, however, was convincing the Soviets that the West was really serious in its concern for the security of sea lines of comunication, that is, shipping. Soviet analysts and policy makers, taking at face value public pronouncements by successive SACEURs on the inevitability of early nuclear escalation and making pessimistic forecasts of the performance of their submarines against fast convoys had apparently considered a campaign against Atlantic shipping both irrelevant and impossible. Public concern with SLOCs in the West was, therefore, just seen as a pretext for the forward deployment of long range land attack maritime striking forces. This perception clearly changed as all Western participants clearly and honestly expressed their primary concern with defending shipping for reinforcement and sustainability. Having established basic points such as this the way has been prepared for more specific informal and unofficial discussions, both on the perception and reality of each side's naval force structure and how confidence at sea can be built.

APPENDIX III

Adderbury Maritime Strategic Dialogue 17-19 November 1989 Report of Conversations

Contents

Session 1:
The US Maritime Strategy 118

Session 2:
The US Maritime Strategy in the Pacific 122

Session 3:
The US Maritime Strategy in the Pacific (continued) 126

Session 3A:
The US Maritime Strategy in the Atlantic 128

Session 4:
The Development of Soviet Maritime Strategy 132

Session 5:
NATO Maritime Strategy 137

Session 6:
Recent Changes in Soviet Maritime Strategy 144

Session 7:
The Current Debate on Soviet Maritime Strategy 148

Session 8:
The Current Debate on US Maritime Strategy 152

Session 9:
Summing up and Ways Forward 156

Session 1: The US Maritime Strategy

The US Maritime Strategy was described by an American participant. He made it clear that it had three fundamental elements:

1. It was based on deterrence, the employment of naval forces to deter threats across the spectrum of conflict from peacetime to global nuclear war. This was *not* new: US naval power had been a deterrent agent of choice since World War II.
2. It was based on *joint* operations with the full participation of *allies.* There was nothing new about combined naval operations with US allies and emphasis on joint cooperation with the other US services. The story of the US Navy in World War II was filled with such combined and joint operations. Recent US Fleet Commanders had all emphasised joint operations, indeed, NATO's Supreme Allied Commander Atlantic had refined allied concepts for over thirty years. The initial drafting of the Maritime Strategy had owed a great deal to (a) NATO's CONMAROPS, first drawn up in 1980, (b) Admiral Hayward's concept in the Pacific, and (c) CINCUSNAVEUR's Mediterranean Concept. All these had been important sources in articulating the *global* concept of operations now called the 'Maritime Strategy'.

   The above three concepts were the basis of the original draft completed in 1982 by Commanders Stan Weeks and Spencer Johnson. Valuable insights also came from Captain Manthorpe and Commander Ken McGruther. Overlaps in force priorities between the Atlantic, Mediterranean and Pacific concepts were deleted. The Maritime Strategy was also put in the framework of national policy, Department of Defense guidance and policy and Joint Chiefs of Staff guidance. It was a way of describing both the peacetime crisis uses of US naval power and the worst case of a global conflict. This combination of the existing three operational concepts (plus the extra insights) put into the framework of the three phases, peace, crisis and war, was what became the 'Maritime Strategy'. The latter was a clear articulation of the historical experience of the United States and its allies, and critical strategic insights collected and refined by the respective theatre commanders. It was fully accepted because it was so fully consistent with current strategic theory. The emphasis on taking the initiative was also fully consistent with the approach of the Navy's civilian leadership, Secretaries Lehman and Weinberger and ultimately President Reagan.
3. The third key element in the Maritime Strategy in addition to 1) deterrence and 2) joint and combined operations is 3) *forward deployment.* This has firm historical precedent and an overwhelming geopolitical

rationale and is not meant to pose a hostile threat to any nation that does not attack US forces or allies. The US Navy has always been forward deployed. John Paul Jones operated around the British Isles and President Jefferson deployed US naval forces to deal with pirates based in Tripoli. This was an early demonstration of the major US commitment to the freedom of the seas also shown by more recent clashes with Tripoli.

The concept of the 'home fleet' never took root in the USA. This was for geopolitical as much as for historical reasons. The USA is a maritime nation, as emphasised by Mahan. American isolationism ended with the two World Wars. It ended because German submarines and Japanese aircraft attacked US forces and not vice versa. In the modern world the USA has many overseas allies and a greater than ever reliance upon the seas for her economic life. Both America's own principles and her allies must be defended forward. This was clearly recognised in the immediate post war period. Recent historical work has demonstrated how Admiral Forrest Sherman briefed President Truman with a global concept for the employment of US Naval forces very similar to that which Weeks and Johnson drafted in 1982.

The Maritime Strategy is *not* a war plan but a *concept of operations* for US Naval forces. It reflects the best naval experience and the advice of the responsible theatre commanders covering contingencies from routine peace to global war. Equally it is *not* a 'go it alone' US Navy strategy but the maritime component of national strategy. It reviewed and restated the explicit thinking of US civil leaders and their tasking to the naval forces deployed (a) to defend US and allied interests, (b) to control vital sea lines of communication with allies and (c) to conduct counter offensive operations, if necessary, in both US and allied defence. The Strategy was not 'go it alone' as it was consistent with *Allied* concepts of operations and emphasised the role of joint and combined forces in the event of war. It recognised from the beginning that navies alone cannot win wars but they can lose them.

The Maritime Strategy was not designed as a US Navy force building strategy. This is best understood by examining its origins. In the Autumn of 1982, two years into the Reagan defence build-up and the Lehman naval build-up, the strategy was drafted in response to specific tasking by the Vice Chief of Naval Operations, Admiral Small, who wanted a clear statement of naval strategy for the annual budgetary decision making process. The strategy was a *current force* strategy, updated yearly, to be used as a framework and benchmark against which future programmes were to be judged (in other words programmes were judged on how they fitted into the Maritime Strategy: the Maritime Strategy did not provide new force goals). The authors succeeded in their basic tasking. They provided the Navy's internal benchmark for assessing its programmes.

The authors did not expect the rapid degree of acceptance of the Maritime Strategy, nor its resulting utility for naval leaders to explain and justify naval forces to Congress. They did not foresee the way the Maritime Strategy would combine with the War College and gaming community to stimulate tactical and strategic thought within the Navy. Neither did they force the Strategy's international impact nor the misunderstandings that made this strategic dialogue so valuable.

As for these *misunderstandings*, these needed to be frankly stated and considered. First, why did the principle of *forward deployment* receive greater emphasis? 1982 was a time of much greater concern with the Soviet threat. It was the era of Afghanistan and the Soviet SS20s threatening Europe. The USSR had built up her conventional forces, including her navy: she was engaged both in a build-up of strategic forces and in stirring up elements around the world hostile to the USA. The USN was faced with the problem of how to deal with an increased threat with a fleet half the size. The strategic answer was to emphasise forward deployment more. The logic was similar to that of a basketball court: emphasise area defence forward rather than point defence in the rear. This was only a change in *emphasis* (not the adoption of forward operations or the abandonment of direct defence of shipping). The change of emphasis did, however, begin to be reflected in exercises both in the Atlantic and the Pacific.

The second misunderstanding is the confusion of the offensive with the initiative and the emphasis on the latter in forward deployment. Combined with the distribution of offensive power (for example, SLCMs) through the fleet this seemed to threaten the USSR. Actually the overall threat to the Soviet Union was much less than it had been given the decline in the US Fleet by half and the diminishing number of US land bases, not to mention the increased capability of the Soviet Fleet. The US has distributed cruise missiles through the fleet because of the increased power of the Soviet Naval Air Force to destroy American carriers. The Soviet Navy in general devotes lots of conventional capability for anti-ship use.

The speaker had considerable experience with US planning. He had never seen a plan to initiate attacks on the Soviet forces—or anyone for that matter. The strategic concept in the Maritime Strategy was one of deterrent, joint and combined operations. There was no offensive threat—unless allies or US forces were attacked. In this case the attacker would be rightly concerned with the distribution of offensive power through US forces. Any prospective attacker should be concerned, and thus deterred. The US Maritime Strategy harnesses the offensive capabilities of a maritime nation and its allies to fundamentally defensive purposes.

As Admiral Chernavin said in his Pravda interview, to be defensive does not mean to be passive. If a conflict breaks out, he went on, submarines and surface ships must fight before the enemy enters one's own territorial waters. Such is not 'old thinking' or 'new thinking' but realistic professional thinking.

Dialogue should build understanding the speaker concluded. Navies were good at increasing understanding as they operated in an international environment in all areas of the world. There were already common understandings, notably the 1972 Incidents at Sea Agreement, the most effective and long standing arms control agreement between states. Exchanges of visits by military personnel and port visits all help to lessen misunderstandings. The development of better understanding and trust is the best guarantee that Western and Soviet forces will only meet at sea or on friendly passage. Opportunities like this one had to be used for a dialogue that was above all *realistic*.

The discussion first covered the impact of a CFE agreement and Soviet defensive restructuring on the Maritime Strategy and the importance of sea lines of communication (SLOCs). The Western view was that as forces reduced the ability to re-introduce them became more important. Hence the defence of SLOCs would become *more* important after CFE. The Maritime Strategy would, however, develop with changes in funding, force levels and the international environment. The US-Soviet conflict was only the worst case end of a broad spectrum.

The next topic was that of horizontal escalation and its importance as a concept in the Maritime Strategy. The group was reminded that discussion of horizontal escalation had preceded the drafting of the Maritime Strategy. The latter has just re-stated the obvious fact that naval forces are inherently global in nature with no fixed boundaries. It was incredible that SACLANT's forces could be fighting and dying in the Atlantic with the two sides waving to each other in the Pacific. There was, however, no automaticity. It was not the theatre commanders but the political leaders who had the final decision. A decision on horizontal escalation would be made in the context of de-escalating the conflict and restoring deterrence. Horizontal escalation remained a realistic option given the global context of naval forces and would be judged on its merits.

It was re-emphasised by an American speaker that the decision was one for the national command authority. There was some Soviet-American consensus about the difficulty of stopping a local war between them escalating to something wider.

Soviet speakers asked if they were entitled to an offensive superiority on land if the West was entitled to one at sea. An American speaker said the situation at sea was very different. The West needed superiority at sea to defend its allies, all but two of which were over a thousand miles away by sea. Defence at sea was different: there was no terrain and were no fixed frontiers; the defender was at a *dis*advantage. Also to deter one had to be able to threaten.

A Soviet speaker concluded by raising the impact of possible confidence building measures on the Maritime Strategy. If navies were an integral part of national strategy how could they reflect current political aims (i.e. to de-escalate the East-West conflict) and build on the 1972 Incidents Agreement. An American speaker replied that the global nature of naval forces and global asymmetries made concluding such agreements difficult, but not necessarily impossible. The fundamental factor was that diminished forces and confrontation made forward defence, if anything, even more vital. We had, however, to lessen the perception of imminent threat. One contribution to this might be the reductions in naval funding on both sides that would result from the national decisions of governments and legislatures.

Session 2: The US Maritime Strategy in the Pacific

The Pacific was not well known or appreciated by Americans, and with all the events currently taking place in Europe, the opening speaker thought that he was at something of a disadvantage. Attention was riveted to other issues: European economic integration; the 'Common European Home'; CFE. All these were potential opportunities for enhancing peace through greater stability. There were also opportunities to do this in other areas. The USA needed to reappraise its view of the world but it should not rush into anything. Pragmatism was necessary for a number of reasons.

The Eurocentric focus of US policymakers should not persist. The USA cannot ignore its interests in the Pacific-East Asia region. Soviet military power remains as capable today (if not more so) than it was in the recent past. Ships of new classes have replaced older units and added to overall strength in a building programme that has not been reduced. These factors cannot be ignored, indeed they must be considered in the implementation of the US Maritime Strategy.

In every year since 1982, US trade between the USA and Europe has been less than that with America's trading partners in the Pacific-East Asia region. Trade in the Pacific (both ways) totals over $270 billion, $110 billion or so more than the $160 billion of US-European trade. Pacific states will provide 50 per cent of the world GNP by 2000 and the combined GNP of Japan, South Korea and Taiwan will be $6 thousand billion by 2010. Portland, Oregon is already America's most important port in terms of tonnage, and Los Angeles in terms of value. Vancouver is Canada's major port in both value and tonnage. The next 100 years will be the Pacific century. The economic integration of Europe in 1992 will be a great step forward but the economic engine of the twenty-first century will be the Pacific-East Asia region. One cannot, therefore, see the events of today or tomorrow exclusively in Euro-centric terms.

Pacific SLOCs were crucial. All passed within 50-200 miles of Adak in Alaska. This was, therefore, more important than Keflavik. The US was fundamentally interdependent with the nations of the Pacific. She depended on goods (computers, communications equipment, etc) all from the East Asian region. East Asia's industries were also an important part of the defence industries of the United States and of the entire free world. Ninety-five per cent of the world's micro elements were assembled in Asia. Technological development is likely to increase this interdependence still further; it certainly will not change.

The speaker regarded the Pacific Ocean/Indian Ocean/Persian gulf areas as an entity when implementing the maritime strategy. Countries like Japan and the Philippines had bilateral treaties with the USA but the region is too diverse for full political economic integration. The need was for a coalition strategy, forging a Pacific partnership in which Europe had a real role.

China was going to continue her economic modernisation and her opening to the West. She cannot reverse her modernisation and will play a positive role in enhancing regional and global stability and sustained by the role of the US Maritime Strategy in helping underpin that stability.

The US-Japanese relationship was the most important bilateral relationship in the world between the world's first and second most important economic nations. The potential for world economic development is great. The US Maritime Strategy is sound and working in relation to Japan. The Japanese Maritime Self Defence Force is ready to accept greater responsibilities in defence of SLOCs within the 1,000 mile area.

There is a need to ensure greater investor confidence in the Philippines to help solve its economic problems (complicated by continued insurgency). The forward US diplomatic presence helps produce confidence. Negotiations on continued US base rights are beginning. The Philippine government wishes to keep all its options open. The ASEAN nations wish to keep US power strong in the area. Singapore may offer presence rights to the USA if negotiations with the Philippines fail.

South Korea remains threatened from the north. The Seventh Fleet helps ensure stability in the area. It was a key factor in providing stability during the 1988 Olympics. Anti-Americanism in South Korea is on the wane.

The Maritime Strategy projected both power and humanity. Sending the hospital ship *Mercy* to the Philippines, Solomons and Kiribati created more goodwill than the previous decade's economic aid and was well worth the effort. The Maritime Strategy in the Pacific was meant to underline confidence, deterrence, nation building and compassion.

The Maritime Strategy had three tenets, 1) deterrence; 2) alliance relations and coalition; 3) forward deployed forces, principally naval, of especial importance given the great distances involved in the Pacific (San Diego to Subic Bay was 7,000 miles, to Tokyo 6,000 miles, Subic to the Straits of Hormuz 4,400 miles). The future Maritime Strategy in the Pacific region would be determined by a number of factors.

The first was the threat, regional and global, conventional and non-conventional. The threat included terrorism, drugs and piracy. Regional problems were also important in forming the threat, along with political developments in Japan, the Philippines and China. Many countries and problems were involved, including across to the Gulf. The changes in how the Maritime Strategy is carried out in the Pacific depends on changes in the USSR. There are two prospects. The first is a continuation of considerable uncertainty with regard to the USSR's evolution, uncertainty about events, no real shift in the budget and no shift from heavy to light industry (not just a shift in heavy industrial production lines to lighter products with the heavy infrastructure still in place). If this is the atmosphere of the future then there will not be much change in US deployment or force structures.

The second factor is stable and peaceful future evolution in the Soviet Union. (The US cannot dictate the form.) This should be tied together with a shift from heavy to light industry. There needs to be a genuine reduction in Soviet force structure; just retiring some old equipment and replacing it with new will fail. To be specific. In 1989 nine new submarines were built by the USSR, the highest tonnage figure in the 1980s. Although old submarines have been scrapped the continuation in current building and scrapping rates promises a 30 per cent increase in strength by 1996. As for surface ships, 40-50 have been scrapped and 30 new ones added, but the latter are much more capable. By 1996, at the current building rate 25 per cent of the Soviet Navy's surface ships will have been constructed since 1989.

As for current operations the speaker was puzzled by the almost weekly simulated bomber attack profiles carried out against Okinawa, Japan and Alaska. Some of these aircraft carry air to surface missiles. One can only conclude that this is intimidation. The US carrier battle group commanders also appreciate the free, unprogrammed air activities with which they have to deal. Another puzzling operation was the recent firing of several strategic missiles coordinated with strategic bomber flights into the Arctic and Gulf of Alaska. This seemed a strange way to demonstrate a reorientation of force posture and only wanting to contribute to peace and tranquility in the Pacific. There were also other indicators like the USSR's base structure. Another good indication of Soviet willingness to end the Cold War would be to return the northern territories to Japan.

Once it becomes clear that the USSR was making changes then the USA would make a significant reduction (say, 25 per cent) in both the military budget and the active force structures. The changes would be in deployed forces rather than unilateral withdrawals and all changes would be in consultation with allies and friends. The last thing the USA would wish to do would be to create a vacuum with all the uncertainty and instability that involved. One cannot ignore the proliferation of nuclear weapons and ballistic missiles to many countries, nor the threat of terrorism. (The USSR might act to prevent North Korea becoming a nuclear power, a major blow to stability.) The future threats would require maritime forces to maintain both deterrence and stability. Proposals involving cuts to naval forces would therefore not be looked on with favour by the USA.

The American speaker foresaw a Pacific partnership with a US Maritime Strategy evolving according to changes in the threat, and greater Japanese and South Korean roles in maintaining overall defence requirements. There would be a continued 'mini-Marshall Plan' for the Philippines. Vietnam and North Korea would be encouraged by similar aid to join the Pacific Community. Economic and humanitarian assistance would continue, with the hospital ship deployment being repeated. An increasingly more integrated East Asian community would cooperate to deal with trans-national problems like drug trafficking and piracy. The challenge was big enough for everyone to have a cooperative role. One could be optimistic for the future of the USA and the Pacific nations producing stability and prosperity.

A Soviet speaker expressed support for the idea of joint activities to fight narcotics and ballistic missile proliferation. He also suggested cooperation to keep vital SLOCs open. The USSR was also interested in sea communications; more than half the material sent from the western Soviet Union to the east goes by sea. The Soviet Union wished to be an active member of the Pacific Community (within her economic limits) but part of this meant defending the SLOCs in the Pacific and Indian Oceans. There was some disagreement from American participants in the importance of SLOCs to the USSR and Soviet vulnerability to SLOC interdiction. The Soviet speaker insisted, however, that parallel action to protect SLOCs would be in the spirit of Pacific partnership.

Discussion then moved to the activities in late October-early November and the launch of the seven missiles coordinated with a regimental attack by Soviet aircraft into the Arctic and Gulf of Alaska. An authoritative Soviet speaker said these flights were the result of a major 'PACEX' by the US Third and Seventh Fleets in coordination with allies. The Soviet Naval Air Force had been grounded but the Soviet Air Force felt forced to illuminate the situation. As for the ballistic missile launches (ICBMs and SLBMs), each one had been notified as agreed with the US and in accordance with standing procedures: he did not therefore understand the concern. The need for so many missile shots was that the test programme for the year had been delayed and the operating forces were catching up.

Another Soviet speaker emphasised the importance of agreements like the Incidents at Sea Agreement to prevent these misunderstandings that were liable to happen despite the intentions of political leaders. Why, he asked, should there be pre-conditions for future CSBMs? He also emphasised the threat felt by the Soviet Union when three carrier battle groups exercised off Kamchatka, with weapons capable of reaching deeply into the Soviet Union. Yet the USA was worried only by routine Soviet modernisation. If both sides were worried there was surely even more reason to cooperate on Pacific confidence building measures. The American side stated their exercises were in support of their allies in meeting treaty obligations for defence purposes; they failed to note any Soviet allies in the Gulf of Alaska.

After another exchange when the American promised a 25 per cent US force cut if the Soviets restructured, and the Soviet requested no preconditions be put on the USSR, the chairman called the day's proceedings to a close by pointing out what an excellent example the meeting had been provided with of each side's exercises being seen in the worst possible light. It proved we do need CBMs as international agreements and then perhaps move towards naval reductions on a unilateral basis. (It was later decided to continue discussions on the Pacific for the first part of the next session.)

Session 3: The US Maritime Strategy in the Pacific (continued)

The second part of the discussion opened with the American speaker reiterating his point that if the conditions he had outlined were satisfied the USA would re-evaluate its policy, reduce its forces by 25 per cent and change its deployment patterns. There was no need to garrison the Indian Ocean with a carrier battle group, as if it was an army division. The whole object of being able to move naval forces was to send signals. As for the increasing role of the Japanese MSDF it would continue to limit its operations to a 1,000 mile arc so as not to raise fears of the past. One did not want to inject destabilising elements.

A Soviet speaker suggested using the Northern Pacific as an interim testing ground for CBMs. The area was less highly charged politically than European waters, but there were nevertheless important pressures for a forward naval policy on both sides, to defend allies and secure communications. A hot line between fleet commanders might be one idea and more transparency in naval movements. If this was done the Maritime Strategy would not look so dangerous.

There was some debate over the need for such a hot line and CBMs in general. American speakers said that there was already a hot line between Washington and Moscow; navies were subject to national command authorities and communications were already good when required. A torpedo fished up by the Russians had been returned on request within twelve hours. The Americans also argued that there was already notification of naval activity through NOTAMs (but the Soviets did not notify their simulated bomber profiles).

In answer to a question on horizontal escalation, an American speaker said that an incident in Korean waters might trigger horizontal escalation if it were a global crisis.

A Soviet speaker then made four points: 1) that the discussions so far had been both very important and very interesting; 2) that the time had come to change the relationship between politico-economic interests and military forces—it was not clear how far shipping necessarily required military force for its defence; 3) reform of military policy was going on in the Soviet Union but it could not be made a precondition for further progress in dialogue; 4) Soviet restructuring was being carried on for much more important reasons than arms control or confidence building measures.

An American speaker responded that US Naval power in the Pacific was concerned with more than just SLOCs. The main point was their role in the maintenance of overall stability. He reiterated that the concept of forward deployments would not change but their scope could change depending on reduction in Soviet force posture and operations. He denied that the USA targeted the Soviet Union. Soviet activities sent the wrong signals: the USSR should use allies like North Korea for their exercises. He was also sceptical about CBMs for their own sake. The best such CBM would be signs in the 13th Five Year Plan of a shift away from military production. Discussion then turned to the differences between how the Maritime Strategy was understood in the Atlantic and the Pacific. Geography mandated a much greater naval role in the Pacific. Was the Pacific also more important for the US Navy? Doubts were also expressed about whether the Pacific and Indian Oceans really were a single entity.

A Soviet speaker said that we could not equate the Atlantic with the Pacific. The USA justified its forward basing with reference to SLOCs but Soviet sea communications with the Far East were no less important than those from the Far East to the USA. Fifty per cent of all goods flowing to the Soviet Far East came by sea through the Pacific. Sea lines of communication were important to both sides. The Soviets could count the US allied orders of battle, they could easily disrupt Soviet SLOCs in the Pacific. The Americans had an exaggerated view of what the Soviets could do against Western sea lines of communication.

As for simulated attacks on Japan, the Pacific Fleet had not carried out such manoeuvres for a long time. Soviet operations bore no relation to the scale of operations carried out by the US Navy. He could not comprehend why the Americans wished to send three carrier battle groups into the Sea of Japan. There were no sea lines of communication in the area. The Soviet Pacific Fleet did not do such things to the USA or her allies in that area; its structure does not allow it to carry out such aggressive activities. The three American carriers came within 30 kilometres of Vladivostok. The Soviet Pacific Fleet deployed 27 submarines and a surface squadron into the Wonsan area and carried out 20 simulated missile and naval air attacks. In the circumstances these precautions were understandable; the Soviet Pacific Fleet needed to make a point. Both sides have a common responsibility for security and ought to negotiate without preconditions to remove mutual distrust. It was impossible to understand why the Americans would not even talk on the subject. One was not talking about scrapping ships and submarines but a structure of confidence building measures.

An American speaker repeated that he did not regard Soviet SLOC requirements as the same as American. The USSR had alternative internal communications. Although the meaning of the Soviet sea communications was not the same as American, the USSR had a forward deployed infrastructure at Dahlak Island, Cam Ranh Bay and Aden. The USA also had security treaties with South Korea and Japan that required forward naval deployment: the only way to South Korea was by sea. He denied, however, that US carriers had come within 30 km of Vladivostok—although some aircraft may have intercepted Soviet strike bombers in this area.

The Soviet speaker denied that the Soviet bases mentioned were as significant as Subic Bay was for the Americans. No ships were based at these minor facilities, as the USA did at its bases. These facilities were only for replenishment with provisions, rest and recreation and similar low level support. These facilities were in no way comparable to American bases.

Discussion finally returned to the question of the relationship of the Indian Ocean to the Pacific. A Soviet speaker said the Soviet Foreign Ministry did not regard them as one region. The Asia/Pacific region was divided into a number of sub-regions and the Indian Ocean was not part of the Pacific. The Northern Pacific area is of vital interest to the USA and USSR, being of military significance to both sides. The Indian Ocean was different. Here both the USA and USSR were 'guests' with a common interest in freedom of navigation. Local actors, India and Pakistan, were important. The Indian Ocean, therefore, ought to be expelled from the military relationships of the USA and USSR. The Northern Pacific could not be. A sub regional approach was therefore essential in any régime to build confidence in different areas.

Session 3A: US Maritime Strategy in the Atlantic

The American speaker began by stating that he considered the focus of the Maritime Strategy remained the Atlantic. In this area the strategy was not just a US but a NATO strategy. The US Maritime Strategy was designed to use US naval forces most effectively to support US national strategy and objectives, and to use maritime power or forces in combination with sister services to bring about termination of war (if one should eventuate) on favourable terms. The US Maritime Strategy was stated formally by Admiral Watkins as CNO in 1984-5. It was never fully understood by many who saw it as a means of creating support for 600 ships. As had been emphasised the previous day, the Maritime Strategy was not designed as a political tool to create a '600 ship navy'. The '600 ship navy' and the Maritime Strategy did, however, have a relationship. The Maritime Strategy was initially 'sold' as a broad plan for the unified and specific commanders, the CINCs, for their use of maritime forces. It was not, therefore, a detailed war plan with specific time lines, dates and targets. Because of pressure of business the Maritime Strategy was not sold properly to other services or allies; it therefore seemed unduly 'independent'.

The principles of the Maritime Strategy are deterrence, forward deployment and alliance solidarity. Deterrence needs to be credible, capable and ready. Forward defence is essential to meet threats far beyond US borders and to signal by presence American solidarity with her many allies. Forward presence is absolutely essential to America's allies.

What of the NATO context? The North Atlantic Treaty was signed by 12 nations in April 1949 to provide for the collective security deemed necessary to deter aggressive action by the USSR. As a result we have had forty years of relative peace, a remarkable record. This was related to a perception of how the two world wars started. The Alliance's political cohesion and its strategy to deter have assured safety and stability.

NATO strategy has always been *defensive*. Those who have served in NATO's military structure have no doubts as to its defensive strategy. It has evolved in response for the offensive posture of Europe's predominant land power, the USSR, with its 400 divisions. The Soviet Union has maintained a significant military advantage on the ground, an advantage that still remains. Geographical realities in Europe greatly favour the dominant land power. It can only be balanced by alliance with North America, but North American ability to make the difference is dependent on the ability to transport the means of making a difference across the sea. Over 90 per cent of the economic and military goods in crisis or war must come by sea. The Atlantic lifeline thus forms the very foundation of the NATO alliance. Put another way it is a bridge or highway between Europe and North America.

NATO developed flexible response as its strategy. SACLANT's and CINCHAN's role in flexible response is control of sea lines of communication (SLOCs). Without control of the Atlantic one cannot reinforce or resupply Europe. NATO's Maritime Strategy is also consistent with the principle of forward defence. The objective of forward defence is to deter war and show the resolve not to relinquish an inch of allied soil. NATO forces need to respond to conflict before conflict begins. This is practised through exercises when forces are trained and made available.

Forward deployment may be seen as offensive or defensive depending on one's point of view, but NATO always insists on the *strategic* defensive. No single aggressive act has been made by NATO forces. Forward defence is applicable to any situation from tension to crisis to local hostilities. It implies that in all these circumstances NATO is prepared to respond. It does not signify that the Eastern bloc is an enemy; it is only prudent military strategy. Forces will be deployed forward in an attempt to deter conflict. Forward deployed forces are in the best position to defend, indeed they *must* deploy forward to defend efficiently. If they defend to the rear more forces are required in a battle of attrition.

Clausewitz argued that all forces should be put against the enemy's centre of gravity. His ideas were developed in the strategic framework of land warfare on the Continent of Europe in the eighteenth and nineteenth centuries. The Atlantic is NATO's centre of gravity. Without control of the Atlantic NATO cannot prevail in any conflict. The need to maintain this centre of gravity is thus absolutely essential. The USSR is in an unchallengeable position unless the USA comes to the defence of Europe. North America cannot come to the defence of Europe without naval forces designed to control the Atlantic.

Gentler breezes are now blowing from the East but the negotiations have not yet altered Allied military doctrine. In response to the offensive potential of the Warsaw Pact, the Alliance must remain sufficiently strong to provide for the common defence as today's situation unfolds. NATO's Atlantic Strategy remains as valid today as it was twenty years ago. Before the US Maritime Strategy was devised NATO's naval leaders were working on the Concept of Maritime Operations (CONMAROPS). The two concepts are interactive and both have the same aim, the use of maritime forces most effectively.

Collective security works but collective security depends on NATO's Maritime Strategy. It is unlikely that arms reductions will result in a situation where the Atlantic is no longer the Alliance's centre of gravity. Indeed, as we reduce land forces in Europe the importance of SLOCs is magnified. The Alliance *must* remain strong at sea. It is imperative for SACLANT to protect reinforcement, sustainability and resupply; this is dictated by geography.

At the Sealink '89 Conference, both Secretary General Woerner and General Altenburg pointed out that substantial reductions in Europe *increased* the importance of NATO's maritime strength. While the Soviet Union operates on interior lines naval forces must rely on naval forces to protect *exterior* lines. Tanks in Georgia, USSR are different from tanks in Georgia, USA.

Is forward defence credible for the future? If it is executed it makes the Atlantic a bond not a barrier. Recent events in Europe truly boggle the mind but we need time to assess them carefully as we move to a more peaceful world. One is greatly encouraged. It is necessary to find areas of greater understanding to remove the tensions that have been endured collectively. If we move ahead in a pragmatic and well defined manner suspicions can be removed.

A Soviet participant began the discussion by commenting that the speaker had logically developed his assumptions but that these could be questioned. The defence and interdiction of SLOCs was clearly based on the idea of protracted conventional war in Europe. This justified western naval programmes and actions. But would a war not be terminated or escalate quickly. SLOCs might be important for political reasons but they were not important for real war fighting.

In answer the first speaker re-emphasised the need for forward presence as a form of deterrence and support for allies. NATO conducts exercises to demonstrate the capacity to reinforce Norway. US Naval exercises in the Mediterranean are also a continuous requirement as the USA has interests there, like the USSR. Confrontation in Europe is not unthinkable and weapons, foodstuffs and other supplies have to be provided. The emphasis on conflict in which maritime power is relevant has increased over the last decade. War need not necessarily be short. It would be cheap but unwise to leave oneself in a situation where one was forced to terminate hostilities because one had run out of supplies. Going nuclear was more basically unthinkable than before; one should not be *forced* into it from any level of conflict in Europe. The USA provided the largest contribution of equipment to the Alliance but it was removed geographically from the main theatre. Europe could not be left to go it alone; this was a commitment the USA had made forty years ago. The capacity of the West to deter was thus dependent on its capacity to protect the Atlantic SLOCs.

Another western speaker made the point that should the CFE negotiations result in a treaty where Soviet forces were primarily East of the Urals and US forces in the Continental US, the importance of the capacity to reinforce if things turned sour would be even greater.

A western questioner asked what were Soviet perceptions of the length of a possible war. Were there new perceptions as to the likelihood of rapid escalation?

A Soviet participant commented that the West was arguing for superiority in the maritime area because of its greater maritime interests. This was, however, inappropriate as the Vienna talks moved to parity in ground and air forces. In response a western speaker said that the CFE talks would have some impact. Their success would lead to changes in reinforcement and alert times and alteration in the reinforcement equations. An extension in warning time might allow the West to make some response at sea. Another western speaker said that Western naval preponderance was not assumed. As we move to greater security in Europe we may move to efforts to reduce the naval confrontation.

Finally, there was discussion over the relative vulnerability and speed of land and sea lines of communication. It was suggested that railways were more vulnerable. Soviet participants compared seven days for a merchant ship to get from the USA to Europe with 12 days for movement by land from the Urals to Central Europe.

Session 4: The Development of Soviet Maritime Strategy

The Soviet speaker began by saying that the USSR did not have such a concept as maritime strategy. Instead the concept was the operational and strategic use of the navy. The Soviet Navy was an integral part of the Soviet armed forces as a whole: the old name of the Red Navy, RKKA, meant the naval forces of the Red Army. In the Second World War the navy was subordinated to corresponding front commanders. Tasks were defined by the front commander with reference to tasks set on the maritime flanks. From 1940 to 1949 there was a Navy Ministry but even then the operational use of the navy was planned in the Ministry of Defence.

Throughout the Soviet period the roles and designated tasks of the Soviet Navy have not changed. The fundamental role is the prevention of seaborne invasion. More specifically, this means:

(a) the destruction of groups of surface ships; in the first phase strike carriers and missile armed ships in those areas where they are capable of inflicting strikes on military and industrial targets.
(b) carrying out strikes against groups of amphibious ships during transit at sea and totally destroying such forces and any beach-head they might make in coordination with ground forces defending the shore. Missile, air and artillery strikes would be made against ships attempting to carry out a landing. A landing force would be broken up prior to its elimination.
(c) defence of maritime trade and sea lines of communication and disruption of enemy SLOCs. This prevents an enemy from conducting a long war against the Soviet Union.
(d) search for and tracking of enemy SSBNs and defence of the USSR's own ballistic missile submarines.

All the above missions are defensive. They thus correspond to the adopted defensive military doctrine. This defensive orientation is also reflected in the order of battle of the Soviet Navy. Only 12 per cent of its ships are capable of oceanic operations against 65 per cent in the USN: 52 per cent of its units are coastal ships and craft against 6 per cent in the US. On 1 July 1988 Soviet naval strength was announced, 61 nuclear missile submarines, 280 other submarines (of which about 150 are nuclear powered), four air capable cruisers (with one more in trials), 96 cruisers and destroyers, 174 escort vessels and small anti-submarine ships and 106 amphibious craft. One must take into account in these overall numbers, that they have to be divided into four separate fleets, Northern, Baltic, Black Sea and Pacific, that none of the fleets is reinforceable and that all face straits under NATO or other US and allied control. Even in peacetime each fleet requires sufficient vessels to carry out wartime tasks alone. The US navy on the other hand can concentrate at the required point. The structure of the Soviet fleet therefore reflects its defensive nature.

Soviet naval programmes, the strategy, tactics and tasking of the fleets and the views of the military and naval leadership, are conditioned both by the threats facing the Soviet Union and the overall economic and technical capabilities of the USSR. In 1922 the Soviet Union had 140 ships, 44 of them major vessels. Principally these units had been built during the Tsarist period. After the Civil War the fleet had been reduced. Given the probable threats at that time and the conditions of a weak economy and a weak industrial base, the main initial thrust in the re-building of the navy was on the construction of smaller vessels and ships, a 'mosquito fleet'.

In the mid-1930s the rise of the Axis block with its large naval forces, the new strength of the Soviet industrial base and the influence of traditional western theories of decisive battle led to the development of two opposing views on naval construction. One argued that priority should be given to submarines, the other defended the major surface warship. A commission of the Red Army resolved the discussion: 'We will build various types of ship necessary for defence... and not for supremacy at sea.' Nevertheless under the dominant theory of Colomb and under the personal influence of Stalin, construction of battleships and heavy cruisers was undertaken. The Second World War slowed down this programme but afterwards it was continued. In the mid-1950s the missile appeared and this caused Khruschev (not without support within the navy) to take out of service the large, gun armed ships. Several large cruisers were scrapped and future construction concentrated on submarines and smaller missile armed craft. An oscillation in construction programmes began, and continued until the recent past, governed by the decisions taken at various times both by the state leadership and the heads of the armed forces, especially the navy.

The Sixties and Seventies were the Cold War years. The USSR was drawn into an arms race. Without regard to the economic capabilities of the nation, the leadership set as a goal catching up, if not overtaking, the USA and the other leading maritime nations. Mistakes were made in building up and using the fleet. As is well known Admiral Gorshkov joined the leadership then. No doubt Gorshkov was well intentioned but he made a series of serious mistakes. Air capable ships made their appearance, and big nuclear missile cruisers. They were very expensive and in the speaker's view not based on rational calculation; they did not fit cost effectively into defensive tasks. The external effect of these ships and Western propaganda helped Gorshkov and carried him away, together with the leadership at that time. It was also more advantageous to the military-industrial complex to have a single expensive ship than several smaller ones.

A large number of submarine designs also emerged, as Gorshkov strove to catch up with the West in the technical sophistication of its submarines. A particular contribution made by Gorshkov was the institution of 'combat patrols', lengthy deployments by groups of ships into distant ocean areas. This was not really brought about by threats to the USSR and brought about in the West, in turn, mistrust and counter action, just as the unbridled actions of the US fleet evoke distrust in the USSR.

One cannot blame Admiral Gorshkov for all of this. These actions were dictated by the whole military leadership structure. One should not exaggerate Gorshkov's role as an individual. It is wrong to see Gorshkov's period as a dividing line. He did that which appealed to the military leadership.

At the moment a new Soviet shipbuilding policy is being worked out. As long as there is a seaborne threat, and this still exists, the Navy should have everything it needs to defend the country from the sea. The refusal by the USA to negotiate naval CBMs and reductions is interpreted by many in the Soviet Union as an attempt by the USA to gain military supremacy. Even after stability is achieved on the basis of parity in ground and air forces, the West still strives to achieve naval and therefore military superiority. The Soviet Union gets very alarmed when American naval forces carry out exercises in the vicinity of our coasts. Each carrier has forty nuclear capable aircraft on board, with a 1,300 km radius of action. Tomahawk has a 2,800 km range, the non-nuclear variant 1,300 km. It is this forward basing of the navy that is a cause for concern when one works out the fields of fire for attacks on shore targets not ships. The Soviets are not convinced that this capability is justified by the need to defend SLOCs.

The USSR has a great interest in reducing the Navy. Ship construction programmes will, it appears, be reduced. Navies cannot, however, be treated in separation from ground forces. If a balance of ground forces is created, and the naval forces of the USA remain as they do today, they will exceed by many times the combat capabilities of the Soviet Navy. It is absolutely essential to begin an official dialogue, beginning with CBMs. The USSR can believe the US Navy is not directed offensively against the USSR. Both sides should get together and discuss what we want out of CBMs: mutual seeds should be sown.

The speaker was asked how far the Soviet Navy was drawn into forward deployment by the threat of Polaris. Also had there been sudden changes of policy, as argued by Mike MccGwire? It was also asked how far the lessons of the Great Patriotic War demonstrated that forward defence at sea, and therefore a return to the Stalin programme of big ships, were necessary? The speaker answered that indeed there had been a direct relationship between the development of Polaris and Soviet forward deployment. The anti-SSBN mission was added to the anti-carrier mission in the 1960s. The Soviet Navy had to go out to the range required to meet the threat.

It was confirmed that designing a carrier was envisaged in Stalin's programme. As for the influence of Russian theorists like Klado, it was stated that the naval leadership did not listen enough to its subordinates, especially the scientific naval establishment. A case in point was the air capable cruiser programme. Institutions made reports on the lack of cost-effectiveness of these vessels but the leadership pressed on with these ships, disregarding the advice. The speaker himself had categorically objected to them although the situation then was not as it is now, when each can give his own opinion.

Objections were raised to the use of 'forward defence' with reference to Soviet deployment. The Soviet Navy is not based at Aden. There is a repair and support facility at Dahlak. As for Cam Ranh Bay, provisions and certain spare parts can be supplied and there is a floating dock but no ships are permanently based there and the territory belongs to Vietnam. Only depot ships spend much time there. The speaker claimed responsibility for the Cam Ranh facility which was required by the long passage from Pacific Fleet bases to the Gulf, a passage which takes a month even if there are no problems. A port was necessary to take on water and vegetables. The USSR had said it would eliminate Cam Ranh Bay if the Americans eliminated Subic. It was commented by an American participant that the Soviets had strike bombers at Cam Ranh, while the Americans only had defensive fighters at Clark. (The bombers at Cam Ranh were in fact withdrawn shortly after the meeting.)

In answer to the initial questions it was stated that foreign bases owed more to Gorshkov than to any lessons of the war, and as for radical changes the basic politics had remained the same for forty years. Western naval activities had, however, led to changes in Soviet procurements over this period.

One western participant said that it seemed that the combination of combat patrols, the doctrine of the 'battle for the first salvo' indicated a doctrine of first use of nuclear weapons at sea. Was this true?

Soviet participants said this was absolutely incorrect. The role was shadowing US CVBGs and tracking them, maintaining the capability to reply to a strike. The emphasis was on retaliation not pre-emption. This had been the view of Gorshkov and all other Soviet commanders.

In answer to a question on the structure of the Soviet fleet in the 1990s, it was stated that this would depend on the future activities of NATO navies.

Another Soviet speaker then made an extended commentary on the first speaker's presentation. As to the structure of the Soviet Navy, it is currently about 45-47 per cent ocean going and 53-55 per cent coastal. This is about the optimal structure for the Soviet navy whose doctrine has always in principle been a defensive one. State policy never envisaged pre-emptive strikes by anyone, including the navy. Neither does the navy have an independent role. In World War II fleets carried out missions given by the front commanders. Nowadays the navy consitutes a more independent part of the armed forces and it will retain this greater independence in the future.

As for the Western Europe region, land forces, including air forces and ground forces, are moving towards reductions and leading to stability. The importance of navies is therefore growing as the Vienna talks take place without reference to navies. Soviet calculations show that by 1995 the contribution of navies to the carrying out of *all* military missions will go up by approximately 20 per cent. This is just as valid for the US and other NATO navies as it is for the USSR.

It is therefore essential to undertake measures to secure the reliability of defence. One need not blame or justify Gorshkov. Strategy was still defensive then, but until 1985 navies as mobile assets could not just be passive. They had to be in the areas of sea and ocean from which the threat was posed, where there might be a danger to territory. From this period came the forward basing and the move to the open oceans. The worries of both sides were reflected in the bigger naval formations that started to appear in the North Atlantic, south of the Greenland-Iceland-Faeroes gap, in the Indian Ocean and in the Mediterranean.

Now, in relation to the current officially announced defensive doctrine, the movement of ships close to Soviet territory causes concern. Neither the Indian Ocean nor the Mediterranean are of military significance so why are modest and small groups of the Soviet Navy deployed there? The Soviets feel worried and apprehensive about the movement of ships with long range striking weapons beyond lines drawn through the northern part of the Arabian Sea, from southern Greece to the Eastern Mediterranean and up the Norwegian coast from Trondheim to Bear Island. When US ships cut across these lines they cause apprehensions of Pearl Harbor-type surprise attacks. The attacking side has many advantages in these circumstances. It is necessary to put up aircraft (including strategic bombers) to monitor such activities although such aircraft do not carry weapons; they are purely reconnaissance aircraft. The Soviets find it useful to deploy against such movements one or two reconnaissance vessels. Carriers can get their aircraft into the air quickly: the Soviets have observed this many times; 12 aircraft plus an escort in minutes. These aircraft fly towards Soviet territory and then return. As such the possibility of surprise attack cannot be excluded. Soviet ships hinder US forces in carrying out their tasks. Soviet aircraft may bother the Americans or adjacent states but in the present climate they cannot act in any other way, otherwise the political masters would dispense with their military commanders.

As to forward basing, the Soviets understand that the US Navy will carry out its missions, but to intercept such forces the Soviet Navy may require the appropriate infrastructure. The requirement to operate in distant seas results from the need to support the lines of alert, off Norway from Trondheim northwards, from the Peloponnese to south of Crete and from Karachi to Muscat (see map for the speaker's drawing of these lines). The Soviets regarded the USA as having similar lines, the Greenland-Iceland-UK gap and from Attu to Midway. When such lines are crossed the country and its populations feel threatened. This was the pragmatic Soviet view of forward basing.

The 'Battle of the First Salvo' had been misunderstood. The Soviet Navy had never prepared for such a battle. A better translation of the Soviet term was that 'destruction begins with the first shot'. The main point was the *single shot kill capability* of modern weapons.

Session 5: NATO Maritime Strategy

The Western speaker began by arguing that discussions on doctrine were a good way of leading into discussions on force structures. This was less the case with naval than with land or air forces as naval strategy links less directly into the structure of forces given that ships take a long time to build and last even longer. Confusion is also created by the connection between doctrine and procurement. Military organisations sometimes create doctrines to obtain money for procurement, and the latter is in turn driven more by what is technologically feasible than what is actually required conceptually.

Doctrine and strategy provide a hierarchy of plans and concepts first to deter war and then to fight it. NATO's maritime strategy emphasised initially transatlantic reinforcement and the projection of carrier air power, both concepts developed and proven in World War II. With the advent of nuclear weapons a gap opened up between SACEUR's Central European strategy and SACLANT's Atlantic Strategy. Even with the strategy of Flexible Response the expected length of a conflict in Europe was too short to allow the American reinforcement of Europe. It seemed therefore that emphasis on navies was mistaken and they tended to receive lower priority. This disagreement was removed over a number of years. Successive SACLANTs argued that maritime forces had to support ground and air forces in Europe.

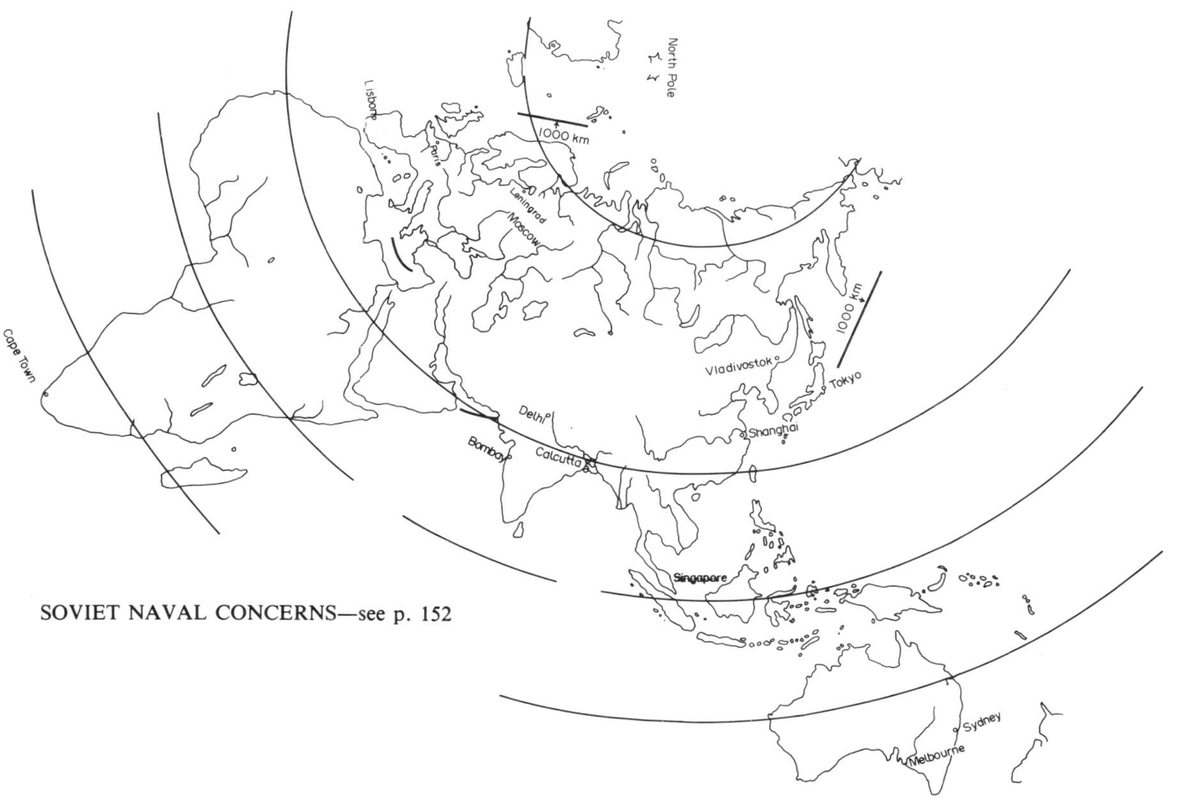

SOVIET NAVAL CONCERNS—see p. 152

In the late 1970s questions were asked by a senior British NATO commander about what *was* NATO's maritime strategy. Was there a NATO equivalent of the forward defence doctrine on land? He questioned some of the statements made in certain circles about defensive barriers at the Greenland-Iceland-UK gap. The answer was that NATO did not have a distinctive maritime strategy. There was a General Defence Plan, and a number of subsidiary and contingency plans but no overarching concept. As a result of this enquiry SACLANT therefore began to formulate a comprehensive *Concept of Maritime Operations* (CONMAROPS). This did not just look at forward defence but *defence in depth*. The full length of the Norwegian Sea was to be exploited properly for the defence of shipping. If this area was to be exploited forces were to be deployed as far forward as possible.

Maintenance of the initiative was also crucial. NATO remains a defensive alliance but attack is the best means of defence. This is not a matter of wanting to make war but a proper sense of how one exploits the effectiveness of one's forces. In the event the concept stressed *containment, defence in depth* and *maintaining the initiative*. CONMAROPS also referred to the differing characteristics of the naval campaigns in different parts of the NATO area and it also pointed to the economic vulnerability of the Alliance's southern flank to the interruption of sea communications. In some ways NATO's CONMAROPS resembles the US Maritime Strategy.

The speaker concluded by arguing that from the political point of view there is a requirement to develop maritime measures to extend the régime of confidence building measures (CBMs) at sea, some of which have been modestly agreed. Other proposals are on the table at Vienna and these must lead to discussion of numbers and naval force structure. There is a need to decide on the limits and structure of these dicussions. The structure of CFE is common ceilings, but common ceilings in the naval area are very difficult to agree upon. Such ceilings might be practical in the submarine field but not for surface ships. Like does not fight like. The concept of common ceilings thus has limited application in the naval field.

There was a need to explore the limits of these sorts of discussion in practical terms before we enter official discussions. We also have to ask which is the correct forum for such discussions. Global negotiations are too difficult but regional fora also pose difficulties. A number of countries in the CSCE framework have no navies. The Group of 23 discussions do not cover CSBMs. Twenty-one countries in CSCE have navies. How can one relate naval negotiations to those on ground forces? It was, however, important to make a start on this process in the context of wider European security.

In the discussion a number of extra points were raised. One western participant argued that threat-based strategies were dying a slow death.

One had to look at other bases of strategy. Threat-based strategies made sense in an atmosphere of deep Cold War when threats were high, when it was known that it was a Soviet aim to reach the Atlantic coast in 14 days and the USSR could fear German ravanchist forces.

Threat-based strategies are less appropriate now and should be replaced by *interest*-based strategies. Instead of beginning with the 'threats' it faces each state should start with its *interests* and then see if these interests are likely to be threatened. Strategy should be based on the latter assessment. The interests of two sides might well often coincide and only clash at certain points. Maritime forces are particularly useful for interest-based strategies, for example, those based on interests in using the sea for various purposes.

Another western speaker then went on to develop the theme in a diagrammatic form. He argued that the three elements of national interests, deterrence and cooperative security all overlap and are all moving closer together. Traditional security through threat-based deterrence is now being supplemented by supporting national interests through co-operation, and cooperative deterrence based on dialogue (like this meeting). This structure might look something like this:

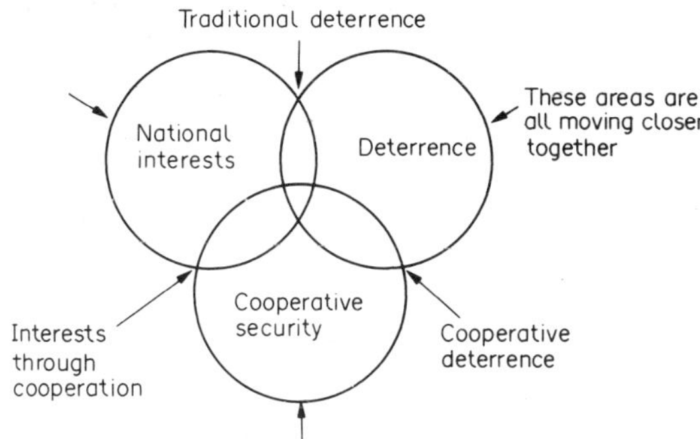

A Soviet speaker then unveiled his own diagram on how he viewed the situation with CFE in place. NATO will lose 10 per cent of US forces which will be withdrawn from Europe. On the other hand, 70 per cent of Soviet forces in WTO areas will have to be withdrawn. In addition, the Soviet Union is making unilateral cuts, while non-Soviet WTO forces are weaker than non-US NATO forces, and half of Soviet forces guard the Chinese border. The situation might thus be rendered like this:

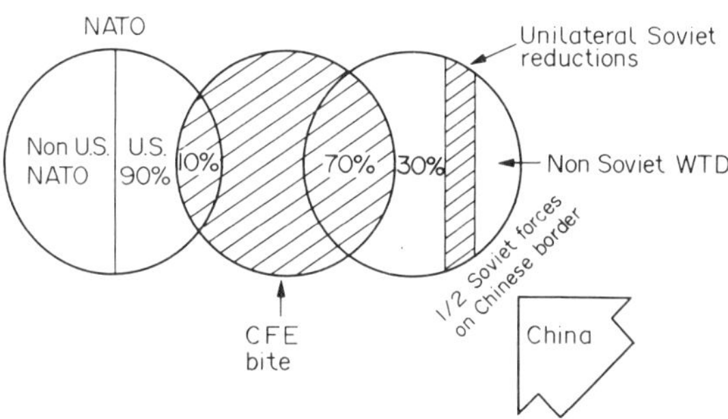

The diagram illustrated how the Soviet capacity to reinforce East of the Urals was limited and thus how, to the Soviet military, the large number of US forces not covered by CFE plus the unrestricted potential of the USN and the protected US SLOCs, had a very threatening and offensive character.

In reply a western participant pointed out that the Soviet Army East of the Urals was larger than the total US Army. With 500,000 Soviet troops remaining East of the Urals, the US has only a small army and 2,000 tactical aircraft. A Soviet participant then pointed out that the Soviets were having a reduction treaty with China. This would leave little room for any build-up of the Soviet armed forces even if it were desired. Most Soviet troops were concentrated in the Far East. The southern and eastern frontiers of the eastern USSR were the only region in which forces could be deployed. The rest of Siberia cannot be used. It is impossible to create new infrastructure on the terrain.

There are two groups of Soviet forces in the Far East. One, orientated against the sea has been reduced already. Both will be radically reduced. The aim is the full demilitarisation of the border. Soviet forces in Europe will be covered by the CFE ceilings. In Siberia the usable territory will be covered by the treaty with China. The rest will give security from the sea. Reductions East of the Urals will total 200,000 (including the 120,000 cut already). In Central Asia the 150,000 men will be reduced by 60,000. With these limits there will be no reinforcements to shift. There is not enough infrastructure to build up. This situation, equality in Europe, Soviet inability to reinforce from beyond the Urals, and NATO's ability freely to reinforce across the Atlantic, significantly favours NATO. Indeed, unlimited forces in the US plus a capability to reinforce could be perceived as an offensive strategy for the USA. Sea lines of communication as such were neutral, it all depended what happened on land.

A western participant countered that it was difficult for NATO to think reinforcement was not necessary. The West would need a great deal of convincing that the Soviets did not have real advantages with trans-Ural reinforcements. It was also added that it was not just a question of troops but of supplies.

A Soviet participant agreed with the first speaker that it was important to agree on a forum to talk, and to agree on subjects upon which we could start realistic discussions. Subjects would include doctrines and strategies, force structures and mutual concerns. One might begin in 1990 with the seminar on doctrine where military experts, officers and scholars would meet to discuss problems of mutual concern. If the West cannot discuss officially then this would be done unofficially, or simultaneously officially and unofficially. There were problems: naval forces were indeed global and one could not draw strict lines. The situation in the Mediterranean was different from that in the North Atlantic. It was very difficult for the US to discuss the Mediterranean as its fleet there was multi-purpose. The easiest case was the North Atlantic where the USN was entirely geared against the Soviet Union. The Pacific situation was more difficult. After general discussion on doctrines one could move to discussion on doctrines in the North Atlantic, then to naval measures in this area such as limits on weapon systems, trust building measures, perhaps some restrictions. The North Atlantic area would be a test area.

The original speaker pointed to parallels between western sea lines of communication across the Atlantic and the importance of land lines of communication across Eastern Europe. There was a need to appreciate the concerns of the Soviet military. NATO's requirement to defend SLOCs resulted from the perceived threat to NATO's interests. If one discusses reducing that threat then NATO's response to the threat can be reduced.

Possibly, he went on, the Gulf might be a good area to begin with a move to more cooperative forms of security. Here, as elsewhere, there were very considerable common interests between East and West. If threat was the only criterion the rationale for armed forces, necessary to maintain stability, might wither away. It was vital, however, to develop common interests and look more carefully at where these interests coincided.

The chairman pointed out that political relations were fluid. The three nations represented in the room had all been friends and enemies. We were entering a situation where one will not have a specific immediate threat but navies would exist to cover unforeseen contingencies. Maritime forces have the ability to stabilise situations and keep the peace.

A western participant agreed that naval forces were hedges against threats which one could not currently identify. One should not confuse what one would like to see with things that have actually happened. Incredible steps had been taken in the previous three years. We had made a very good start in building common understanding and trust. One had to build step by step. In, say, seven years' time, after five years of CFE implementation then there might well be different attitudes towards SLOC protection and the cooperation that might be possible. Another western participant emphasised the need to have time to evaluate indicators.

Discussion moved on to the tendency of navies to be built to deal with the worst case threat, and then be used for other purposes that might not require such a force structure. The transfer of technology to 'Third World' nations meant that high quality equipment was necessary to deal with many countries' forces. There might therefore be changes in force *structure* to reflect the changing situation if not in force *quality*. Forces would still have to be structured to face the worst case threat.

The original speaker warned that it might be difficult to control the timescale. Pressures of both public opinion and the budget would be strong. The fundamental concept, both on land and at sea, was not how much force was necessary to deter war, but *how much force was necessary to preserve peace*. This meant more CBMs, measures to promote transparency, stability and *predictability*. Then the discussion might move on to numbers of men or ships, or the size of one's forces. Maritime measures were, however, more difficult than those on land or in the air.

Returning to CONMAROPS, the speaker said that both sides would have to adapt. They also had to understand each other's concepts better so we knew where we were now. The political situation had fundamentally changed and there was a need to seek something new emphasising a cooperative approach. Soviet ideas on reasonable sufficiency led to discussions on how little was necessary rather than how much. Another Western speaker concluded that the NATO and WTO structures were no more important than they had ever been in order to provide a framework for the process of change in Europe. Military-political concepts had to become political-military, but a military voice was still necessary as we moved towards reductions in Europe and dealt with the problems involved.

Session 6: Recent Changes in Soviet Maritime Strategy

The Soviet speaker commented first on the nature and speed of the changes taking place. Clausewitz said that politics defined strategy; politics came first then strategy. One should not, however, expect rapid changes in naval strategy. It was not realistic at the moment to expect mutual naval reductions at the present time. But the problem of mutual confidence at sea continued to be important. The first priority was to develop means to remove mistrust and suspicion. This was more realistic than reducing manoeuvres or exercises. It was unhelpful to concentrate on the negative side of forward basing. One had to accept realities and use them as one's point of departure. One should therefore discuss what one can do in this situation.

The first priority was to work out a package of measures to reduce mutual distrust. These might include:

1. To ensure the survivability of sea based strategic forces. One could mark out fixed geographical areas in which strategic forces could operate without interference. Such regions would not impinge on the principle of the freedom of the seas. There would be no limits on freedom of navigation, just limits on the presence of certain forces of the other signatories.
2. In order to lessen the apprehension about the dangers resulting from manoeuvres, the number of ships and aircraft engaged, the lines on which they move, the areas in which the manoeuvre is due to take place and the operations it will simulate should be notified to diminish misgivings. This information could be communicated by better utilisation of existing channels. Details communicated would include how big the exercise would be, the number of ships and aircraft included and the principal missions they were carrying out.
3. As both sides had approximately the same weapons one could talk about the establishment of boundaries beyond which certain weapon platforms could not be deployed. This would be within range of targets of vital importance. This would greatly reduce concerns even if one could not eliminate them.

These three proposals were, of course, subject to modification during discussion at various levels, formal or informal, bilateral or multilateral, NATO-WTO or in a wider framework.

Western participants all expressed their scepticism at the idea of SSBN sanctuaries. One, who had spent much time considering the problem, had concluded that such sanctuaries could be destabilising. It would be difficult to select which units to exclude. The list becomes longer and longer as many platforms could carry underwater detection equipment. Sanctuaries were also unequal in effect as the US relied on wide ocean deployments. Sanctuaries would thus greatly help the USSR.

Then there was the question of violations and potential violations. ASW detection and classification was a very inexact science. There would be lots of false alarms but if sanctuaries were declared such genuinely suspected, but mistaken, violations would be seen as violations of a solemn treaty. Every time there was an alarm commanders would have to decide whether to begin a diplomatic incident. It would be a destabilising nightmare.

What could be done to reassure the Soviet Navy? The US Navy should state its intention not to conduct the kind of campaign that would constitute a pre-emptive strike against the Soviet SSBN force at the start of confrontation.

As for CSBMs on the Stockholm model these could be negotiated in due course. There is no reason why observers should not be allowed in close proximity to exercises, on the non-combatant ships of the exercising nations. Other CSBMs might be applied as extensions of the bilateral Incidents at Sea Agreements. General agreements in the UN framework might be very difficult to work.

There was one possible addition given the danger of submarine incidents. Unilateral statements might be made that any submarine assessing the likelihood of a close encounter would transmit on active sonar and underwater telephone. The declaration might also include an undertaking to avoid incidents.

As for the third proposal made by the Soviet speaker, it was important that all weapons crossing the coast *in both directions* should be dealt with, i.e. aircraft and cruise missiles. All have to be taken into account.

Another western speaker commented on the proposed sanctuaries. There was an assumption that these would be located from choice close to home bases. There was no distinction between one area of sea and another. If such a régime was introduced there could be American SSBN havens in the Black Sea or Soviet bastions off the coast of Norfolk, Virginia. If bases are placed close to home bases, the advantage is asymmetrically in the Soviet Union's favour. Waters off the coast of the USA, UK and France are among the busiest in the world: the Arctic Ocean in comparison is the equivalent of a maritime Sahara Desert. It is thus much easier to detect a violation in the Arctic Ocean than in other areas.

In response, the Soviet speaker reminded the participants that he had emphasised that rights of free passage would be upheld. These would include those merchant vessels that might be equipped with sonar. The actions of merchant ships equipped in such a way cannot present a serious threat to the other side. Limitations should relate only to submarines. As for the areas where zones were located he was not after one sided advantages. He would suggest:

(a) for the USA: the Gulf of Mexico; off Alaska.
(b) for the USSR: the Sea of Okhotsk, the Barents Sea and the western side of the Bering Sea (which could be split down the middle).

Measures affecting conduct in these areas would be appropriate as these areas were within the 200 mile economic zone.

As for notification of exercises, the Soviet speaker said he had not mentioned numbers or quantities. These would be a subject of negotiation. The intention was *not,* however, to limit exercises by both sides. Each side would simply inform the other about what was going on. It was useful to know which forces were going to move and in which directions. Notification would take place using existing channels. As for limitations on weapons that cross the coast, the range of aircraft and cruise missiles and the threat they pose to vital shore installations would suggest lines being drawn 800-1000 km from the coast.

A western participant reiterated that a better way to solve the SSBN problem was to state an intention not to eliminate Soviet SSBNs in a pre-emptive strike at sea. Another western participant emphasised that the USN engage in 'strategic anti-submarine warfare'. ASW was a generalised task. It was impossible to distinguish submarines in war (the Soviet speaker interjected that he was not talking about war but peacetime). Prudent submariners would not put their submarines into dangerous situations. As to boundaries, it was wrong to think a strike out of the blue was likely if there was no crisis. There was no problem with current unilateral monitoring of exercises. US commanders welcomed the participation by Soviet aircraft and submarines. Soviet speakers reminded him that in a previous session concern had been expressed about Soviet aircraft creating tension in recent exercises. The western participant replied there was a difference between exercise monitoring and simulated strikes against Alaska and mainland Japan.

Another western participant emphasised that an agreement to maintain SSBN sanctuaries would be meaningless when it mattered, in war. In war it would be vital to the West to attack Soviet SSBNs in order to draw down other forces.

It was next suggested that CBMs might be usefully broadened from operational matters to what proved a powerful source of tension before the First World War, each side's building programmes. Uncertainty in planning could be a considerable source of tension. The Soviet speaker was asked for his reaction to the idea of notifying future and intended construction programmes, what ships and submarines were to be built, where and when. In reply the Soviet speaker said he could tell what was building this year but the next Five Year Plan had not yet been presented to the Supreme Soviet. The reduction in allocated funds would mean a reduction in the programme. The Soviet military budget was published in the press. The western questioner emphasised that it would be useful to know what ships were projected. The Soviet speaker replied that publication of data differed from government to government. He could not say if the published figures would give precise numbers.

One western participant likened the Soviet ideas on SSBN sanctuaries to declaring fixed areas where mobile ICBM platforms would be deployed. Was this necessarily stabilising? In answer the Soviet speaker said land and sea were different and he was only talking about SSBNs.

He went on to explain Soviet concerns about the dangers currently posed to submarines. In about 1968 the USSR lost a ballistic missile submarine with its missiles on board in the Pacific. They believe it collided with something. Such occurrences may happen again. Submarines can hear surface ships and take countermeasures but with other submerged submarines it is a different matter. All sorts of local conditions at a particular moment might lead to a very close encounter. Two years ago in the Barents Sea two submarines collided: one was Soviet. Neither commander had wanted to hit the other and the collision took away part of the submarine's plating. Submarines with a high degree of silencing can approach each other without being detected. This and the resulting collision causes alarm. They should therefore be prevented.

Another Soviet speaker said it was premature to talk about major changes in the American forward strategy. It was also too early to talk about limiting naval activities. However, one should begin to discuss CBMs and how to work them out. Prior notification of exercises had been done twice by the Soviet Union unilaterally. Only newspaper correspondents came to the Baltic exercise and not everyone invited came to the Pacific exercise. Thought should be concentrated on CBMs. Strategy can only be changed if we remove mistrust and suspicion. Until that happens no one will limit their actions.

A western participant emphasised the need to maintain stability. SSBNs had operated for almost 30 years without serious trouble. Abrogating a 'sanctuary' treaty in crisis would be destabilising and the agreement would be irrelevant in war.

A Soviet speaker stated that to him SSBN sanctuaries were not related to collisions but to strategic stability. START would mean dramatic reductions in SSBN numbers. If ASW techniques improved and forces increased they could threaten the reduced force. SALT had deliberately encouraged both sides to shift their nuclear forces to sea. Hence it was necessary to take measures to reduce the risk of surprise attack on these forces to provide strategic stability.

The chairman concluded that it had been made clear that the SSBN sanctuary issue was non-negotiable to the west. One ought, therefore, to concentrate on areas where we might get some agreement.

Session 7: The Current Debate on Soviet Maritime Strategy

The Soviet speaker began by pointing to the differences and similarities between US and Soviet terminology. In the USSR there was no concept of a 'strategy' for a particular branch of the armed forces. The USSR had an integrated military strategy derived from overall military doctrine. 'Naval strategy' is the operational art of a particular arm. Into this concept of naval art comes working out how naval forces should be employed. The basis, the overall defensive military doctrine currently obtaining in the USSR, is well known.

Using the western term, however, Soviet 'naval strategy' rests on three main principles:

1. Soviet naval strategy is based on the resolution of conflict primarily by peaceful means. Goals should be achieved not so much by military as by diplomatic means. If success is achieved in this first principle one can reduce one's deployed assets.
2. Realistic account must be taken of the changes resulting from nuclear weapons. Experience of Chernobyl, where a huge area will be out of use for many decades, shows that a nuclear war cannot be protracted. In no circumstances would the USSR use nuclear weapons first. The Soviet government is committed to use all means to avoid the use of weapons of mass destruction.
3. Soviet maritime strategy is totally defensive. Forces are not intended to undertake large scale offensive naval actions.

All these principles existed previously and they guided policy. However, mistakes and global ambitions led planners to build ships of such size and capability that they were seen as a threat not only to maritime communications but other nations' coastlines. However, it was the defensive principle that forced the forward deployment of naval forces in areas from which threat could be posed. From this came the principle of ocean deployment with fully worked up ships capable of carrying out their tasked missions at short notice. The overall principles of employing ships in this way are not changing. What will change are:

(a) reduced numbers of ships on such deployment.
(b) the reduction of their activities to reconnaissance and intelligence tasks.

There have been two great periods of decline in the post-war history of the Soviet Navy. The first was 1956-7 which virtually eliminated all major warships and concentrated on building up primarily submarine forces. The second period of decline is now and we are all witness to it. It has been recognised that only peaceful means will solve current problems. Both periods were connected with cuts in the overall defence budget including the naval budget. An evaluation of the naval budget is critical for evaluating naval power and capability. The Soviet Parliament will be concentrating on possible reductions in the military budget. Because of the special nature of the economic system these changes will only become evident in 1990-1.

The backbone of US naval strategy is forward deployment. The USSR has no such system: geography does not allow it. Cam Ranh Bay, Dahlak, Luanda and Tartus are repair and support facilities for the rest and recreation of ships involved in the reconnaissance task. These four 'points' do not really have the facilities for logistical support of warships. For ships to enter any of these ports one has to obtain permission of the host. Moreover, fuel supplies, stores, provisions and spare parts do not exist in large quantities. There are only sufficient stores and supplies to service 2-3 medium sized ships, frigates or destroyers. Stocks are replenished strictly as they are run down. Host countries have the right to prevent ships coming in or indeed to order the Soviets out, as at Valona, Berbera and Sollum. The Soviets thus have no system of forward basing or deployment. As for boundaries/lines, the west has specially equipped lines, e.g. Midway-Aleutians. These specially equipped lines do not exist on the Soviet side. The four main Soviet fleets have as their main task the conduct of defensive operations adjacent to home territory. Another task is preventing the build-up of ship groupings in these areas in peacetime: the Barents Sea, the Baltic, the Black Sea, the northern part of the Sea of Japan and the Sea of Okhotsk. In the light of the present naval situation these areas are very sensitive to the Soviet Union. Any danger coming from sea areas, as well as adjacent areas alarms the USSR. This is the basis of Soviet naval strategy.

The previous day the speaker had mentioned that the movement of vessels armed with cruise missiles or aircraft across certain lines causes the USSR to take action the US perceives as threatening, notably sorties of military aircraft and a build-up of submarine forces. Obviously the USSR is forced to send out forces to intercept and keep an eye on threatening groups of surface ships. Such events that caused alarm were the manoeuvres of the Pacific Fleet, PACEX 89. The Soviets had a year's warning but the *size* of the exercise was unexpected. Tactical surprise was achieved. The Soviet Navy did not deploy submarines in the exercise area and even forbade flights by naval aircraft. In order to clarify what was going on Soviet Air Force aircraft were sent out. Even this caused the

Americans alarm and one can understand their concern. The USA in turn should understand Soviet concerns. Ships can conduct full combat operations within 5-10 minutes. To take defensive measures the same amount of time is required. The USSR is very sensitive to the dangers of a sudden first strike. 1941 is something that cannot be allowed to happen again.

The USSR would be prepared to remove its ships from the Mediterranean and Indian Ocean if the West removed theirs. There was no strategic reason to keep warships there other than to watch the ships of the other side. The presence of Soviet warships came about because one side's moves were mirrored by the other's. One needed to be fair and trust each other.

The USSR does not threaten anyone or wish to deploy large naval forces outside Soviet waters. Why, therefore, are there such a large number of submarines? The emphasis on submarines, begun in the 1956-7 reassessment, continues today. Submarines can be regarded as offensive or defensive weapons. The tasks set Soviet submarines are the prevention of the build-up of large groupings of surface ships. Submarines can monitor, and in war, attack such groupings.

As far as large scale surface combatants are concerned, the large air capable cruisers (called carriers in the west) have as their main task the area air defence of Soviet ship groupings in the operational areas mentioned above. Their key role is *defence in depth against air attack*. The role of *Kiev*, *Minsk* and their successors is to extend the reach of land based air cover, to take it some distance out to sea. Putting *Kiev* out in the Atlantic to disrupt communications is a senseless idea: the ship would be certain to be destroyed. Using *Kiev* and her 5-6 successors in an offensive role would be certain suicide. The Soviets only had four such ships in commission with a fifth on trials. These were divided between the fleets. They did not have strike aviation for use against the shore. Their aircraft were purely for the defence of ships.

Submarines can bring about justified concerns, in particular those capable of operations against sea lines of communication. There was, however, no system of forward basing of large concentrations of submarines across SLOCs. In the last four years no submarines had been sent out to work against communications. Surveillance systems can monitor with some reliability the entry and exit of units into the high seas.

Discussion first centred on Soviet views about the length of a possible war. The Soviet speaker said their policy would be to try to bring the war in Europe to a rapid end. The longer a war lasted the greater the possibility of nuclear weapons being used. Both sides might use such weapons for defensive purposes against targets in the rear. This would cause serious damage to populations. The USSR does not exclude the possibility of selected nuclear strikes against Soviet targets, but it would never be the first to use nuclear weapons. In the event of selective nuclear strikes governments would be forced to the negotiating table.

Tactical nuclear weapons were next discussed. The chairman said that we in the West think that the Soviet Navy sees nuclear weapons as a means of making up for Western naval superiority. Both the submarine grounded in Sweden and the *Slava* carried nuclear weapons. Yet the US has eliminated nuclear SUBROC, ASROC, nuclear Terrier and the nuclear torpedo. All have been withdrawn. Will the Soviet Union also start to withdraw tactical nuclear weapons at sea?

The Soviet speaker replied that the American move was not unilateral. The USSR could learn from its mistakes like the submarine on the rocks incident. *Vessels deployed in the Baltic, Black Sea and the Sea of Japan operate without nuclear weapons* but they carry standard dual capable weapon systems. This problem of dual capability applies to both sides, hence the problem of long range sea launched cruise missiles. Verification is a problem and in such a situation one is forced to depend on trust. The *Slava* in the Black Sea was specially fitted with a nuclear weapon for the verification experiment. Nuclear weapons are part of the war loads of some vessels deployed in more distant areas where the chances of tragi-comedies like the submarine incident are less.

A western participant said that he understood the Soviet concerns about certain types of forces crossing certain lines and the responsibilities of commanders with central authorities asking what was going on, but to be a real *threat* there would need to be other indicators of a possible surprise attack. Another western participant found Soviet concerns with PACEX 89 odd, given the world situation with no tension or confrontation. The exercise should not have been a problem as it was carried out in US waters. In a situation of high tension, and if there was a good probability of the outbreak of hostilities, it would be a very different situation. It was necessary clearly to differentiate between the two scenarios. It was thus difficult to see where CBMs would help.

The Soviet speaker said that peacetime activities could cause public concern. There was a need for direct navy to navy contact in these situations. The Soviets therefore supported such CBMs at sea.

Another Soviet participant said that while unilateral measures were helpful in creating the right atmosphere, they could not radically solve the situation. There had been proposals for the limitation and reduction of tactical nuclear weapons at sea. But these had two weaknesses. First, it was very difficult to verify limitations on tactical nuclear weapons. Second, tactical weapons were connected with SLCMs. Given verification problems it would be better to settle the problem by banning nuclear weapons on all sea-borne non-ballistic systems.

Discussion then turned to the alert lines (see previous map). The concerns reflected by the lines could be removed, it was suggested, if movement across the lines was notified. The Soviet speaker made it clear that the Soviets regarded the Iceland-Faeroes and Attu-Midway 'lines' as analogous to their own lines. He made clear using the map that the Soviet Union has concerns resulting from Tomahawk range, about US naval activities in proximity to the Soviet homeland. The areas so defined were: from Trondheim to Bear Island 1000km from the coast, the Barents Sea, the Black Sea, the Mediterranean and Aegean from the Peloponnese to the south of Crete, the Muscat-Karachi line, the sea of Okhotsk and the northern part of the sea of Japan within 1000 km of Soviet territory. *Within these lines* the Soviets have serious concerns and would like to have notification if they were to be crossed by aircraft carriers or ships with cruise missiles. The Indian Ocean is of less concern than the Barents and the Far East although agreement on notification would be useful. The Soviets saw the Attu-Midway line as the main US line of defence, although there were other lines further back.

Western participants denied that such lines were the basis of western naval deployments but the Soviet speaker said he regarded the Attu-Midway line as the one behind which western forces would not retreat and the one used for monitoring. The chairman concluded the discussions by saying that there were clearly fundamental differences of view on sea power between the Soviets and Westerners.

Session 8: The Current Debate on US Maritime Strategy

The Western speaker said that when first published the US Maritime Strategy had led to tremendous controversy. There was controversy over the potential of naval forces to trigger a war, controversy over naval forces engaging in strategic missions beyond SLOC protection, controversy over the declared intention to attack SSBNs, controversy over the uses and survivability of carriers, controversy over the relevance of the Maritime Strategy to overall US Naval and military strategy. Much of the controversy has now died down and it was useful to point out what had happened to the Maritime Strategy over the last few years, partly as a result of the controversy. The US Naval leadership, while not altering the strategy, had placed additional emphasis on things that had not been emphasised so much before.

This was evident in a speech Admiral Trost made in 1987 at the Naval War College. Trost said that there was much confusion about what the Maritime Strategy was about. This confusion existed inside the US Navy as well as outside. He therefore wanted to clarify the USN's position. In particular he wanted to emphasise that the options in the Maritime Strategy were not the strategy itself. Options such as anti-SSBN attacks, operations against the Soviet homeland and horizontal escalation are all *consistent* with the maritime strategy but not *required* by it. He realised that confusion had arisen over this. In Trost's opinion this confusion was not wholly undesirable: it contributed to deterrence by heightening uncertainty. This confusion was also a natural outcome of the ongoing process of revising the Maritime Strategy. Trost used Marxist terminology when he called developing the strategy a dialectical process: it was both 'dynamic' and 'evolutionary'. He also gave his point of view. One needed to return to an emphasis on *general principles* rather than specific options. One needed to avoid 'set piece' thinking and 'rigid intelligence estimates'. Soviet strategy was in a state of flux. It was therefore necessary to avoid having just a single picture of what the Soviets were doing. One needed to concentrate on principles to be applied by US operational commanders no matter what circumstances they were facing.

The speaker defined these principles as:

(i) In a period of crisis, naval forces must be moved early and in strength to the point of the crisis and also to other areas if this contributes to deterrence;
(ii) If conflict arises US and Allied forces should seize the initiative and maintain it;
(iii) These forces must look to achieving strategic leverage beyond merely protecting sea lanes;
(iv) They must employ *conventional* weapons alone: this is *not* a nuclear strategy;
(v) Operations will be with sister services and allies, i.e. be joint and combined.

The above five principles were continuations by Admiral Trost of Admiral Watkins' thinking, but Trost put emphasis on an additional principle, something that had always been understood but was not put forward as a principle:

(vi) One must be reasonable and flexible in the employment of forces. Circumstances would determine how forces would be used. There is a possibility that in a major war the Soviet Navy might do something unexpected in terms of our understanding. The intelligence picture has generally expected a defensive Soviet Navy posture. But what if the Soviet Navy does something very different? The Americans were bothered by two exercises in which the Soviets engaged in major deployments of attack submarines into the Atlantic. Such an action might precede the commencement of hostilities. As a result the CNO implied, but did not specifically say, that his advice to the JCS in these circumstances might not involve large numbers of forces being sent north, because the immediate threat would be in the south.

In short, the Maritime Strategy has consistently called for the early, decisive and offensively orientated deployment of maritime forces but especially in the last 3-4 years there has been a strong emphasis on developing multiple options so that one could most effectively regulate and moderate according to circumstances how forces ought to be used. There has also been additional emphasis within the last few years on non-general war concerns.

In 1989 the CNO's staff produced an unclassified briefing which compared to earlier statements placed much greater emphasis on the contribution maritime forces might make to protecting national interests in an era of violent peace and at lower levels of conflict. Compared with other conflict the global war possibility was extensively addressed but it was also described as *extremely unlikely*. The speaker believed that this trend towards flexibility and non general war contingencies would continue.

Admiral Trost intends to publish a new unclassified variant of the strategy to parallel that published in 1986 by Admiral Watkins. Some of the above ideas will be in the new document. The speaker re-emphasised that what he had said was a personal opinion that had not been able to cover a complex subject in any depth.

The chairman re-emphasised the speaker's point about flexibility. NATO had just exercised the Shallow Seas Campaign emphasising convoy protection rather than forward operations in the Norwegian Sea Campaign. CONMAROPS meant what it said about defence in depth. When the new statement of US Strategy came out the British First Sea Lord would provide an Alliance perspective.

Another western participant commented that the first speaker's account had been very accurate. He had seen the draft of the new unclassified version on flexibility and the need to be prepared for other contingencies. Unlikely options had been *de*-emphasised.

A Soviet participant said that he found the principles expounded by the speaker as completely reasonable and no cause for concern. The principles enunciated and Soviet maritime strategy were a good basis for confidence building measures. Another Soviet participant agreed that this evolution of the Maritime Strategy was less destabilising than the earlier version. It was closer in conception to Soviet operational art/maritime strategy but it only addressed the political role of strategy. It was vital to discuss jointly and in some detail the military technical side of Soviet and US maritime strategy and the military technical risks both posed by and facing each side's forces.

A third Soviet participant agreed that the general softening of the maritime strategy, and the greater flexibility being shown was very encouraging. But Admiral Trost's greater emphasis on flexibility was a good illustration of the inadequacy of unilateral changes. These could send the wrong signals and have opposite results. It implied that rapidly deploying Soviet submarines across Atlantic communications was the best way to alleviate the danger to the Soviet shore and secure the safety of Soviet SSBNs. Not sending units into the Atlantic was therefore the best way of inviting forces close to the shore. It was important therefore to have agreement not to deploy in Atlantic communications. One should trade off an offensive against SLOCs against an offensive against the Kola peninsula.

A fourth Soviet participant made the point that attacks on SSBNs or land based targets were still *not excluded.* The new emphasis on flexibility by not excluding these options made the situation more vague. The publication of a new statement therefore need not stabilise the situation. It was difficult to analyse the situation 'by post'. It was better therefore to find a vehicle for discussions by serving people, to compare and ask questions. Otherwise vagueness could have a negative effect. CBM is a dirty word to many: therefore we need a new word for maritime measures ('measures of transparency and predictability' was suggested by a Soviet colleague).

A western participant emphasised that the CNO had nothing to do with the initiation of operations. This was a matter for the national command authorities and the CINCs. The original speaker confirmed that the CNO said himself that the Maritime Strategy is a set of recommended options. He was not an operational commander. Indeed his version of the Maritime Strategy had not been submitted for approval to the Joint Chiefs of Staff or NATO. This allows the navy to make revisions and changes as naval leaders see fit and to make new offerings in the market-place of ideas.

A western participant said that many asked why the USN should publish anything. It was being done in a spirit of 'glasnost' honestly to develop certain measures of confidence. It also clarified basic principles. This is necessary as people have lost sight of key concepts. The Maritime Strategy is not a plan. The debate it generated focussed on options at the *outer limits* of the concept, at the expense of the principles of using naval forces in a more relaxed environment. Other threats including terrorism and drugs have come to the fore. The Maritime Strategy has been seen in too specific items: the flexible and situational aspects of it have been lost. The basic concepts are of long standing and have suffered distortion in the debate. The Naval leadership therefore thinks it is important to re-state the Strategy clearly, not as a strategy of the previous administration but as a consensus strategy with broad principles of continued validity. This is more important than a debate.

A Soviet participant said that concern over the Maritime Strategy had not subsided in the USSR so the corrections and clarifications were very welcome and very important. They were also very correct given unilateral Soviet force reductions and American reluctance to discuss formal new CBMs.

Another Soviet participant agreed that it was very heartening to hear about the changes in the Maritime Strategy in the light of the current situation. Concepts were, however, one thing, what would follow on? He would like more illumination on how forces might be used. There seemed to be no great differences between the new and the old versions. The principles were the same as before. The Soviets did not know what to expect from 'flexible use of naval forces'. How did the classified version differ from the unclassified version?

The western speaker said that uncertainty cut both ways. Trost's remarks reflected western uncertainties about the Soviet Navy (a Soviet speaker interjected that this reflected the genuine pluralism of thinking in the USSR). The unclassified version was very much along the same lines as the secret version. This flexibility made discussions between navies even more important as uncertainty exists in both sides' minds. If one got down to what US or UK officers were really worried about it was sea lines of communication. Hence Trost's example about SSNs sent south.

Session 9: Summing Up and Ways Forward

The chairman first said that the discussions had made clear that the Maritime Strategy was very different from the common caricature. As had been made clear, important changes were being made in the presentation of the Maritime Strategy that would counteract the original journalistic 'hype' and over-emphasis on high level options. The current re-articulation was a useful CBM in itself. It should allay Soviet fears and have a positive effect on the US debate, although such unilateral statements were not substitutes for formal naval dialogue. Even the old strategy was not as offensive in its orientation as some of its supporters and opponents thought. Defending exposed allies such as Norway needed forward deployment. When one examines actual exercises one sees US carriers forward deployed in powerful *defensive* positions forcing the opponent to mount attacks upon them. This puts the ball in the opponent's court if he wishes to operate offensively against either Norway or Atlantic shipping. By the defender thus taking the *initiative* the side on the strategic offensive is forced to take on powerful defensive forces where the defender has many advantages. Corbett would have approved of this exploitation of the defensive form of war, as Clausewitz argued, the inherently stronger form. Corbett, the greatest classical maritime strategist, was always suspicious of the fetish of the 'offensive' and its confusion with the *initiative*.

The discussions had made clear that different nations think about maritime forces and strategy in different ways. Even the US and UK have had different approaches since 1945. Americans have emphasised power projection and operations against the shore, whereas the British tended to think primarily of the use of the sea for movement and the defence of shipping. Soviet thinking with its lines and areas is, in its turn, a very land-orientated way of thinking. American commanders find the Soviet imposition of lines on their strategy very strange. The Soviets clearly see the GIUK gap in the Atlantic and the SOSUS line in the Pacific as final lines of defence. We in the West just do not think like that. This demonstrates a real problem as we impose our thinking on each other, interpreting the ideas of others in our own intellectual terms. It is, therefore, important that we have meetings like this so we can see how others see us. We need to discuss what our ships, etc., can do and what others *think* they can do. The 'lines of alert' demonstrate just how differently we think. A look at other problems may also surprise us both. This should be on the agenda of our next meeting. Also we must discuss more fully the nature of the threat maritime forces pose to the other side. What worries us most? What makes certain activities threatening? The discussions clearly demonstrated a perceived threat to both sides from the others' exercises. Can we avoid that? We need to think about this in detail.

People may react adversely to the term 'confidence building measures' but 'naval arms control' is even worse, and should be dropped. We must clarify our thinking about confidence building measures, disarmament and arms control. The three concepts overlap to general confusion as they have very different logical centres. They could be visualised as three overlapped circles:

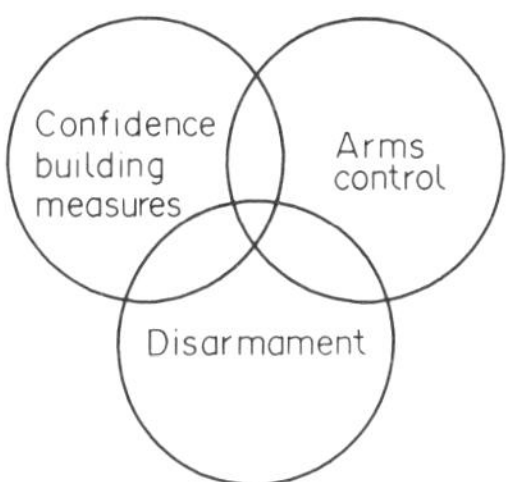

The logic of *disarmament* is that arms cause war and that without them we have peace. The logic of *arms control* is that a stable balance of forces can be agreed between potential adversaries who do not want to fight each other but do not trust each other. It implies some level of hostility or potential hostility between the participants. Arms control was relevant to British-USA relations from the end of the War of 1812 to the late 1930s when Anglo-American antagonism faded and became cooperation against greater common enemies. *Confidence building* is a dynamic process leading to the situation where one is not worried by another's armed forces, no matter what their size or notional superiority to one's own. In a post-CFE world, where relatively high levels of naval power will remain necessary to maintain international security, it seems most appropriate to emphasise the confidence building route to international security. So the future agenda must emphasise CBMs, not just notification and observation but exchange of information in specific areas (for example building programmes). This approach does not of course rule out those measures of arms control or disarmament that come within the confidence building circle, for example the mutual abolition of the sub-strategic nuclear weapons that make naval forces unnecessarily threatening. There was much to talk about when the group next met probably in six months' time. It would be useful to analyse the revised statement of the US maritime strategy. It would also be useful to discuss a range of maritime CBMs and, perhaps, think up new names for them.

The rest of this session was devoted to a discussion of the maritime aviation issue in the CFE talks. A western expert (who had not been present at previous sessions), pointed to the counter-offensive elements in western maritime strategy and the offensive potential of Soviet naval aviation; even the fighters in ships of *Tblisi* class could be used to escort land based strike aircraft. Soviet staff doctrine included the Soviet Naval Air Force in the forces used in offensive air operations. The western position was therefore that land based air must be included in the CFE talks. These threatened not just the Northern Flank but the United Kingdom itself. He was optimistic about the prospects for a CFE 1 in 1990 and obtaining an acceptable compromise in training aircraft and Soviet interceptors. The Western view on land based naval air would remain rigid but it would be accompanied by a great, honest awareness about Soviet concerns with western maritime air. CFE would be followed by further negotiations which might cover both side's maritime air. These might impose restrictions on the movement of aircraft carriers in proximity to Europe but would safeguard the world-wide freedom of movement for carriers.

Soviet participants made it clear that they did not regard the splitting of maritime aviation into two parts, land based and sea based, as making sense. Naval forces were excluded from the CFE talks by mandate.

The speaker said that attempting to include sea based aviation in the talks would jeopardise them. As agreement was reached at CFE 1 there could be a formal request to continue negotiations. These might well include all naval aviation.

A Soviet participant made it clear that the western position on land based naval air undercut the principle of *reciprocity* central to the Vienna talks. In areas where one side was superior it would engage in asymmetrical reductions. All Soviet naval strike aviation was ashore and US naval strike aviation in carriers.

The speaker agreed in principle but argued that it was impossible to reach a comprehensive agreement on maritime air in a year or eighteen months. A CFE agreement including land based naval air would make an agreement on sea based aviation and other issues much easier.

In answer to a question a Soviet participant stated there were about 500 Soviet naval strike aircraft in Europe. Western participants with naval backgrounds also expressed reservations about the inclusion of land based maritime aircraft of either side in CFE. Opposition was also expressed to including carriers, the basis of US maritime strategy in arms control. Reductions in numbers of US carriers would take place as a result of the budgetary process but substantial naval forces would remain for the USA's world wide commitment to maintain deterrence and stability in a situation made more dangerous by the proliferation of weapons of mass destruction. One participant therefore agreed with the chairman's suggestion to drop the term 'arms control' as it applied to naval forces.

The speaker emphasised that he was only talking about the deployment of carriers within striking distance of the USSR. If the Kola defences were reduced some restriction on carrier deployment (necessary anyway because of budget cuts) might be possible. One was only thinking of peacetime restrictions.

The chairman pointed out that restricting carrier deployment in European waters was a fundamental attack on NATO's current maritime strategy. Carriers were there to attract submarines as well as air strikes.

One western participant expressed frustration as the Western position was the result of an alliance compromise on the definition of 'land based aircraft'. NATO, especially the European allies, had legitimate concerns about Soviet land based maritime aviation, notably the Backfires in the UK air defence region. The US conceded the inclusion of its land based naval aviation to get the Soviets to come half way by including Backfires. There was some concern that having opened up the issue the West was getting no response.

A Soviet participant said he was in favour of configuring medium range bombers to have no effective capability to attack land targets. The West was not sure that naval strike aircraft were incapable of delivering strikes against land targets. Currently there was much overlap between naval aviation and the Soviet Air Forces. Naval bombers were escorted by PVO Flankers. The Smolensk Air Army had a secondary maritime role. However, it might be technically possible to separate the maritime from other strike roles and to reduce naval aircraft to visual targeting of land targets alone.

It would be best, he argued, to include *all* naval aircraft in the *next* stage of the Vienna ngotiations. This need not mean reduction of carriers but quantitative limits on numbers of deployed aircraft in the European arena and adjacent waters. Land based aircraft could be withdrawn if carriers were brought in, so as not to exceed the ceilings. CFE would thus remain a European negotiation in conventional forces not a naval arms control negotiation. Some western participants expressed disagreement with the inclusion of carrier based air in any CFE talks.

The chairman concluded by saying that although it was a pity the meeting was ending on a note of disagreement, at least it demonstrated how much there remained to discuss at future meetings of this kind.

Notes

Chapter 1. Europe's Maritime Security Interests

1. Figures provided by the British Maritime Charitable Foundation (BMCF).
2. J R Hill, *Maritime Strategy for Medium Powers* (London, Croom Helm, 1986), p. 31.
3. Figures from H Peltor, *A Global Strategy for the Western Alliance*. Paper prepared for the 1987 Royal College of Defence Studies Course, kindly made available by the author.
4. Energy figures from *BP Statistical Review of World Energy*, June 1987.
5. *Europe in Figures* (Luxumlery, Office for the Official Publications of the European Communities, 1988), Section 19.
6. British Maritime Charitable Foundation figures.
7. General Council of British Shipping Statistical Brief, No. 24, p. 3.
8. *Supplement* to *Why Ships Went*, British Maritime Charitable Foundation, 1988, p. 6.
9. British Maritime Charitable Foundation figures.
10. 'Shipbuilding', *Britannia Book of the Year, 1989*, p. 225.
11. Supra, notes 8 & 9.
12. Supra, note 8.
13. 'Fisheries', *Britannia Book of the Year, 1989*, pp. 121-2.
14. Hill, ibid, Chapter 10, pp. 149-156.

Chapter 2. The Forward Maritime Strategy and Extended Deterrence

1. *The Maritime Strategy* brochure, p. 15, issued with the January 1986 issue of U.S. Naval Institute *Proceedings*.
2. Taken from the headings in the brochure.
3. N Friedman, *The US Maritime Strategy* (Jane's, London, 1988), p. 33. This book is by far the best intellectual justification of the Maritime Strategy.

4. 'The Role of the Navy', 13 September 1957, Public Record Office CAB 131/18.
5. Main sources for the above were J J Sokolsky, 'Canada and the Cold War at Sea 1945-68' in W A B Douglas (Ed.), *RCN in Transition 1910-85* (University of British Colombia Press, Vancouver, 1988), p. 229, and *Seapower in the Nuclear Age: NATO as a Maritime Alliance*, thesis presented to the Department of Government, Harvard University, August 1984, pp. 213-221; 226-7.
6. The best source on CONMAROPS is Vice Admiral Sir Geoffrey Dalton, 'NATO's Maritime Strategy' in E Ellingson (Ed.), *NATO and US Maritime Strategy: Diverging Interests or Co-operative Effort* (Norwegian Atlantic Committee, Oslo, 1987).
7. The account of the development of the Maritime Strategy draws heavily on J B Hattendorf, 'The Evolution of the Maritime Strategy 1977-87' in *Naval War College Review*, Summer 1988, pp. 7-28.
8. Note 1, p. 8.
9. Ibid, p. 9.
10. Ibid, pp. 11-13.
11. Ibid, p. 14.
12. General P X Kelly, 'The Amphibious Warfare Strategy', ibid, pp. 18 and 26.
13. Watkins, ibid, p. 14.
14. Quotation from 'Maritime Strategy from the Deckplates', US Naval Institute *Proceedings*, September 1986.
15. Vice Admiral Henry C Mustin, 'The Role of the Navy and Marines in the Norwegian Sea', *Naval War College Review*, March/April 1986, p. 5.
16. Quoted in Hattendorf, op. cit., p. 16.

Chapter 3. The Atlantic Link—NATO's Merchant Fleets and Extended Deterrence

1. Unclassified EASTLANT briefing, Northwood, 30 January 1987, supplemented by I C Kidd, 'NATO Logistics System Stands in Danger of Collapsing Under Strain of Conflict', *The Almanac of Sea Power*, 1989, p. 62.
2. EASTLANT briefing.
3. Vice Admiral Sir Geoffrey Dalton, 'NATO's Maritime Strategy' in *NATO and US Maritime Strategy: Diverging Interests of Co-operative Effort* (Oslo Norwegian Atlantic Committee, 1987), p. 45.

4. *Sealink 86*, report of Conference, SACLANT, Norfolk, Virginia.
5. The Organisation of the Joint Chiefs of Staff, *United States Military Posture, Fiscal Year 1987*, p. 68.
6. Sokolsky, *Seapower in the Nuclear Age* (see previous chapter note 5). Chapter V contains an excellent account of the development of NATO Sealift policy.
7. A copy of the unclassified sections of the 1987 PBOS report was made available to the author.
8. Kidd, ibid.
9. Dalton, ibid.
10. C H Whitehurst, Jr, *The US Merchant Marine: In Search of an Enduring Maritime Policy* (Annapolis, Naval Institute Press), pp. 131-133.
11. 1986 PBOS Report: copy made available to British Maritime Charitable Foundation.
12. 1989 Defence White Paper, Cmnd. 675-I, Table 1.4.
13. 1986 PBOS, op. cit.
14. *The War at Sea: History of the Second World War*, Volume III, Part II (London, HMSO, 1961), p. 402.

Chapter 4. Europe's Premier Navy: Problems and Prospects

1. See author's, *Vanguard to Trident* (London, Bodley Head, 1987).
2. See House of Commons Defence Committee, Session 1987-8, *The Future Size and Role of the Royal Navy's Surface Fleet.*
3. *The Economist*, 6 June 1981: quoted in Sir James Cable, *Britain's Naval Future* (London, Macmillan, 1983), p. 127.
4. Mr Mottram before the Defence Committee, Note 2, Minutes of Evidence, p. 15.

Chapter 5. NATO's Continental Navies

1. 'N Atlantic role for Spanish Navy aircraft carrier', *Jane's Defence Weekly*, Volume 11, No. 17, 29 April 1989, p. 730.
2. Martin Deleare, 'Dutch seek naval specialisation', *Jane's Defence Weekly*, Volume 11, No. 82, 3 June 1989 and S Hobson, 'Europe studies defence of Norway'; ibid, Volume 12, No 1, 8 July 1989.

Chapter 6: The Gulf Precedent—Birth of a Western European Navy?

1. Captain W C Mabesoone, 'European Co-operation—Naval Lessons From the Gulf War', *NATO's Sixteen Nations*, Volume 34, No. 1, p. 68.

2. Western European Union, Secretary General's Note C(87)162, 17 September 1987.
3. Mabesoone, ibid, p. 73.
4. Ibid, pp. 73-74.
5. Ibid, p. 74.
6. Ibid.
7. Western European Union, *Platform on European Security Interests*, The Hague, 27 October 1987, p. 1, paragraph 3.
8. The quotation comes from an official who cannot be named.

Chapter 7. Soviet Naval Policy in the Gorbachev Era

1. P V'yunenko, B N Makeyev and D Skugarev, *The Navy: Its Role Prospects for Development and Employment* (Moscow Military Publishing House, Moscow, 1988).
2. Statement by Rear Admiral William O Studeman, US Navy, Director of Naval Intelligence, Before the Seapower and Strategic and Critical Materials Subcommittee of the House Armed Services Committee on Intelligence Issues, 1 March 1988, pp. 36-37.
3. Statement by Rear Admiral Thomas A Brooks, US Navy, Director of Naval Intelligence, Before the Seapower and Strategic and Critical Materials Subcommittee of the House Armed Services Committee on Intelligence Issues, 23 February 1989, pp. 13-14.

Chapter 8. Conventional Arms Control in Europe— the Naval Dimension

1. W H J Manthorpe, 'Why is Gorbachev Pushing Naval Arms Control?', US Naval Institute, *Proceedings*, January 1989, pp. 76-77.
2. Johan Jorgen Holst, 'Confidence building measures—a conceptual framework', *Survival*, Jan-Feb 1983, p. 2.
3. J R Hill, *Arms Control at Sea* (London, Routledge, 1989), p. 199.
4. Speeches at the 'Sea Link 89' conference at Annapolis, Maryland, USA, 13-15 June 1989.
5. Speech, 'Speaking for NATO', quoted in *Arms Control Reporter*, 1989, 402.B.212.
6. Ibid.

Index

AAW (Anti-Air Warfare) systems 49, 55, 57
ABM Treaty 108
Afghan war 120
Alaska 124-6, 146
ALCM 99
Arctic 125
Arms control, naval 72-85, 97, 101, 103, 105, 111-13, 157-8
  asymmetrical reductions 113
ASEAN nations 123
ASROC (Anti-Submarine Rocket) 70, 151
ASTOR (Anti-Submarine Torpedo) 70
ASW (Anti-Submarine Warfare) capability 41-6, 48-50, 55, 69-70, 86, 95-6, 99-100, 145-7
Atlantic 109, 113, 129, 142
  US maritime strategy in 120, 128-32
Aviation, naval 158-60

Baltic 111, 149, 151
Barents Sea 109, 149
Barnett, Captain Roger 21
Belgium 50
  and cooperation in the Gulf 60-1, 63
  navy 55-6
Benelux countries 63-4
Black Sea 149, 151
BPKs (Large Anti-Submarine Ships (Russian)) 70
Brezhnev, Leonid 68
Brooks, Admiral Thomas A. 69
Brosio, General Manlio 17, 19

Canadian navy 56
CBMs (Confidence Building Measures) 80, 98, 100, 103, 105, 108-14, 122, 126-8, 134, 139, 143, 146-7, 151, 156-8
  see also CSBMs
CFE (Negotiations on Conventional Armed Forces in Europe) 73, 76, 85, 106, 114, 121, 131, 139, 141-3, 158-60
Channel, the 55
Chernavin, Admiral 120-1
Chernobyl 148
China 109, 124
  Sino-Soviet border 141
  Soviet treaty with China on reduction of forces 141-2
CINCHAN 129
Clausewitz, Carl von 144, 156
Colbert, Rear Admiral Richard 17
Command 8288 42, 46
Concertation 61-6
CONMAROPS (Concept of Maritime Operations) 20, 26, 118, 130, 139, 143, 154
Conventional warfare/capabilities 27-9, 39-58, 100, 120
  arms control 71-85
  forces (NATO) 1, 73, 76, 85
  see also CFE
Corbett, Sir Julian 24, 156
Cruise missiles 26-7, 71, 95-6, 99, 112-13, 120, 145-6, 151
CSBMs (Confidence and Security Building Measures) 72, 77-81, 84, 125, 139, 145

Data on operational and technical matters 104, 111
Denmark 33
  navy 54
Denuclearisation, naval 70-1, 82, 92, 100, 102
Disarmament 157-8

Eastern Europe, political events in 130
EASTLANT 30
East-West confrontation, past effects of 88
European naval cooperation 'out of area' 59-66
  see also Gulf, the
Exchanges of visits
  by military personnel 121
Exercises/manoeuvres, naval 72, 80-4, 95, 97-9, 111, 115, 126, 130-1, 144, 146-7, 153, 157
  PACEX 89 149, 151
Experts, meetings of 101, 103, 115

Falklands War 12
FAMS (Family of Anti-Air Missile Systems) 57
Fleets, fishing 55
Forward deployment 15-28, 118, 120, 122-3, 127, 129-30, 135
France 109
  and cooperation in the Gulf 60, 63, 65
  navy 48-50, 56, 59

Germany, West 52-3
  navy 53-4, 56-7, 64
GIUK Gap 19-20, 43, 137, 157
GLCM (Ground-launched Cruise Missile) 26
Gorbachev, Mikhail 72, 74
  navy policy under 67-71, 127
Gorshkov, Admiral S. G. 67-8, 93, 98, 115, 134-6
Greece 52
  navy 52
Gulf, the 13, 46, 59-66, 108, 143

Hayward, Admiral Thomas B. 20, 118
Hill, Admiral J. R. 78
Howe, Sir Geoffrey 77, 84

ICBMs (Intercontinental Ballistic Missiles) 96, 125
  mobile platforms 147
Incidents at Sea agreements 77-8, 84, 97, 99, 108-10, 121-2, 125, 145
Indian Ocean 115, 123, 125-8, 136, 150, 152
Information, exchange of 108, 158
Inspection of naval exercises 98
Iran 59, 62
Italy 51
  and cooperation in the Gulf 60-1, 63-4
  navy 51-3, 56, 64

Japan 123-6, 146
  US-Japanese relationship 123
Jefferson, Thomas 119
Johnson, Commander Spencer 21, 118
Jones, John Paul 119

Kelly, General P. X. 23
Khrushchev, Nikita 133
Kola Peninsula 113, 159
Komer, Robert W. 21
Korea, North 125
Korea, South 123

Manthorpe, Captain W. H. J. 118
Maritime trade dependence 2-3, 10
McGwire, Mike 135
MCM (Mine Counter Measures) vessels 56, 59-62, 64
Mediterranean 64, 80, 100, 115, 136, 150
  CINCUSNAVEUR's Mediterranean Concept 118
  incidents in 98
  US naval exercises in 131
Merchant fleets (NATO) 3-9, 28-39
Moreau, Rear Admiral 21
Mottram, Richard 43
Mustin, Vice Admiral Henry C. 24-5

NATO 13-28, 42, 58, 129
  CONMAROPS (Concept of Maritime Operations) 20, 26, 118, 130, 139, 143, 154
  Continental navies 48-58
    see also under individual countries
  maritime strategy 15-28, 113-15, 129, 137-44, 158
    flexible response 17, 20, 129, 137
    forward deployment 15-28, 118, 120, 122-3, 127, 129-30, 135
  merchant fleets 3-9, 28-39
  SNFL (Standing Naval Force Atlantic) 17, 54-5, 58, 86
  SSGs (Strategic Studies Groups) 20-1
  striking fleet 16-20, 43-5, 86
Naval activities, conversations on limitation of 106-14, 152
Naval aviation, Soviet 158
Naval cooperative security 97-101
  Soviet ideas on 97-8
  Western ideas on 98-100
Netherlands 50
  and cooperation in the Gulf 60-1, 63, 65
  navy 55-6
Nitze, Paul 27, 92, 112
North Sea 55
Norway 19
  border with Soviet Union 77
  navy 54-5
  Norwegian International Ship Register 33, 38-9
  reinforcement of 19, 21, 25, 42, 44, 46, 55, 81, 131, 156
Norwegian Sea 86, 109-10, 112, 115
  campaign 154
Nott, Sir John 40
  defence review 40, 42, 46, 87-8
Nuclear strikes, selected 150-1

Observation of exercises 97-9, 145-6, 158

PACEX 89 149, 151
Pacific 94, 115, 118
  Pacific-East Asia region, importance of 122

US maritime strategy in 120, 122-8
Pacific Community 125
Pacific states 122
Personnel, maritime 35-6, 46-7
Philippines 123-5
Polaris 135
Portugal 51
navy 51
Pre-emptive doctrine of naval nuclear use 27, 113

'R' Day, preparations for 29-31
Railways 132
Reagan, Ronald 118

SACEUR 137
SACLANT (Supreme Allied Commander Atlantic) 17, 30, 34, 36, 129-30, 137, 139
SALT (Strategic Arms Limitation Talks) 148
Sea of Japan 95, 127, 149, 151
Sea of Okhotsk 149
Sealink '89 Conference 130
Shallow Seas campaign (NATO) 154
Sherman, Admiral Forrest 119
Shipbuilding 9, 47
Soviet 134, 147
Shipping
NATO's PBOS (Planning Board for Ocean Shipping) 32-8
Norwegian International Ship Register 33, 38-9
Siberia 142
Singapore 123
SLBMs (Submarine Launched Ballistic Missiles) 27, 92, 112, 125
SLCMs (Sea-launched Cruise Missiles) 27, 71, 95-6, 99, 120, 151
SLOCs (Sea Lines of Communication) 121-3, 125, 129-32, 134, 143, 150, 152, 156
Small, Admiral William N. 21, 119
Smith, Adam 36-7
SNAs (Sous-marin Nucléaire d'Attaque) 48
SOSUS line, Pacific Ocean 157
Soviet Central Asia 142
Soviet Union 57, 124, 129
Army 141
home defence 21
land power 91
maritime strategy 92-3, 113-14, 132-7, 144-52, 157
American concerns with 93-5
Naval Air Force 158
naval policy in Gorbachev era 67-71, 127
navy 57, 124, 129, 132-7, 149
Spain 50-1
navy 50-1, 56
SS20s 120
SSBNs (Nuclear-powered Ballistic Missile Firing Submarines) 1, 21-2, 25, 48, 68, 92, 94-6, 99, 110, 113, 132, 155
sanctuaries 145, 147
SSNs (Nuclear-powered Attack Submarines) 40, 68-9, 97, 156
Stalin, Joseph 133, 135
START (Strategic Arms Reduction Talks) 70, 96, 147
Stewart, Ian 61
Studeman, Rear Admiral William O. 68
Submarines 108, 110, 124, 132, 134, 145-7, 150
incidents 147, 151
see also ASW (Anti-submarine Warfare)
SUBROC (Submarine Launched Rocket) 70, 151
Swartz, Commander Peter 21

Tactical nuclear weapons (TNW) at sea, use of 99-100, 103, 114
withdrawal/limitation of 151
Terrorism 125
Thatcher, Margaret 63
Third World countries 93, 100
transfer of technology to 143
Train, Admiral Harry B. 21
Trost, Admiral 152-4, 156
Truman, Harry S. 119
Turkey 52
Turner, Admiral Stansfield 19

UK 37
cooperation in the Gulf 59-61, 63-5
maritime strategy 156-7
navy 40-7, 56-9
USA 22, 25-6, 53, 57, 70
budgetary pressures on 58, 102
cooperation in the Gulf 59, 63-4
maritime strategy 15, 91-2, 115, 118-32, 152-8
Soviet concerns with 95-6
unilateral initiatives 70-1

van Eekelen, Willem 61
Verification 111, 151
Vial, Admiral Nardiz 50-1
Vietnam 125

Warsaw Pact countries 29, 36, 53, 113
proposal on transfers of naval forces 80-1

Watkins, Admiral James D. 21-2, 129, 153-4
Weeks, Lieutenant Commander Stan 21, 118
Weinberger, Caspar 118
Western Europe 2-3
and maritime trade 2-3, 10-11
as importer/consumer of energy 2-3, 11
as producer of food 3
WEU (Western European Union) 60-3, 65-6
World War II 39

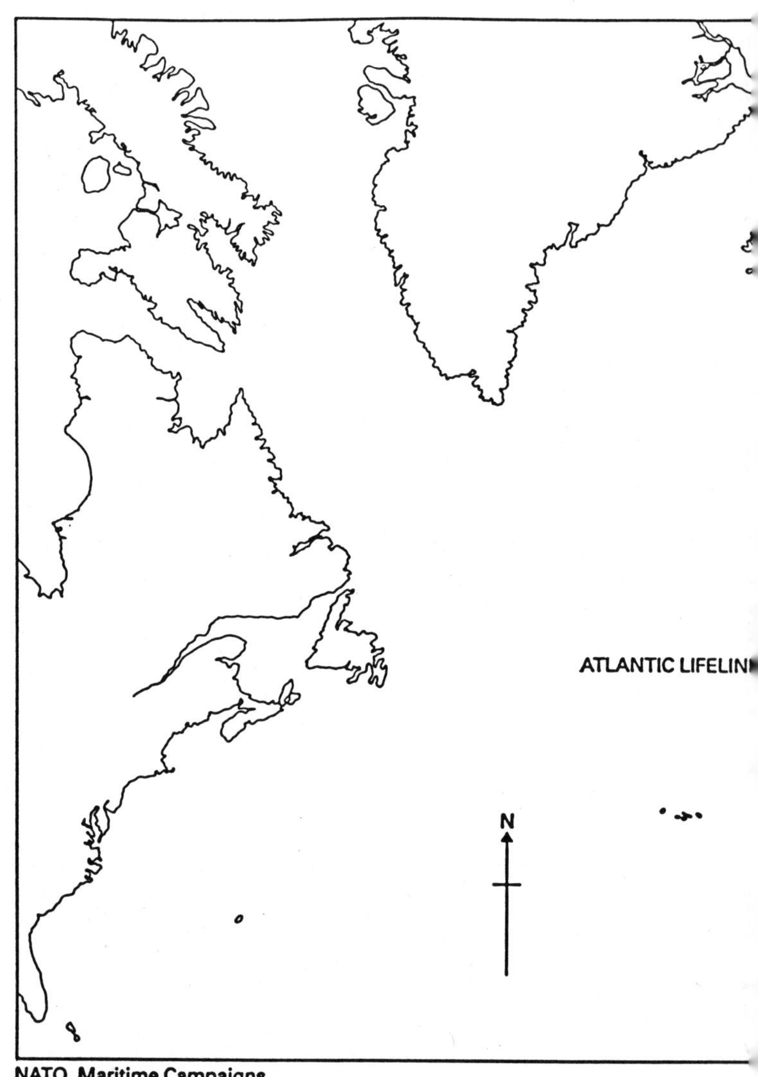

NATO Maritime Campaigns